Other Works on
THE AWARENESS OF REALITY
by WILLIAM SAMUEL

THE MELODY OF THE WOODCUTTER AND THE KING
THE *AWARENESS* OF *SELF*-DISCOVERY
TWO PLUS TWO EQUALS REALITY

A Guide To
AWARENESS AND TRANQUILLITY

Gift from William Morgan

William Samuel

A Guide To
AWARENESS
AND
TRANQUILLITY

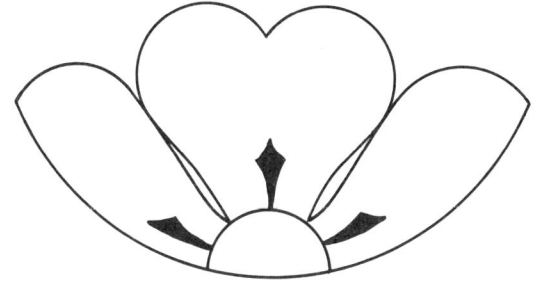

SEED CENTER
Palo Alto • California

A GUIDE TO AWARENESS AND TRANQUILLITY
Copyright © 1967, by William Samuel

*All rights in this book are reserved.
No part of the book may be used or reproduced in any manner whatsoever without written permission except in the case of brief quotations embodied in critical articles and reviews.
For information address Seed Center, Box 591, Palo Alto, California 94302*

ISBN 0-916108-06-6

This softbound edition published by
SEED CENTER
Box 591
Palo Alto, California

First printing 1976

MADE IN THE UNITED STATES OF AMERICA
BY BANTA WEST, INC. AT SPARKS, NEVADA

The world is not as it appears to the busy, troubled mortal. A beautiful and magnificent harmony is spread over the entire face of the land; perfection permeates everything. This perfect Harmony is readily discernible and immediately available to anyone willing to acknowledge its presence and pay the small price demanded of it.

What is the price? Surrender of the personality! Only the personality, the prideful, intellectual ego, denies the totality of Reality and the presence of a perfect experience.

Contents

Section One — AWARENESS

I	Special Notes for the Study of This Volume	3
II	Now	9
III	At the Beginning Is Awareness	14
IV	The Lollygog Lectures	27
V	Vignettes of the Within	36
VI	Selections from a Lollygog Lecture About the Christ and the "Virgin Birth"	40
VII	About Religion and Science	45
VIII	A Discussion of the "Prerequisites" to a Knowledge of Truth	52
IX	About the "Old Man" Who Is to Be "Put Off" and Exactly How to Do It	56
X	The Real Identity	64

Section Two — TRANQUILLITY

XI	Judgment—A Key to Tranquillity	87
XII	About Experience and Our Daily Affairs	120
XIII	Practicality	126
XIV	A Lollygog Lecture on Thinking, Thought, Meditation and Miracles	138
XV	The Way to *Experience* the Miraculous	146
XVI	Boundless Energy, Effortlessness and the Rediscovery of Youth	153
XVII	More Selections on Effortlessness and Energy	161

CONTENTS

XVIII	The Return of Youth, Expanding Awareness and Death's Death	165
XIX	Concerning Dualism	180
XX	A Lollygog Class on "Feeling" and Transcendent Tranquillity	188
XXI	Identity Is the Center of Being	207
XXII	Selections on Supply	227
XXIII	*Ending* the "Seeming"	247
XXIV	Simplicity	259
XXV	A Discussion of Church Membership	266
XXVI	About Love	275
	Conclusion	283

Introduction

The declarations of the heart can be presented intellectually only with the greatest bumbling. I forthwith warn the unwary reader that the intellect will *never* understand the full meaning of the heart's declarations. "The two are at enmity, one with the other."

Therefore, reader, to the best of your ability, examine this book with your heart, leaving the intellect out of it. With each subsequent reading, the heart will recognize more—and the intellect argue with less.

I assure you that if you but touch the hem of the Truth written of within these pages, you will discover *practical* Tranquillity with an ensuing happiness *beyond your greatest expectation!*

This book is composed of short, interrelated selections taken from the works of the author, including his classes, lectures and the wide correspondence he invites from all who are interested in discovering Tranquillity.

Insofar as possible, the selections have been grouped into instructive sequences so readers unfamiliar with the concept of the "Absolute" will find the subject matter easy to comprehend. The selections within the chapters are not necessarily related.

Names have been changed for obvious reasons.

SECTION ONE

Awareness

CHAPTER I

Special Notes for the Study of This Volume

1. PURPOSE, SCOPE AND PROMISE

Reader, I have discovered a peace of mind and tranquillity that are utterly beyond belief—and with the discovery has come the ability to communicate it to others!

By "peace of mind" I do not mean the ecstatic ebbing and flowing "happiness" of religion. I have discovered an unfluctuating, unchanging, *permanent* sense of well-being that transcends every human concept. I call it Transcendent Tranquillity.

It is not new. It is the "peace beyond understanding" spoken of by the saints and sages throughout history. No, it is not new at all, *but I have found it;* and, miraculously, with the finding has come the ability to give it to others. Indeed, to the special few who want it and are willing to listen, I find myself able to speak of this Transcendent Awareness such that they are able to understand for themselves—and be it!

Listen: The purpose of this book is to give this Awareness of Tranquillity to you. More than that, this volume is intended to prove to the reader that the awakening to Reality and its experience of Peace does not, contrary to the popular belief among the students of metaphysics, require the difficult, step-by-step processes of metaphysics, education, experience and "unfoldment." Instead, simplicity and honesty are its keynote.

Tender, childlike *simplicity* and *honesty* are the hallmarks of Reality's Tranquillity.

If this sounds presumptuous, I will make it more so. I tell you that the nearly effortless *practice* of the tender precepts spoken of in this work will open the reader's door to a tangible, practical, down to earth bedrock, *unfluctuating* Tranquillity such that nothing the world has to offer can prevail against it!

This is not another idealist's vague promise of happiness; not another metaphysical system nor philosophic fantasy intended to explain away despair, disease and death! This is not another fanciful theory. These words are written such that you may prove them and see for yourself if they are honest.

Tranquillity—call it Equanimity, Serenity or Peace, if you like—has little to do with education and less with religion. Even metaphysics, that esteemed (and disparaged) higher religion of the intelligentsia just coming into its own in the highest places of human authority—even that "metaphysics of the Absolute"—has little to do with the Transcendent Identity destined to survive the upheaval already begun; yet, the Reality which is its warp and woof is effortlessly available to the childlike, right here and now. How do I know? Because I have found it! I am it! It is I!

The days have already begun when we shall see the world as it is presently perceived come tumbling about our feet in a strange sickness and inscrutable insanity. Within a personal concept of self, it is inevitable that we shall see what appears to be a mysterious mental madness eating away at the victuals of a society holding itself separate and apart from Reality. Indeed, soon to make its appearance under the guileful label of individual and collective freedom will be a searing, drug-abetted, uninhibited and nearly unrestrained metaphysical upheaval of such masochistic proportions that it will lay bare, dismember and devour everything conventional and familiar. It is our inescapable obligation to help as many as are willing to discover, uncover *and be* the Tranquillity untouched by

Special Notes for the Study of This Volume 5

turmoil—a tranquillity as effortlessly available as our own Identity. Those who find it are enabled to be passers-by, tall and untouched by the world. Those who find it are healed.

Such is the scope of this book. Make of it what you will.

2. ABOUT METHODS AND PROCEDURES

Many have asked for a method and procedure to "work in the Absolute." The earnest seeker wants something to sink his teeth into. He wants a set of rules to follow, a step-by-step procedure at the end of which he will arrive at "cosmic consciousness," "illumination," or the solution to his problem.

Well now, who can write such a set of rules? The attempt is tantamount to a declaration that the Absolute is not absolute, that Reality is not real, that perfection is not perfect; in short, that God is not God. A "procedure" is virtual acknowledgement that within Finished Perfection exists an ignorant, arrogant ego that needs something in order to understand Reality.

As usual for such subject matter as this, the problem appears to be *how* to teach the unteachable, how to define the undefinable, how to write the unwritable. We find ourselves saying, "How shall we picture the Kingdom of God, or by what parable shall we describe it?" (Mark 4:30, The New English Bible). It is not really possible to make a scholastic breakdown of the Absolute into an instructive order of presentation, so what has been done here is only one of many possible presentations. It contains much repetition because the same ideas are presented from varying directions in an effort to make them crystal clear.

Within every conversation about Truth there is a sentence or an idea, sometimes just a word or two, which appears to be the spark of the entire discourse. Perhaps it is an illustration or merely a rhythm of words and warmth of expression; but whatever it is, the successful conversation has a specific "something" wherein comprehension bursts through with new light, new understanding, new illumination. When this happens we feel it within ourselves and see it in the eyes of others. Over the years I have made it a point to mark these occasions of especial comprehension and understanding, given or received, and have recorded the exact words that appeared to be the spark. They comprise the body of this work.

> *It is important that this book be read from the beginning since it is not likely to be understood otherwise.* If, at first, you do not understand every selection within the chapter, do not be alarmed. Without struggling too hard, go on to the next selection. Our subject matter becomes easier, not more complex, as the book takes the reader out of the world's maze of metaphysics into the tender simplicity of Transcendent Awareness.

3. ABOUT WORDS

It has been said that the Absolute should be expressed without resorting to "dualistic" words and examples, but from experience I have found this to be nonsense. To write in such a way is to write like an engineer who uses a jargon understood only by other engineers, or to write as a poet who writes only to other poets. It seems unwise to so limit the range of a discourse about Infinity.

Those who have come to know who and what they are, are not fooled by words! The old sage, Laotse, said, "The truly wise work diligently without allegiance to words," which, after all, are only ink spots or sounds. Since I appear to have a choice of words to use, I choose the simple, unpretentious phrase—the happy sound—because its noise is an *understood* melody, the *joyful* noise that David would prefer.

4. A FINAL NOTE

None of these words is intended to jolt or shock, but this is not to say that what is said here will not precipitate a controversy between the intellect and the heart. It oftentimes takes a mighty kick in the britches to end our thraldom with the world dream. An old saying goes that the flower must burst its bud before it blossoms, blossom before it seeds, and scatter its seed in the summer wind before it rests.

The artist who stands in the midst of an overwhelming sunrise may attempt to portray it on canvas for others to see and enjoy, but the picture is not the sunrise itself, and the painting is bound by the limitations of canvas and oil. If it has purpose, it is but to exist. Existing, say some, it appears to have the ability to lift the gaze of a passerby from scenes he thinks less beautiful and to point a finger to the overhead beauty he is too busy looking at his feet to see. In any event, this book is merely a canvas. The artist (or viewer) is foolish who forgets that the value is in the real Sunrise and not in an essay that only haltingly portrays the Deific Reality.

Absolute perfection is at hand! Deific Tranquillity, like the principle of music or arithmetic, is eternally omnipresent; and hence, it is right here and now spread over the whole face of the land! When this is seen and understood —*when this is felt within the heart*—one is not long tempted to believe his own putrid picture of poverty, only a partial picture of peace, but is able to "be a passer-by," shake the dust from his feet and return again to his Father's house where there are many aspects of perfection—and from which, in actuality, he has never wandered.

The Heart doesn't speak of misery; it tells of *perfection*.

The Heart tells us all is well. The Quiet Place says, "Tranquillity is the *real* nature of our Being!" The Still Small Voice whispers, "It is so! It is true! God is ALL, and God is Good!"

This is a fact. It is a fact that embodies Absolute Perfection as the only presence *already—and the consequent end of every seeming ill in one's experience!*

I have been admonished to write these facts; picture them; tell them to all! It is stated, "Write the vision, *and make it plain* upon the tables, that he may run that readeth it."

These pages are the happy and joy-filled effort.

CHAPTER II

Now

Note: The following lecture is as good a place as any to begin. It has served countless times to call home the prodigal wandering in the pigsties of worry, frustration and fear. Just as much of the work in this volume, it serves well to be read aloud.

TO DISCOVER REALITY AND UNCOVER TRANQUILLITY WE BEGIN WITH THE NOW

Now is the only "time" one is ever concerned with. Reader, consider this a moment, because here and now, a magnificent first fact of Truth begins to unfold. It has to do with *now;* the primacy of *now;* the allness of *now;* the absoluteness of *now*.

When do we see a flower? That is, what time does the seeing take place? I see the flower now, we say.

When do we see the picture of a flower in a book? Now. When do we smell the fragrance of a rose? When do we touch it, enjoy it, experience it? Now.

When does one hear a voice or a melody? When does one experience the occurrence of any event? Now!

Listen carefully: When do we *remember* the event? When do we reminisce about the event? When do we think about the past? Now; always now!

When do we dream of a future event? When do we plan and calculate concerning future activities? Now. *All* experience, all activity, all memory of the past, dream of the future, thinking and thought taking are inevitably, invariably "happening" in the now. Isn't this so?

So you see, it becomes evident to anyone who stops long enough to acknowledge it, *now* is the only time we are ever concerned with. It is always now! We cannot escape it.

Even so, what has humanity done to *now*? What has man done to this ubiquitous, all-inclusive, ever-present *now*? He has made it the most infinitesimal part of a great time system. He has sandwiched it between a past that stretches infinitely in one direction, and a future that extends forever in the other. He has relegated it to the merest razor's edge on a sliding scale *between* a past and a future. Is this not so? To humanity, *now*—*this* very moment of Awareness—is so fleeting, so ephemeral and transitory, that one cannot find it on the very device used to measure it. Try to point to *now* on your watch and it is instantly past, a memory.

Ah, but when do we recall the memory? *Now*. When do we see the watch? *Now*. When does one speculate about the fleeting nature of humanity's time? Now. When does one awaken to the fact that he is never concerned with a past or a future except right *now*? *Now!* When does one experience? Now. So, reader, *when do you expect to discover Reality?* When do you expect to experience a "healing" or a "demonstration"? When do you expect to experience completeness and happiness? *Now!*

THINKING ACTS LIKE A VEIL

Look at a flower. We see it now. We behold its form now. We are *aware* of the flower, right here, right now; but suppose we think about something else while looking at the flower. Think about that big bill that is past due and worry a little. What seems to happen to the awareness of the flower? We are not as aware of it as before, are we? We are looking at it with eyes that hardly see. It seems fuzzy, hardly noticed, but the same rose is there; the same beauty, the same form, the same grace and magnificent delicacy is right before us to be beheld and enjoyed, but we hardly see it. We are too busy worrying about the bill. We are too busy *thinking.*

The bill is not now. All that is now is the awareness of the rose. The *rose* in all its loveliness is now. The bill is nothing more than a memory that is not in this now-awareness *unless we choose to put it there.*

We see that *thinking* is like a film spread over the eyes; like a mist that covers the whole face of the land; like a veil; like looking at the flower—and everything else—through a glass darkly.

NOW IS ALWAYS ALL RIGHT!

We view the rose again. It is here, within Awareness which is aware *now.* The time of Awareness is always *now.* Right *now,* Awareness includes a rose. Look at it closely. See it with rapt and undivided attention. Behold with enthusiasm! This is beauty *here and now!* While so aware, can we be aware of worry, fear or grief in the same *now?* Are we? Absolutely not! The "return" to "now" is an automatic departure from the not-now, past and future.

As we shall point out in the coming pages, *now is always all right!* It is filled with beauty, grace and magnificence, containing neither sight, sound nor sensation that is not absolutely harmless and altogether perfect. You shall very soon see and understand—even before you finish this volume—*now* is filled with peace, serenity, sassy and sparkling happiness. It is filled to running over with everything one thinks he needs.

So, as we turn from the memory of the past and dreams of the future—as we turn from thinking—we are neither ignoring Reality (as the world contends) nor burying our heads in the sand to escape the "press of circumstances." Contariwise, we find ourselves returning to the perfection at hand, to discover anew that *now* is all that is real and all we ever need be concerned with!

Here "troubles" are not ignored, nor is a home or business neglected. Here we see with the clarity with which the rose is seen when we are not weighted down with fear and consternation. Here we see things as they *are,* and accordingly, *know better what to do.*

Have you heard these words?: "Behold, *now! Now* is the time. *Now* is the day of salvation. *Now* I am with you always. The kingdom is here and *now.* You can tell the signs in the sky but you do not know to test this *now. Now* are we the sons of God. Now! *Now!* Here and *now!* I will never leave you nor forsake you."

Reader, *this* now, here and now, is a basic fact of Isness, God, Reality. There is no need to be over-concerned with a past or future when the transcendent NOW exists to enjoy and be.

"BUT WHAT IF . . . ?"

Those who have just begun to hear about and ponder the transcendent nature of *now* are ever anxious to create hypothetical situations and present them to us in the gravest tones to see how "this new way of looking at things" will take care of it. "But, what if such and so . . . ?" they ask, picturing something they think most awful. "Suppose you should see this or that horrible mess, what would you do *then?*" they ask, to see how we will rationalize or *explain away* a situation that is not even a part of this *now* in the first place—except as a harmless dream!

Over-concern with the not-now is a portion of the farcical foolishness that has us so in the habit of overlooking the beauty, wonder and perfection of the moment. Jesus admonished those who questioned Him along these lines to "look on the living One (the now-awareness) as long as you live . . ." He likened their concern about the not-now to a corpse.

Reader, before I found Tranquillity, I had to concede *honestly* that I was ever concerned with the *present* now-awareness, alone and only. I had to see that all speculation about a not-now was a silly waste, tending to hide the beauty of the moment. It is the business of dreaming, wondering and worrying, so to speak, that appears to present a confused *now* in need of correction. *To stick to the now is to find it perfect, without need of correction—and containing nothing to fear!*

When these hypothetical situations are tossed into my lap, I can only ask where is any of it happening in this here-and-now? To those who persist in struggling with the not-now, I say again as it was said before, "You have dismissed the living One-Now that is before you and have spoken about a corpse." (Thomas, Log. 52.)

CHAPTER III

At the Beginning Is Awareness

It is foolish beyond measure to stand buffeted and blown by the world's vicissitudes when an undisturbable, unshakable Tranquillity is as close as breathing.

There is a means by which one comes to make a practical, concrete discovery of this Tranquillity for himself. He can lay hold on this Truth and take it unto himself—without struggle and without traveling the long road of intellectuality.

The following pages are all about this immediately available Tranquillity. There is no educational, theological or metaphysical route to its doorstep. If there were, we would be the first to agree with the organizational dictum that states there are no short cuts to Truth. Indeed, there are no short cuts to the *intellect's* wisdom! It struggles for every miserable morsel it gets—and with all of its getting, ends with a straw dog. Certainly there is no short cut to the Tranquillity about which we write. It is *already* here and now, the only fact of existence. Consequently, there is no *path* to it. As the prince was told concerning the kingdom of his heritage, *"There is no way there, but to be there!"*

The old idea that we journey from ignorance to enlightenment is the cornerstone which the builders have accepted and use to create their silly systems and imperious institutions. Peace and Perfection, *already at hand,* is the stone they have rejected.

At the Beginning Is Awareness 15

QUESTION: Mr. Samuel, if it is true as you and so many others have said, that Perfection is the *only* fact of being, why is it that all of you turn right around and write books obviously intended to correct personal pictures of imperfection and ignorance? If Perfection *is* all, is it not a bit hypocritical to write something there could be no *actual* need for?

ANSWER: I asked this question of others many times, but now I know the answer. Listen softly and you will see, to write such a book as this is not a concession to the appearance of inharmony. I write simply because, at the moment, it seems to be a happy thing to do—like breathing. I have no motive. I have no intentions of trying to heal and make over a perfect universe. While I am here, it seems good to write of the Identity I have found. As appearances go, the words seem to help others discover *their* Identity.

However, whether I write or not, it is not up to me—but to the Isness being Me. I have no responsibility for the appearing process. I am in tow, so to speak, simply blooming and seeding in the summer sun. It makes no difference to the blossom whether or not it scatters its seed before Fall's frost or the wail of Winter's wind. Perfection is already perfect and Peace is already here. Whether I write a single page or not, green leaves will burst forth in the Spring and busy ants will trail along garden walls and over walkway stones, very much as usual. Clouds will still billow on hot summer afternoons and showers will refresh the air. It makes no difference, large or small, if more vain sounds have been written into print. The words I fail to find will be found by another, and when they are sounded they will say nothing that has not been said before. Words, sounded or not, written or not, the universe goes on being the universe; the earth still spins; the swallows still soar and sing, and the simple sparrows go on twittering. Any tome I might write—or read—would have no more authority *in itself* than yon sparrow's twit.

Does this sound as if I have a motive in mind? When the tree gives its leaves to the earth each Fall, does it have a purpose? Is it wrestling with itself or trying to correct its own picture of impoverished soil? No—the tree is just being a tree—and I am busy just being me.

TRANQUILLITY EXISTS BEYOND APPEARANCES

I do not go out into the world with the intention of changing it. I am not attempting to take the facts of life to people with argument or contention involved. Where the Truth is (and there is no place where it is not), all is true and perfect already, consequently, Truth has no mission. It is motiveless. Perfection has no need of healing. There is nothing you or I can do to make it more perfect. It has been said, "The world is a perfect vessel and cannot be improved. Whoever tries to alter it, spoils it; whoever tries to direct it, misleads it."

Yet, Truth can and *does* change the appearances of everything for each of us individually. To the human way of looking at things, the Truth about which we are writing appears to be the most momentous power in the Universe. To those who have found the Heart, the secret place within, this same power is understood to be the very presence of God—an ever-powerful peace and tranquillity beyond belief.

Truth is the power one is—not the power one uses.

TRANQUILLITY AND WORLD PEACE DEPEND ON THE DISCOVERY OF REALITY

QUESTION: When, where and how do we start to discover Reality? How do we begin our search for Truth, Wisdom, the Absolute?

ANSWER: This now-awareness is the starting place! We

At the Beginning Is Awareness

begin with this here-and-now consciousness of existing called Life, Awareness, Consciousness.

The consciousness reading this page is an undeniable and inescapable now-fact. We call it "Awareness" and Awareness is present for the simple, self-evident reason that we are conscious—even as we are conscious of these words.

Let us define Awareness and have our meaning carefully understood. This is not a mystical term and there is nothing difficult to understand about it. As we refer to it here, Awareness is *the simple consciousness of being*. We are speaking of the conscious awareness that smells flowers, hears sounds, sees trees, bees and dogs scratching fleas—the selfsame Awareness (awareness) reading the words on this page.

This is the Awareness, Life, Consciousness of Being that is the starting place. Here is where we begin. Where else can we? And *when* else but *now?*

AWARENESS IS BASIC

Awareness is the common denominator woven through all else that is called experience. Surely, all we know about *every*thing comes to us by way of consciousness, Awareness. Every sight we have ever seen, every sound we have ever heard—every dream, every idea, every anything from the infinitesimal to the infinite—has been noted by way of Awareness!

AWARENESS IS SINGLE

How many "Awarenesses" have we been concerned with during our lifetime? This one only. Everything, including that which we call the Awareness of mother, husband, daughter, friend, or humanity comes to us *within* (and *as*) *this* single Awareness that reads these words. *This* Awareness is the *only* Awareness we have ever known.

There seems to be a time in our spiritual development when we awaken (sometimes very suddenly) to the wonderful realization that *this* conscious Awareness, right here, right now, *really is all-inclusive!*—that no "thing," no object of perception, no idea, thought or feeling is *external! Indeed, they are everyone included within this Awareness-I-am!*

Though we may have heard these words thousands of times before, quite of a sudden, when the intellect is relaxed, the Heart-within declares their simple, inescapable *factuality*. We discover their *significance*. Just as we perceived that now is the only "time" we are ever aware, we begin to comprehend that Awareness is *single, only* and *all-inclusive*.

AWARENESS IS ALL-INCLUSIVE

Dear reader, have we ever been conscious of anything that was not included within *this* Awareness that is right here? Have we ever said "you" to "another" without addressing an object of perception that appeared within and as *this* Awareness? Have we ever seen a sight or heard a sound that did not come to us as this present consciousness?

What is the smell of a rose, the taste of a berry, the feel of a rock if it isn't the Awareness one is? Are not all the arts and sciences, the figures and events of history with all their stories, every sprig of grass, every grain of sand, every star in the heavens, *everyone* included in and as this Awareness, being "I" right here, right now? Of course!

This is a simple, though seldom perceived, fact of existence. We live alone, so to speak, as an all-inclusive Awareness of existence. Friends, relatives, trees, mountains and the throngs of humanity who keep us company are actually aspects of this Awareness we are. They are images, objects of perception,

At the Beginning Is Awareness

ideas *within* this consciousness-I-am. We are concerned with *this* single Awareness, alone and only!

A LETTER ABOUT THE SIMPLICITY OF AWARENESS

Dear David,

Awareness is not *here* and the tree *there*. The tree is seen *within* Awareness, just as all sights are. The sound of the wind is not in the tree *there*. The tree, the wind and the sound are here, within this Awareness that is aware right now. An island or a continent, whether seen with the eye, or thought of as an idea, is included within this here-and-now consciousness. So is the "sea" that surrounds the island. Abraham, Moses, Jesus, Buddha, Mohammed, the mountain, bird, tree, Mary, Bill, George Washington or Next-Door-Nelly are not images *out there*, not entities separate nor apart from us.

Do we see people and things differently when this point is understood? Not immediately. The tree looks just as it did before—so does Nelly—but we comprehend that they are not separate nor apart from the Awareness-I-am. They never have been. We perceive that they and this Awareness *are one and the same!* Indeed, they *are* the Awareness I am!

I will never forget when I first came to understand this. Picking up a pen, I wrote:

> NOW I look across the way and see a tree—that tree is ME!
> It is not separate nor apart from me—my very Self I see!
> This is MY Kingdom! My Kingdom is ME!
> All "things" have their being "in" this Awareness I be.
> Why, it truly *has* been my Father's good pleasure to give the Kingdom to me!
> (From The Melody of the Woodcutter and the King)

This is what Jesus meant when he declared:

> ... I am the ALL, the All came forth from Me and the All attained to me. Cleve a piece of wood, I am there; lift up the stone and you will find Me there.
> (E. J. Brill, *The Gospel According to Thomas*, Log. 77. c, Harper & Bro., 1959.)

David, this idea of the onlyness and all-inclusiveness of Awareness need not be strange and unfamiliar to you. Consider the screen on the television set. All the images are included within a single and all-inclusive screen. All the people and things being depicted as stories, news programs or commercials are actually shadows and images on a single screen. Everything is included *within* the screen, *as* the screen. Exactly so, each of us lives forever alone with (as) a single conscious Awareness, *within* which all things—all the sights and sounds of experience—are included. It is in this sense we state that an object of perception is not separate from the perceiving.

Inspect this idea for a time; you will find it is absolutely true—and very simple!

LETTERS TO ONE JUST BEGINNING THIS STUDY

Dear David,

We "begin" with this now-awareness, but the beginning must be a new and genuine *redetermination* of Isness. We start from scratch, but this is not being done until our previous beliefs, ideas and cherished opinions are loosed and let go. The practice of humanity, the intellectual temptation, is to carry them with us to see if our new discoveries coincide with our old ideas.

No, we let go *everything* and start again like new babes, with the first and basic fact about which there is no uncertainty—the isness of this present now-awareness. All else

At the Beginning Is Awareness

must go. Without regard or regret, without fear or consternation, we stand in a void, naked, childlike, innocent. *As* this now-awareness, empty of the ego, we open our eyes and awaken!

David replies, "This sounds as if I will lose my identity. I certainly don't want to do that. As a matter of fact, I am *searching* for identity."

Dear David,
When we begin with Awareness we find we lose nothing that is real, most certainly not the Identity. Rather, we let go the notions of an identity we have never been. We lose the unhappiness, loneliness, lack, poor health and fear inevitably associated with a misidentification called "the old man," his intellect, his cherished common sense and his high opinions of himself.

So, we shuck the old ideas and let them go, David. We bring attention back to this real and present fact of Awareness. Awareness *is* a fact; we know it; we are it; *nothing* is outside of it. Here, we discover the true Identity!

When one looks at the television and sees things on the screen, he is not tempted to believe the screen is in one place and images in another. He knows they are *one television screen*. Exactly so, awareness and the images of perception are all one *Awareness*.

WHEN WE KNOW, WE KNOW!

There are no words we can read that will convince us of the *allness* of this now-consciousness; there is no one to whom we may listen or talk who can do more than persuade us *intellectually*. We know—and we know, we know—only when we find it and feel it within the Heart.

Reader, this will happen for you much sooner than you

expect. Your "awakening" is inevitable, irresistible and certain, because the fact is—as you shall see and have been told many times—you are not sleeping to be awakened now. Despite the appearances on the world's stage, you are *already* all you could ever hope to become. You are already in the Father's house. The nearly unanimous pronouncements of classical theology and education to the contrary, your real Identity is neither sinful nor fallen; you are not a prodigal acting the profligate and wandering in the pigsties of a far country. The Identity you are *this instant* is Harmony's Now-Awareness being aware. Our heritage, effortless and divine, is to acknowledge this fact!

Right now, bring yourself from an overconcern with *things* within Awareness to Awareness *itself*. Here you will find that all bodies, all images, and everything Awareness includes, are aspects of your own Identity! Here you will find that you are happiness, completeness and joy itself.

A BIT OF ZENNESS

I saw a little boy looking at a tray of donuts in the bakery window. His eyes sparkled and his thoughts were an excitement that moved his lips to half-spoken words.

I saw an old man looking into a cake box at a gift. His eyes sparkled and his thoughts were an excitement that brought a smile to his face.

I looked into a mirror on the wall and saw a little boy and an old man watching me. They heard me wondering to myself, "How strange that I should see their images in the mirror instead of my own."

But then, it isn't strange really. The Isness being the cake and the tray of donuts is the same Isness being the little boy, the old man and the mirror on the wall. Is not the Awareness of them all, the selfsame Identity being me?

At the Beginning Is Awareness

A LETTER ABOUT READING BOOKS

Dear Mary,

With whatever I find myself reading—just as you now find yourself reading this letter—I have found it wise to be very, very wary! Why? *Because our old arrogant, egotistical nature seeks out sustaining agreement with itself and its distorted opinions.* The habitual, unregenerate intellect of us all is seldom interested in aught but shoring up its forged and fraudulent foundations. When it finds a line or a paragraph that agrees with its view of Reality, it says, "Ah hah!" and underlines the words. When it finds an idea repugnant to its already established concept (usually something that tends to demean, diminish or finish the high and mighty ego), it grunts and writes "Bosh!" in the margin. How often we are amused by these notations at a later reading!

When a book is successfully communicating, one may not be as impressed with the same words at the end as at the beginning. Insights are nearly always expanded upon *re-reading*, and very often the boshes of the first reading begin to make sense with the second.

With kindest regards,

P. S. Mary, no two artists paint the sunshine alike, but it's the same sunshine. Take the words of this book and substitute your own familiar expressions for my unfamiliar ones. It will not be long until you grow into the spirit of the new work and find yourself quite certain of its message.

FAITH

"Faith" is the world's designation for that which operates between the intellectual acceptance of Truth and the Heart's declaration that says "It is so!" The Singing Heart speaks such that we know "without mental reservation or equivocation"; then we are enabled to act from the standpoint of knowing instead of faith. The Christ-Heart's declaration lifts faith from a concern over the accuracy of philosophies, the exactness of words or the integrity of people, to the certain knowledge of Isness *itself*. The Heart is the spokesman for Isness, and this Awareness we are is the faith-full witness.

NOW IS TRANSCENDENT

Now transcends the past and the future. Why? Because *now* is the "time" of tangibility; *now* is the time of experience; *now* is when Awareness is concretely aware. No matter how awesome, magnificent or poignantly personal a memory may be, and no matter what it contains, the thought about it is taking place *now* and this makes the nowness of *now* transcendent. No matter what wild scheme we entertain, no matter how beautifully we construct a dream of the future, all the scheming and dreaming is taking place in the now, and this makes now transcendent, quite above and beyond time's past and future. Sharp, fearful dreams and the rough memories that appear to be their causes are smoothed by this transcendent *now* when we let it!

Now is the common denominator of Awareness, just as Awareness is the common denominator for all experience. The two are intertwined in such a way that they are not two at all, but an inseparable one. Because the nature of Isness is singleness rather than multiplicity, we come to equate nowness and awareness as one. *Now* is not a time-frame wherein experience happens. Awareness is the action of Deific Mind and, as such, is not at the mercy of past experiences. This now-awareness is in no way beholden to human chronology.

At the Beginning Is Awareness

Philosophy, religion and education make an effort to understand Reality, but Reality (Deity) stands in confident self-being, already knowing itself. Deity's "knowing" is forever beholding, comprehending and apprehending itself as itself. Here there is no need to learn or to understand anything; here is simple, natural, normal *being*.

Notice the fine line here: to *determine* Identity, to *seek* Self-knowledge, to *strive* for information academically, esoterically or by any other means, is to be the old man still, the misidentity making the effort to understand the identity of another he calls God.

On the other hand, to rest in the infinite Self-knowledge of Being, knowing I am forever beholding, knowing, comprehending and apprehending the Divine Self who is being this Consciousness, *is to live the Identity I am!*

This is not to say that all I am aware of is a dream; not at all. This is to be continually Self-aware. This is to joy in Spirit being all one perceives. This simple action *taken* marks the end of evaluation, the "last judgment." This is the Sabbatical Rest.

THE ILLUSTRATION OF THE CARVER

For just a moment, put yourself in the shoes of the old wood carver. Imagine walking through a forest early on a crisp Fall morning. The air is moist and still. You are alone. Occasional drops of dew fall from the trees above, plummet through the slanting sunshine and enchanting morning mist. They flash like diamonds for an instant, then patter softly into the leaves below. The only other movement is yours and the only other sound belongs to the morning. The air is exhilarating. The moment is holy.

Suddenly, unexpectedly, a deer bounds across your path, leaps a fallen log, and noisily—but ever so gracefully—disappears among the trees! Your heart pounds. You are thrilled by the suddenness and beauty of the animal's leap to anonymity; and then, the silence, more silent now, returns.

"How beautiful," you think. "How magnificent! How privileged I am to see such a scene and feel such emotion! Let me take a piece of wood and carve into it all the tenderness of the moment. Let me carve all I see and all I feel, all I am thinking and all I have thought. Let me take my knife and shape the wood so others will understand the splendor of this morning. Let me carve it with such exactness and precision that everyone who sees it will hear the bounding deer, see the soft sunlight and smell the sweet freshness of the wild earth."

I ask you: Who can tell such a story with a single piece of wood?

Where is the wood that can contain so much within it?

Where are the words that outline Truth?

Who can confine Reality to ten words—or ten million? Such is the job of those who take it upon themselves to write or read a single word and call it Absolute! Yet the simplicity of Deity is less assuming than a single letter of the alphabet.

CHAPTER IV

The Lollygog Lectures

I love the outdoors, the quiet aloneness of the Southern woodland. Here, leaves cracking underfoot are magic potions that entice the heart to sing new songs and reveal new secrets. As campers, Ruby and I and our three sons, Billy, Paul and David, have spent many hours watching nature's grand scheme unfold before us. Then, from out of this love one day, Lollygog came along!

Lollygog is a little houseboat. We think she is lovely because she lets us camp with all the comforts and conveniences of a floating home—in much higher style than the old days. Ever changing the panorama around us, she slips silently along the still shores of the lake, turning all outdoors into our front yard.

Moreover, Lollygog allows Ruby and me to take others with us for what have come to be called "The Lollygog Lectures"—mornings, afternoons and evenings spent teaching (telling) the wonders we have come to perceive; telling our secrets to those of all ages who come from far and wide to spend a day or two, *to those who want to end their search for Tranquillity.* There are few tree-lined banks or rocky cliffs along the way that haven't seen Lollygog stop there for a spell and heard the laughter of Being being lived aboard.

We keep Lollygog on a picturesque and placid lake not far from our Mountain Brook home. A comfortable motel lodge is nearby, nestled among the rolling, multicolored hills of Alabama. When our guests are not aboard Lollygog gliding in and out of the lake's quiet coves, they are enjoying the happy facilities of the lodge—making new acquaintance with old truths.

The Lollygog lectures have been magnificently rewarding for everyone involved. Many wonders have been revealed, many burdens loosed and let go. Many of the selections in this book have been taken from those talks.

The reader is reminded again that the separated selections within the chapters are not *necessarily* related, either in content or sequence. If a selection should seem difficult to comprehend, do not struggle with it but go on to the next. It is important, however, that the *gist* of each chapter be understood before proceeding to the next. With each subsequent reading there will be fewer mysteries—not only in the words of this book but in the reader's experience as well.

A LOLLYGOG LECTURE ABOUT THE HEART

There was a man much embittered by a series of personal disasters. They drove him to a virtual renunciation of everything. "What is all this business about a 'good' God being *all?*" he thought. "How can this be true when the entire world is crumbling around my feet?"

Out of this wonderment—and the answer to it—came the following short play in verse. It commences with the usual venom and vitriol of one grown tired of the ineffectual protestations of theology, but ends with the contrasting soft words of one who has come to comprehend a measure of the Deific Peace.

The Lollygog Lectures

CONVERSATION BETWEEN A MAN AND HIS CONSCIOUSNESS
(Relating the end of a "dark night" experience)

MAN (with fierce bitterness): Battered about and bitter about it,
I baited God one day. God, I said,
Would that I might feel peace again.
What must I do—or not do—
to *stop* this come and go, this ebb and flow
between serenity and sadness?
You are *here,* you say, not far away;
You are *closer,* you say, than breathing;
You are Love, *you say,* that bids me enter the Bridal
Chamber—but here I stand now, seeking a sign, *begging*
a simple sign, that points the way away from this ungodly jungle.
Here I stand with sour stomach, slashing at an
unceasing scene called *experience*—a putrid picture
of poverty and war; *your* picture, God; you painted it, not I!
Why must I rail so, toil and tear so at the terror
in my intestines? Why must I rattle round like a
rat in a rotten tub?
Oh, God, I am tired of a world that so seems to separate
me and mine from a perfection I can only *sense* is
present—and only *suspect* is real.
Listen to my plea, God.
Give me peace.
Give me release from this seeming situation that
obliterates seeing Thee as Thou art!
For Christ's very sake, I would be Thy messenger!
I would be your witness faithful!
I would herald the kingdom—if Thou would but *burst through*
this miserable maze of mind
and make me more apparently Thine!

Then spake God:

GOD: Now see here! I have nothing to do with your mental mist
of misinterpretation. Your misery is a maze of your
own making.

MAN: Then why do you *ignore* my mist and my misery?

GOD: The Light that is Me is Light,
wherein no darkness dwells; wherein no judgment of evil
exists to enter and work a lie.
Principle does not peer at problems on *your* printed page.
How then am I to dispel your "two and two are five"
when no such illusion is?

MAN: But "two and two are five" is an evil injustice to be
seen corrected!

GOD: Principle is—simply is. It exists unencumbered by and
unbeholden to your *evaluation* of symbols that merely
show it forth. It is *your* judgment that call the shadows
good or bad, not Mine! Who ends your judgments? You or I?

MAN (Slowly and with awakening wonder): Then this that
I call experience
either has nothing to do with Isness
or this adventure is not miserable after all, but is
unjudged Being, wholly good, wholly God, Holy Light *itself!*

At this moment, God—at least for a moment—
I sense the futility of fighting a fable—
the foolishness of trying to perfect a fancied fairy tale
that all the time is perfect.

God is Love, they say—well,
God *is* Love—
and Love lingers like a blossom that simply blooms
and gives its beauty without regard or regret

for who looks at it and smiles—
or who blunders by in blindness,
staring only at the earth,
blaming it for a bleakness that isn't even bleak.
Now I see—
Love lets me look and let.
Love lets me see the Love I be, and sing—
or pass it by, and cry in agony—dream inflicted.

THE DIVINE DISCONTENT

For all of us there comes a time when we finally get down to brass tacks, living and *being* the Spiritual Life. Usually, adversity of some sort, health, business, grief, loneliness or boredom, drives us to this decision. Oftentimes it is fear of one kind or another. Perhaps we simply yield to the prodding of others, or to the urge of an intangible feeling within—the "divine discontent"; but whatever the reasons for our action, one fact is certain: the decision that brings it about is very personal. It is an alone experience that takes place *within*. You know this is a fact.

All have discovered that, from the moment we *act* on the decision to discover Reality, we begin to find it. The moment we sincerely begin a determination of the Absolute, it continues of its own accord until Reality is disclosed! The acted-upon decision to determine fact from fiction is somewhat like pushing a canoe into a river where it is quickly caught up in the silent and effortless flow to a happy and Infinite awakening. It is like putting seed in fertile ground.

"Mr. Samuel, be specific! Exactly *what* action is required? Church activity? Prayer? Healing? Self-immolation?"

Here is the answer: our first action is the effortless *turning within* to the Self to *listen* to the Heart. This is it. This is all!

Is this a disappointing oversimplification? Did your erudite nature expect a profound revelation, a metaphysical pronouncement of reason and logic to shake the intellect? Do you, like so many, expect Reality to come forth only from blinding flashes of Light and ecstatic Illumination?

Here is the unadorned Truth, stripped of the ego's covering of abstruseness and intellectualism. Truth is *simple*. It is *always* simple. The Truth is easy and uncomplicated. It is tender and effortlessly available. Its location is not limited to the great libraries, nor to universities, temples and cathedrals. Truth, and the *honest* statements about it, are simplicity itself. It is found within the heart, within the Self, here and now.

For years we have gone outside to teachers, leaders, and holy books, when the entire universe of Truth has been within us all the while. Its confirmation is found nowhere else. Where? Within the Heart! Here! Now!

REALITY IS EASILY COMPREHENDED

Inevitably, intellectual mankind complicates everything and makes a mystery of truth. In intellectual circles the idea is prevalent that Reality is relative at best and can never really be known; that all we can do is get closer to it—and that, say the ministers, philosophers, theologians and educators, takes years of study, prayer, self-immolation, self-denial, suffering, toil and perhaps a death or two thrown in for good measure. Malarky!

Reality is real, not relative, and it can be discovered without labor! Instead of effort, it is the tenderest labor of love; it is happiness beyond belief; it is reward that hasn't even been dreamt of!

> *Prove me now herewith, saith the Lord of hosts, if I will not open you the windows of heaven, and pour you out a blessing, that there shall not be room enough to receive it.*

For this proof, the first action is simply, quietly to turn within to one's Self, there to listen to the Heart, where Truth is and where the answers are!

THE ANSWER IS *HERE*

One's own Heart is *here,* consequently the Truth is *here.* It is comforting to desist from the rat race for a moment and acknowledge that Truth is *at hand.* Truth is the solution to all that seems untrue, hence unreal. How wonderful to realize, no matter *what* the apparent problem, that one is never any farther from the Happiness, Peace and Tranquillity he may think he needs than *himself.* "Himself" is right here, this very *now,* closer than breathing.

> *My sanctuary shall be in the midst of them forevermore;*
> *Neither shall they say, Lo here! or, lo there! for, behold, the kingdom of God is within you.*

HOW DO WE KNOW WHOM TO BELIEVE?

Having been counseled by an entire series of "enlightened ones," each proclaiming his way the only way, a seeker of old threw up his arms in despair and asked:

How do I know whom to listen to or whom to follow?
Which is the Way to go?
Which way is the way to walk?
One says this, another that—then a third and a fourth
  and a fifth.

> *They dispute even amongst themselves and point out their own inaccuracies.*
> *Whom must I follow now, Father? Tell me! Tell me directly! Tell me here in my heart.*

The Heart distinguishes the wheat from the weeds. The Heart recognizes honesty and sincerity—for which words are but symbols, sounds, images on a piece of paper. Once I relished the words spelling out methods and procedures for going from imperfection to perfection, but now the words I choose to read *first* are those that proclaim perfection as the already-fact of existence. Methods that have us work to overcome "error" by contending with it inevitably put us in a position that measures progress by our ability to manipulate and "demonstrate." Manipulative mastership serves no permanent purpose but to keep the basic misjudgment of an overcoming, struggling, self-righteous personality more firmly dream-entrenched in one's daily experience.

"I HAVE GIVEN THEE A WISE AND UNDERSTANDING HEART"

> *I will put my law in their inward parts and write it in their hearts . . .*

Those who have found the Truth have first learned to listen to the Heart, to the "still small voice," to the Holy of Holies within consciousness. The Heart is the place of knowing. External sights and sounds serve only to point a finger in one direction or another. The Heart is the closet Jesus spoke of. Here is where we turn again and again. Here is the quiet refuge, the Secret Place we go, not only when the trials seem too great to bear, or to prevent them from becoming greater, but in joyful moments also.

Those of us who listen to the Heart learn the Truth *directly,* for we

> ... *shall hear a word behind thee, saying, This is the way, walk ye in it, when ye turn to the right hand and when ye turn to the left.*

We declare as another once did,

> *Come, my people, enter thou into thy chambers and shut thy doors about thee; hide thyself as it were for a little moment, until the indignation be overpast.*

—until the trials and tribulations vanish, illusions every one!

Reader, you know where the Heart is, so "knock and it shall be opened unto you!" When shall we do this? *Now! Now* is all we are ever concerned with, and *now*—this now-awareness being I—is perfect!

CHAPTER V

Vignettes of the Within

HAPPINESS IS HERE

No matter what the appearance, there is perfection, tranquillity, harmony and happiness wherever one is, wherever he goes, whatever he is doing or not doing. Perfection is no more present in one spot than another. Tranquillity does not reside more in one place than another. One does not have to seek out the quiet places—mountain trails, meadows and mill ponds—to find the "peace that passeth understanding."

While the world rushes to other places for recreation, we have a place right where we are—a secret refuge wherein we find the end of sorrow and tribulation, where there is rest from every effort. Where is this wonderous place? Within the Self—within—within. What is it called? The Heart, the Shekinah, the Holy of Holies, the Bridal Chamber, the Identity-I-am. Why has it taken us so long to find it? For walking to and fro in the land, looking for happiness out there; for going other places for better viewing.

All the while, peace has been closer than breathing, closer than fingers and toes, here and now within us, not out there at all. All the while, Peace has been the Identity we are.

THE SECRET PLACE

Much has been written about the secret place within. Here is where one goes when something seems wrong in his affairs—because nothing ever appears wrong until this secret Identity has been forgotten, leaving us to wander in a dream world of pseudo-values. When something appears awry in our daily experience, we need only return to the within—to the rightful Identity—to experience perfect comfort and find peace. This Tranquillity is our veritable Identity.

Everything we could ever wish to know is, here and now, included within Identity. The pure Heart finds it. "Secrets" are confirmed in no other place.

Hasn't this always been the case? Even the student who is learning the multiplication tables only seems to be going outside to books and teachers. When the tables are *learned*, it is an inside job, a very personal and intimate action *within*. When this happens, the Heart knows and says, "Now I understand."

SECRETS

The secrets of Life, Reality, Truth and Love—the pearls of great price—are not bits of information that can be passed from one to another. Secrets come from the inside out, never from the outside in. Their meanings are never confirmed outside the immaculate confines of the Heart. No matter how well one defines a secret and paints a picture of it in striking words, the actual import—the honest meaning—comes from the Self alone. A secret for one is gibberish to another until a pure and simple Heart responds to declare, "It is true! It is so! Now I understand! Now I know!"

ABOUT BOOKS

Books, leaders, teachers and all else are objects of perception within conscious Awareness. There is not one particle of value, power or importance in *them*. The value is always the Single Selfhood, the Heart, doing the seeing and listening. The value is the Isness being the Awareness that *includes* them.

QUESTION: Does this mean we are not to enjoy the books of others or that we cannot be inspired by personal visits to those who steadfastly live their rightful Identity?

ANSWER: Not at all. It is wonderful to enjoy the conversation of one who has manifestly discovered the Self (the Heart says who is honest in this regard); yet, we come to see and understand that those we call "enlightened" are not outside *this* single Awareness-being-I; they are not another beside this very consciousness of Being the reader is!

PEARLS OF GREAT PRICE

More often than not, the gems of the Heart are diametrically opposed to the world's proud common sense. Mankind argues loudly about matters it does not understand. Man is ruthless with whatever points out the nothingness of his personal ego. Those still satisfied with their misidentification as great judges of Life are not bubbling over at the prospect of losing their dearest possession, the intellect. Truth is the absolute destruction of all that goes to make up the personal belief and dream of a world filled with intelligent, mind possessing mortals. It marks the end of the old nature, "man with breath in his nostrils," the "old man" to be put off.

The belief of a separate personality capable of possessing this Now-Awareness is exploded and ended in the Heart. Here

Vignettes of the Within

in the Heart one finds Truth, the Eternal Flame, the all-consuming fire destined to overcome the world of fictitious separateness.

First, mankind looked for Truth to come as something from out the sky in the future. Then, it was determined to be from *within* that it would be found, but the "within" was thought to be within a personal mind, contained and controlled by man. Man has been looking for Truth within his intellect, within his reasoning and calculating mind; but no Wisdom, no Truth, no Reality will ever come from the thinking, reasoning, planning, evaluating, judging, opinion-holding *intellect*. It comes forth from the Self-Identity.

How close is the Christ-Truth? Can anything be closer than the Self you are? "The place whereon thou standest is Holy Ground!" Right now! Already! Now is all we are faced with!

CHAPTER VI

Selections from a Lollygog Lecture About the Christ and the "Virgin Birth"

THERE IS NO MYSTERY IN CHRIST!

If one hundred theologians were asked to define Christ, they would likely give a thousand different answers. Why are there so many opinions? Because theology echoes the myriad distortions that spring from the intellect.

Once the intellect has been subdued sufficiently to allow the Heart to be heard, we begin to get the answers; and the Heart's messages are soothing and uncomplicated, nothing like the bedevilling bamboozlement of a befuddling intellect!

So, how does the Heart interpret the Christ? As simple truth! As gentle, unpretentious *truth*. You can spell this word with a capital or not—it is the same truth which is the Christ! The Heart reveals that "Truth" and "Christ" are identical—meaning "the same one."

The dictionary defines truth as "fact; that which is; conformity to reality." "I *am* the truth," said Jesus Himself. "Identity-I (and not the possessor of it) am the Truth, the fact of Reality." *Identity* is the Christ-Truth itself.

This is much too simple and unsophisticated for human theology, of course. Man has a penchant for complicating the simple. He would have the Christ range from a very literal, bleeding body named Jesus of Nazareth, to a metaphysical mys-

About the Christ and the "Virgin Birth" 41

tery of transcending Light and Illumination, or both. The simplicity of "Christ" and simple, lowly, unpretentious, gentle "Truth" *as synonomous terms* is too naive a concept for intellectual churchdom. Erudition is steeped in the esoteric, ego-building disciplines of its man-hewn theological "mysteries."

The world church makes Truth one thing and Christ another; but the fact is, simple Truth (truth) itself is everything meant by the term. The Christ proclaims: "I am the Truth. I, Truth, am come to take away the untruths of the world. Behold, I am with you always. I will never leave you nor forsake you." Indeed, the Christ-Truth is here—not far off, not something we must struggle up a long, rugged mountain to reach. Let us understand this here and now!

If we can comprehend *and admit* that the alphabet is *here* or that the principle of arithmetic is *here,* that the harmonious principle of music is *here,* or that Life, this Now-Awareness-I-Am, is *here*—then we can surely rest, stop fighting it and admit, concede, surrender to the fact that the simple truth—the Christ-Truth—concerning our rightful Identity is right here, right now, present!

Are you willing to make this simple admission? Or will you deny it? The only "second coming" Truth awaits is our individual acknowledgment of its presence *as our very own Identity!*

The mathematical fact that two plus two is four is the Christ-Truth "come to heal" the hellish, devilish notion that two plus two is *not* four—which, as any student will tell you, is pure "sin" on an examination paper. The student laboring over a page of problems in which a mistake appears, uncovers and corrects that mistake *with the simple truth* of the problem. Christ is the tender within-ness that says, "This is correct; this is right; this is so; this is how it is!"

Exactly as Jesus said, the truth does not come to destroy

Reality's world of images, but to fulfill it; to point it out; to edify and clarify. Consequently, truth *appears* to destroy the impostor-ego and his misevaluations of Deity's Universe. (But who is *that* one? No one! No thing!)

The truth of everything—even the small and inconsequential—is the Christ! It is this simple! The human mystery is gone out of it.

THE CHRIST IS HERE

Surely, the truth that is "with us always" and "withholds himself from no man" is not so arcane and difficult that only the Illumined Elect are "saved," as mysticism teaches! Surely, the truth that says "Come unto me *all* who are weary" doesn't withhold itself from all but those who have suffered long years of self-immolation or have died as intellectual churchdom has taught from its conception! The truth withholds itself from naught! It is not out there somewhere else, but *here,* ready and available to separate fact from fiction; *present* to awaken mankind from his prodigal-like peregrinations around his silly misjudgments of Identity. The Christ is here *this instant* to show us all truth.

ILLUMINATION AND ENLIGHTENMENT

QUESTION: Where is the truth first discovered?
ANSWER: Within oneself alone.

When one turns within himself to this secret place and listens to the Heart, something is soon felt as a warmth and excitement, as a joyful Presence. This simple stirring-within is the Christ-experience. It has been called "Enlightenment" and "illumination." But, how many times this simple, tender stir-

About the Christ and the "Virgin Birth"

ring of the Heart has been overlooked, unheeded, unheralded, unappreciated, even denied, because Truth was believed to be a blinding road-to-Damascus illumination.

It is no such thing. "I come when thou least expect, as a thief in the night," the Christ declares. "Behold, I stand at the door. Knock and it shall be opened unto you. I come quickly. I will never leave you nor forsake you. I am with you always. Awake thou that sleepest and arise from the dead, Christ shall give thee light."

LIGHT

Inevitably, the truth puts a new light on everything because Truth and Light are the same Christ. The truth of anything is the light that dispels the darkness (ignorance) concerning it.

"I *am* the light," says the Christ-truth. Furthermore, "I am the light that lighteth every man that cometh into the world." Does this sound as if the Christ were something far removed, nebulous and unattainable? Or that we must *await* its first or second coming?

THE IMMACULATE CONCEPTION AND VIRGIN BIRTH

At the time of this writing, the theological concepts of the "Immaculate Conception" and "virgin birth" are under growing attack by those who can no longer stomach the faltering explanations of churchdom. The pity is that intellectuality believes nothing less than intellectual answers, and this is what the churches are attempting to give; the blind leading the blind, so to speak, unable to explain something they cannot understand. How lucid and understandable are the immaculate conception and virgin birth *in the light of the Christ as truth!*

The Christ-truth is perceived *within*—a personal and intimate experience; an event untouched, untainted by anything out there. When one feels the truth stirring within himself, the experience is pristine, pure and unblemished. It is immaculate. *This intimate and solitary singing of the Heart is the fabled immaculate conception; the virgin birth of the Christ; the coming of Truth that ultimately "waxes strong," "tells us all things" and "overcomes the world" of personal misperception and illusion!*

This feeling-within is the "babe wrapped in swaddling clothes." The manger, the secret place, the Holy of Holies, the Bridal Chamber wherein nothing enters that "maketh a lie" is the Heart!

The time has come to let go the theological history of Jesus of Nazareth, historical Christ. Now is the time to be concerned with the *present* Christ. It is the *same* Christ, the one and only Truth ever destined to be known. More than that, *this is the Christ-truth we be.* We are free to feel its warmth and excitement welling up within us here and now! The very moment one turns to the Heart within, *acknowledging Deific Truth itself to be the Christ,* one has done all that is necessary to do!

"I come quickly," says the Comforter. Sooner or later, in contemplation or meditation, while reading, writing or working; maybe while doing the dishes or having a romp with the children; or while looking at the beauty of a little flower or into the vastness of the night; mayhaps *even as you read these words*—sooner than you expect, the Heart will speak with a feeling of warmth and well being, with a soothing, tender touch of love! You feel a sense of soft excitement, wonderment and awe. *THIS is the immaculate conception, dear reader! THIS is the one "not born of woman"! This is the Christ! This is the Truth!* Acknowledge it! Adore it! Worship it! It will change your experience completely. It has come to declare Reality, to set everything aright and to show forth the wonders of the Infinite Being you are. Joy in it! This is the alone Identity-I-Am!

CHAPTER VII

About Religion and Science

THE MANY PATHS OF RELIGION

Most of us begin an investigation and study of Reality because we are dissatisfied with the half-truths we hear pouring out of the world's institutions, or because we fail to understand the Truth they may be talking about. Something within drives us on if we are sincere, and we progress through the sundry phases of one or more conventional denominations, usually religious, ever searching and finding. Those who persevere may move into (and through) some of the stages of mysticism. This may be a *personal* philosophy, but it is usually the accumulated thinking of an organized body held together by the particular literature of an enlightened leader.

Throughout this literary evolution (how else can we speak of it?) there is an accompanying experience appearing as "states and stages," as levels, each one, in its own view, more arcane, more profound and more absolute than all others. At the same time, however, each is more complex and more difficult to understand. Finally, despite the bewitching, ego-building satisfaction we enjoy from a rare knowledge of the "Absolute" (unknown by those unfortunate unenlightened, of course!), the glaring *absence of Tranquillity* forces us to the simple admission that there is nothing permanently satisfying in these highest orders of religion, or "non-religion" as some are termed. Furthermore, it becomes apparent that whatever morsels of peace we have found along the way become more ephemeral by the day. Ultimately (if not here, then "hereafter") we awaken to find the whole business is, and ever has been, *human intellectualism* carried to its fullest development—an art form even its perpetrator knows is an empty façade, a worthless misperception of Reality.

Today, a growing portion of intellectualism's burlesque resides within the *"metaphysics* of the Absolute" wherein even the use of the term God may be anathema. Within this "highest" strata of human intellectual achievement exists the growing New Theology which says "Humanity is God" at its one extreme and "The individual-I-am is God" at the other extreme—both as far from the *complete* truth as a personal idea can get. This is the sundering dualism already manifesting itself as a human society divided and at loggerheads, either proclaiming or disclaiming the actuality of God—while the god either side speaks of is not God at all, but its own misinterpretation.

Most of us appear to reach one or the other of these pompous extremes (wittingly or unwittingly) only to discover the emptiness of it all in the agony of the effort and the bitter vomit of the attempt. In retrospect, however, we discover that everything has happened as it should have happened and all has been as it should have been; because, out of that dark agony of intellectualism (if not before) comes the Christ-birth of the Truth that leads us to the *actual* surrender of that devilish intellect! And out of this surrender comes *Tranquillity,* fabled Peace beyond belief! Still remaining on the new scene, however, is this simple, childlike Awareness-being-us, very busy being aware. Personal judgments and opinions have vanished; the significance of religion and all other intellectualism is seen in perspective, and God, as God is, appears, leaving neither sight, sound, nor feeling as anathema.

THE FAILURE OF RELIGION

Religious intellectualism is bound to fail us and thereby appear to fail the world. It does not touch the hem of Reality.

About Religion and Science   47

Even though most of us go through its processes to see for ourselves, we ultimately discover that no metaphysical ladder reaches the knowledge of Truth; that systems intended to help the climber, teach the climber, heal the climber, or even to help the climber climb out of himself, are all absurd. The only legitimate "system" is one that disavows the possibility of a *real* climber at all, one that proclaims the already-perfection of Isness to be the only fact, *right now*. Even *that* is meaningful only if the evidence of this fact is actually beheld, understood and experienced, here and now, without ceasing! The totality of Reality—the allness of Isness—does not allow the presence of an unreal ("seeming") is-notness, a separate phantom-ego who must struggle to be bound back to a perfect Only.

But these are just so many words, even to the most sincere, until the time we are willing, or forced, to *make the surrender* of the ego. The simple ones who love Reality enough to do it, quickly find themselves in the presence of landscape, flower, child, teacher, book, morning sun, birdsong, stillness or turmoil proclaiming in clear and unmistakable terms the whys and wherefores of ISNESS as ALL—of ISNESS being the wonder of the Awareness-reading-this!

SELF-RIGHTEOUSNESS

Arrogant intellectualism reaches its peak with the highest states of mysticism and metaphysics. During the time one's status is determined by his works, by his imagined ability to heal or correct the human picture—such metaphysical mastership breeds the deadliest of all personal misidentifications, the opinionated self-righteous. These high priests and practitioners of scholasticism's full bloom are blindest to the tender simplicity and all-inclusiveness of Reality.

Ah, but with the breakaway from the ego, with the *surrender* of the pompous personality (*ours*, not the other fellow's), the bonds of intellectualism begin effortlessly to fall away, to fade away like the morning mist along the river bank. The educated mess of the pseudo-personal mind is left behind, let go, lost. *Then* commences the inspirational instruction of the Heart. This still small voice teaches us directly and honestly. It tells a simple story, a tender story, a warm and gentle story of present health and sufficiency. It tells of unebbing strength and power; of happiness here and now; of tranquillity, peace and deathless life.

QUESTIONS AND ANSWERS

QUESTION: Mr. Samuel, if these ideas about Identity are so revolutionary and capable of doing so many magnificent things for us as you say, why haven't they been recognized by the sciences and by the churches whose business it is to explore such ideas?

ANSWER: The fact is, they *are* being discovered and explored in the fields of science and religion, and many changes are being wrought within the appearances of these institutions. (But so what? Our mission is not to make changes in the world's institutions. Our's is to be what we be, then see what this allows us to see concerning "institutions" or anything else that comes to be seen.)

QUESTION: But why is the scientific world so slow to accept this Identity as Awareness?

ANSWER: Suppose one who is *not* an astronomer happens to discover a new principle of astronomy with which he is able to solve many enigmas, and thereby do wonderous things within his own view of the heavens. Then suppose he sets out to tell the world so it may solve these problems, too. Who does the world listen to in astronomical matters—astronomers or non-astronomers? Astronomers, of course. But how likely are the astronomers to listen to someone unknown in their science and unschooled in their way? There is only the least likelihood

About Religion and Science 49

that they will pay heed to a stranger. The stranger, therefore, must first be *discovered,* happily undisturbed by the enigmas disturbing others. He must be *found* plotting an effortless course through the ponderous mazes so bewildering to those following the programs of officialdom. In short, the stranger must make his mark by *living* his discovery.

Ah, but then—when finally the astronomers come to the stranger to hear what he has to say, how quickly do they comprehend and accept his message? Not until they check every idea against the great mass of detail they already cherish, detail that stands as the time-honored *foundation* of the science that gives them their positions of judgmental authority. Their vast erudition stands in the way—a veritable wall against which every new idea is tested!

Now, when an idea happens to come along that tears at the very *foundation* of the *institution,* there is an understandable reluctance to accept it, most especially by those who have grown to love their institutional positions of judgmental authority or by those who place confidence in those authorities. So, considering humanity's trust in what happens to be a slow-moving and reluctant institution, is it any wonder the educational foundations and the world at large are so slow to accept the Isness they fear will put them both out of business? One day our over-honored institutions will stop passing out crumbs and get down to the business of illustrating meat.

Jesus used a graphic illustration in this regard. Human officialdom, said he, is "like a dog in the stable; it neither eats the oats nor lets the oxen eat."

ABOUT GOD AND SCIENCE

I

QUESTION: Is this philosophy a form of Pantheism?
ANSWER: No. We do not say that the universe is God. We

say that the universe is the total of Deific qualities and attributes perceived within Deity's Self-knowing. Deity is infinitely more than the universe and the Awareness that perceives it.

Now understand this: The Identity about which this book speaks is no philosophy. *Awareness,* this Identity-being-us, is not a philosophy. I suppose an intellectual tag on our words *about* Awareness might be called such, and the *means* by which we awaken to the actual Identity and relinquish the pseudo-identity could be construed as a "philosophic system"; but Identity, this Amness-I-am, this consciousness-we-are, is not a philosophy. It is a fact!

II

There was a time when philosophers called *nature* God. It seemed to them as if all the power of man was as nothing in the face of the eternal seasons, the great cycles and tides. Now man stands on the earth's surface willing and able to change the seasons to suit himself. He has the capacity to alter the course of the earth around the sun. He can make the earth wobble on its axis if he chooses, and alter the length of its days and nights. In the face of humanity's burgeoning technology, it is evident that nature is no longer inviolate. Nature, therefore, is not Isness, not unchanging, unalterable Reality. The pantheist is forced to forsake his view—or have a non-absolute Absolute.

III

The astronomer searching for clues about the origin of the universe looks ever further back in time by looking farther into space. He once reasoned that if he could see far enough, he would see the creation of the universe actually taking place.

Then it was discovered that the most remote galaxies are

rushing away from his viewing telescopes at velocities approaching the speed of light; so it has been concluded, apparently, that the view of the "beginning" of the universe is traveling away from the earth at the speed of light, hence will never be humanly perceived, even by the most powerful instruments.

Inevitably, we find every human footstep *toward* an already present Absolute uncovers ten more steps for the human being to take.

IV

Technology doesn't disprove the existence of God. It merely demands that false gods be forsaken.

Over and above the natural order of being, beyond the mundane, exists Existence, Isness, the Godhead. Advancing technology, spiraling human power and ability, are unable to touch the fount of Being. Rather, Isness is the warp and woof of technology—if technology is anything at all.

V

The appearance of escalating human capability (positive and negative, constructive and destructive) is the inevitable culmination of the human drive to *acquire* Reality, God; it is the attempt to *reach* Perfection and conquer the limitations of humanhood.

The greater our concern with this struggle, the less disposed we are to discover and acknowledge the Fact of the Godhead—*already* here and now.

CHAPTER VIII

A Discussion of the "Prerequisites" to a Knowledge of Truth

QUESTION: Mr. Samuel, why do some people understand the Truth so much more rapidly than I do?

ANSWER: First, let me say, our concern is not with the appearances of *others* understanding or not understanding; we are ever concerned with *this* Now-Awareness-being-I, *right here*—and this, you have seen, *includes* others within it.

Among those who write me or come seeking Reality and its Peace, it appears that I "get through" most quickly (1) to those who are willing to concede the allness of Isness; (2) to those who have come to see that "Awareness" and "Life" are the same, and will *concede* that this Awareness is ALONE, TOTAL and ALL to each of us; and (3) finally to those who possess an eager willingness to *let go the misidentification* once it has been pin-pointed and exposed. These, it seems, are the simple prerequisites to a speedy discovery of the real Identity and the practical Peace it is.

Many who come to us for "healings" or to find Tranquillity are not aware of the onlyness of Isness, the totality of God; nor are they sure that such is even the truth. Many are not aware that Awareness is all-inclusive, or that they may be attempting to act the role of an impossible identity. Consequently, we discuss these things at length. If I were to describe those who most quickly find the truth they are looking for, I would say they are the ones who are most willing to accept these gentle conditions. Really, more than willingness is involved; positive

"Prerequisites" to a Knowledge of Truth 53

action to end the activities of the old man is demanded. Our primary class instruction is to show *how* this is done . . . and to do it.

Now, as you see, these so-called "basics" require no preconditions of their own, no particular mental alertness and no great human education. As a matter of fact, scholarship and erudition have very little to do with the Truth, and lest we are wary they are more detriment than help.

Determination of the "real" Identity involves a process completely different from the usual time-honored processes of scholarship. The world's procedure is to heap facts upon facts. The student is forever adding to a personal storehouse of information. Usually, the more facts he owns, the greater his battle with the ego. Occasionally a new idea comes along that replaces one of his old concepts, but he must take the new idea first and have it firmly in his grip before he lets go the old. Nothing but an *academic* knowledge of the new identity is acquired from these standard processes of education.

Before a tangible, practical knowledge of the new Self is "received," we find it an absolute prerequisite to *let go the misidentification!* The Bible speaks of this in such metaphors as, to empty the container first, to not put new wine into old bottles, or sew new patches onto old garments. Contrary to the ego's many written opinions about it, we find we must let go and stop acting the misidentification *entirely,* before—before—we can consciously know, be, and act the One-I-am.

Well (and this brings us to the crux of religion's failure), we cannot do this until we know exactly what the old identity is, or professes to be; until we know the misidentity's role we are playing right here where the "seeming" is—where there appears to be one less than perfect still contending and still searching for the truth.

This is the area so miserably slighted (or overlooked) by education in general, religion and metaphysics in particular. They would have us end the old man's "sins," but while they go to great lengths to discuss the whys and wherefores of those sins, they never tell us exactly who or what the misidentification is that is doing all the sinning. In its most intellectual presentations, metaphysics merely states the impossibility of an *actual* "fallen" state; but, alas, it still leaves us attempting to play the part of a self-righteous pseudo-identity healing a personal view of the universe, calling everything seen "via the senses" a dream "that isn't going on in truth," and it leaves us still having to see the nothingness of that dream. Well—there is no peace in this. As Jesus related in His parable, every agony swept from the old identity brings seven more in its place.

We say again that as appearances go, many are not aware there is a "real" Identity. Many more are unaware of an identity to "put off." Still others, a particularly agonized lot, speak honestly of the impossibility of that misidentification ("because God is *all* and evil is nonexistent") while they unwittingly keep playing the role of that impossibility, not knowing what they deny. Then they ask why their ills hang on so and wonder about their continuing world at war!

These are the ones who, for a time, call the entire human experience a dream; but their declaration does not end their contention with that dream, nor their attempt to heal it. These are the ones Jesus spoke of who are last to discover the here-and-now-Tranquillity. These are the "first who become last," while the simple, the unpretentious and the childlike are the "last who become first."

Reader, this is not to point a finger at the first or the last, at the most evolved or the least evolved. *We all appear to travel all of these silly paths in what comes as an expanding comprehension of Isness.* Though it seems we search out many views, Awareness itself is ever perceiving new and more inclusive vistas of Isness. Using human terms, there cannot be a first without a last, but there need not appear to be *either*—because, in fact, there *is* neither.

There must be an ending before there can be a beginning.

"Prerequisites" to a Knowledge of Truth

Up to this point, I have emphasized the allness of Isness and the all-inclusiveness of Awareness. Now I will write more specifically about Identity. This, for reasons already pointed out, will also involve a discussion of the identity *we are not*.

CHAPTER IX

About the "Old Man" Who Is to Be "Put Off" and Exactly How to Do It

We have examined Awareness to discover it includes all things. Awareness is the function, the activity, of Mind, Consciousness—but *whose* Mind? *Whose* Consciousness? *Here is the crux of the matter!* Whose Awareness *is* this? Who *owns* the Awareness that is presently reading these words? Is it yours? Mine?

Ask these questions and *answer* them for yourself before reading another word. Stop; put the book aside and consider this Awareness. Have you been considering it "yours"? Have you been acting on the assumption—perhaps unconsciously —that this consciousness is "mine"? Have you been thinking of it as the *activity* of your own mind? Be completely honest.

The perception of this point was basic in my comprehension of Reality, so I want to make it very clear to the reader. I ask you to look at the table across the room or at the blue sky outside your window. This "seeing" is Awareness in action. By now we surely understand that the blue sky and the table, like images on the television screen, are "within" this Awareness that is aware; but listen closely; have we not thought of this consciousness as a personal *possession?*—as "mine," "yours," "ours," "his"? Reader, this is precisely what mankind believes; this is the position from which he has acted since the beginning of time; this is what religion, philosophy and education have taught to this very moment, but it is not true! Such a concept is entirely false, and it is upon

About the "Old Man" Who Is to Be "Put Off"

this false premise that the trials and tribulations of humanity are constructed.

Understand this: this Now-awareness is neither yours nor mine. It does not *belong* to someone called "me" or "us." It does not "belong," period! Awareness (Life) IS!

But who are we?

Awareness is who we are! Awareness *itself!* We are not the ego, the personality or *body,* who says Awareness is "mine." THAT is the incorrect identity, the "old man," the "liar from the beginning," the "deceiver," the devil himself. THAT is the one to be "put off." *That* is the one to "come out from . . . and be ye separate."

Listen carefully: THE BASIC BUILDING BLOCK FOR OUR ENTIRE PERSONAL BELIEF IN AN INHARMONIOUS HUMAN EXPERIENCE IS THE INCORRECT ASSUMPTION THAT OUR PRESENT IDENTITY IS ONE WHO OWNS—POSSESSES—CONTAINS—THE AWARENESS OF THESE WORDS; THE BELIEF THAT AWARENESS IS THE FUNCTION OF "OUR" PERSONAL MIND; THAT WE ARE THE CUSTODIANS OF CONSCIOUSNESS; THAT WE ARE THE RECIPIENTS OF LIFE.

As long as we believe we are the container of Awareness, we identify ourselves, not as Awareness itself, but as an empty ego; as the one who attempts to have Awareness show us the things we want, the way we want them. As long as we believe this, we are acting a role outside the realm of the Real, attempting to make a servant, a slave, a lackey of God's own consciousness of being!

Ponder this basic fact. Once the Truth of it is felt, we do not long continue to identify ourselves as the "old man" who must be put off or as the mortal who must die. Rather, we claim Awareness *itself*—Life, Reality, Truth, Infinite Intelligence *itself*—as the sole and only Identity.

The Awareness that sees these words *is* this Identity! The Awareness-being-I includes the Universe entire! We can never *actually* be the one who claims to possess, contain, imprison, enslave and make a servant of Awareness. When we believe ourselves to be that one, we live as "a house divided," in bondage to our own false sense of Self.
Reader, you are not one who is aware. You are AWARENESS!

Dear Mr. Samuel,
Why in the world did you write to me about the fictitious "old man"? A fiction is a fiction and to write about a fantasy *at all* is not absolute enough for me; it is but foolish delving into duality!

Yours truly,

ABOUT THE MISIDENTITY

For those who wonder why we write about an identity that doesn't even exist in Reality, let me say this again and, hopefully, have done with it. When one has finally put away the old man, the "liar from the beginning," he no longer takes issue with what *appears* to be degrees of attainment, correctness, absoluteness, nor with the *words* another uses.

It appears that many I talk to about their Identity as Awareness fail to comprehend what is being said until *first* they come to recognize the identity *they are not;* until they discover who and what the "old man" *professes* to be *in relation to themselves;* that is, in relation to who and what they *appear* to believe themselves to be.

Simply to be told the human identity is a "nothing claiming to be something," a phantom or "a dream that isn't really going on," does not relax the tenacious grip with which we clutch our personal opinions of ourself. The ego is only a seeming, true, but a seeming is a seeming until it doesn't seem to seem. Seeming ill health and unhappiness, a seeming world filled with turmoil, are only slightly more palatable than the genuine article, if such could be possible. Those who have *had done* with all seeming have discovered its mystery and *know* why these words are written.

TO PUT OFF THE OLD MAN

How long has humanity been trying to put off the old man? Has it been successful? Not at all. Churchdom has been wrong in its identification of the pseudo-ego because churchdom is the *product* of the pseudo-ego, consequently its admonitions as to what to do about it are incorrect and misleading. For instance, classical theology has thoroughly indoctrinated its adherents with the belief that the way to put off the old man is to divest him of his worst qualities, his immoralities, passions and appetites.

Humanly, this is commendable, but even if such a program were carried to a successful conclusion, the old man *himself* would still be left: a paragon of virtue, of course; upright and passionless, but still the old man, the deceiver, the *wrong identity;* and we would still believe ourselves to be that one!

Even the most perfect human attainment leaves one believing himself "born of woman," while ". . . he that is least in the kingdom of God is greater."

The admonition remains to PUT OFF the old man, *then* put on the new. Proclaiming the allness and onlyness of the "new" *first* is like attempting to put new wine into an old wineskin, or a new patch on an old garment. Until the misidentification is seen for what it is *with relation to this Awareness, right here, right now,* our proclamation that "God is all" is so much babble.

The Light declares what *is,* revealing what is *not.* Those who have found the Light to be their Identity know precisely what the "little-I" *pretends* to be. They have the ability to expose it honestly and effectively. *Then,* turning to the Light *as* the Light, one is never more concerned with darkness, with a false identity that only seemed. To the new Identity—uncontained and unpossessed Awareness itself— "the only thing that counts is the new creation." Sorrow, sighing and *seeming* flee away.

THE SURRENDER IS NOT DIFFICULT

The tender simplicity of Reality first comes from the Heart. We have identified the Heart as the "place" of the immaculate conception where the Christ Truth is found. Christ and Truth are the selfsame Awareness beholding these words! Truth is the *real* Identity being you and me!

It is apparent that these concepts are contrary to the high and mighty intellect, contrary to theology and churchdom, but not at all contrary to the wise and tender simplicity of the Heart. While the intellect vehemently opposes Truth and tends toward arrogant self-righteousness, *Truth* remains a very simple, gentle and unblemished Tranquillity, at peace with everything and unmindful of any supposititious opposite concerning it.

As we have pointed out, all one ever needs to consciously *be* and *experience* the Tranquillity of the real Identity is to let go the personality, the pseudo-ego, the mistaken thought and action that *this consciousness, right here,* is an intellect which *contains* Awareness, Life.

This is the classical "sacrifice" of the *entire* old man, not just his passions and appetites, or his worst qualities. This is the axe laid to the root.

TRUTH IS NOT A TOOL

For want of a better way to say it, our love for the personal ego is, to most of us, an insidiously continuing affair. In various wily ways, it tries to reassert itself again and again. Why? Because of our life-long habitual effort to *use* Truth to correct the unpleasant aspects of the human experience. As long as everything is going comfortably with the old man, we have no qualms about playing the part of that *possessor* of Life. When things are not going well, the temptation is very great to settle for the elimination of the misidentity's dis-ease alone. Many metaphysical philosophies are equipped to do this much for the old man. Metaphysics has proven itself an effective flashlight to shine *on* the endless ills of mankind—one at a time.

Within the realm of cause and effect (called karma in some circles) the world concedes that external appearances result from mental causes. Here, all sorts of changes may be effected by altering their supposed source; but if our aim is to do anything at all to an object of perception, especially with the intention of healing it with the Light of Truth, we will not long be satisfied. Why? Because we will still seem *to be* the old mortal who caused his dark spots in the first place. *That* one will be searching for the Light until hell freezes over.

QUESTION: What good is Reality, Truth, Isness, if it isn't to be *used?* What good is Truth if it isn't to help me see better, hear better or conduct my business affairs in a more profitable manner?

ANSWER: Unfettered Truth does everything one could possibly "need," and ten thousand times more! But Truth is not an entity intended to *do* something. *Truth is the Identity we are!* We do not use it; we *are* it!

This fact, honestly understood, acknowledged and *acted,* eliminates the "seeming" and all the misery it contains.

THE FLASHLIGHT ILLUSTRATION

If we wanted to correct a dark spot in the room, we could *use* light to eliminate the darkness, couldn't we? Each time another dark spot appeared, we could go off looking for our flashlight to correct the new darkness. Big dark spots would simply require bigger flashlights—"knowing more Truth." In effect (and greatly simplified), this is how education has us correct "error."

Now listen carefully: When we awaken to the fact that our only identity is Light itself, and claim it and act *as* it, we are never aware again of endless dark spots to be eliminated, healed or corrected because there is no darkness in light itself! Isn't this so?

We perceive that darkness "seemed" in the first place only because we failed to identify ourselves as the Light, believing instead that we were another who could *use* and make a servant of Light by manipulating it in our experience, thereby believing the "seeming" that darkness could be present, even where Light is.

You see, "darkness" and the belief of an incorrect identity are the same. In order to have done with the seeming, it is necessary to stop believing oneself to be the false identity, thus playing its part. This is never done until we recognize how the old identity pertains (though falsely) *to this Awareness we are, here and now!* Otherwise, one goes about declaring, "The personal mind is an utter impossibility," while he goes right on believing himself *to be* that utter impossibility and goes on having to act his belief!

Once the "old man" is understood to be the one who would attempt to make a tool of consciousness itself, then one may consciously *be* the "new Identity," never more contending with an endless succession of illusions. From this time on, we busy ourselves being the Light itself, in which there are no dark spots, no illusions, no lies.

MORE ABOUT "THE SACRIFICE"

Fear, suffering, poor health, lack and limitation—even death—are self-inflicted foolishness. They are an unnecessary unreality which *seems.*

Happiness and Joy are spread over the entire face of the land this instant. There is Contentment and Satisfaction beyond man's greatest dream, to be experienced in the twinkling of an eye—effortlessly—when one is willing to make the sacrifice. What sacrifice? The surrender of the intellect, of one's high opinion of his personal mental prowess and acumen. For how long? Only long enough to discern the Heart for an instant. Whose Heart? Your own!—not *my* words or preachments, nor my opinions or experiences, nor those of any organization or philosophy. The teacher I tell you of is the still small Voice being the very Identity you are.

What have we said here about Awareness? We have said it is not mine; it is I—Me. Awareness is the Identity being I. But who is being aware? Awareness is the activity of Mind: not "my" mind—*God's* mind. This Awareness-I-am (and you are, reader) is *God's* Awareness; it is the Divine Awareness; it is the activity of *God!* NOPE

Preposition makes it an Action of God where in Reality God is Action

If you are not aware of the allness and onlyness of God you can get thrown off balance here.

You've got to know what it is you are standing on.

CHAPTER X

The Real Identity

All who want wisdom, all who wish to have done with problems, *let them discover their true Identity!* All who hope to experience a "healing" of some sort, *let them discover their true Identity!* All who want a respite from fear and frustration, who want permanent health, wealth, harmony or happiness, let them discover their true Identity! Anyone who wants to have done with cycles of depression, with physical and mental disturbances, with problems of any sort, let that one determine who and what he *is,* rather than what he has believed himself to be.

He is not the personality he believes he is! He is not an ego! He is not a mortal, one among many, laboring to make his way in the world; his Identity is none of these things. The actual Identity is not caught up in a web of human woe; is not milling about in a mortal maelstrom of misery. To those who discover their real Identity comes a peace quite beyond the ability of words to describe; and with this peace come works of magnificence and grandeur, just as foretold.

As with the king who believed himself a woodcutter, so for all of us, there is the real Identity to whom the entire kingdom belongs; and then there seems to be a misidentification—an ego, a personality—that one *believes* himself to be. Agony has to do with the dream identity we try so mightily to portray; Tranquillity, Sufficiency and Joy have to do with the real.

QUESTION: Will you describe this misidentification so I may clearly perceive the role in which I have miscast myself?

The Real Identity

ANSWER: We act as the wrong identity when we act as the ego who possesses this consciousness called Life, and when we believe it is our personal property, the "action" of a private mind. We act this misidentity when we think of ourselves as one who is the recipient of Life. We act the true identification when we reckon Identity to be Awareness (Life) *itself*. We act the true identification when we declare that Awareness itself is being this Identity-I-am, when we act from the standpoint that Awareness *only* is being Identity-I, instead of the body-form which is merely the focal point of images *within* Awareness. How much more Identity is than a single shadow-image which it includes within itself!

The misidentification is an image-centered identity called man, mankind, Bill, Mary, you and me. It is like a role we play in a stage production of misplaced values. It is the role of a ghost-dreamer who dreams dreams, judges judgments, evaluates the valueless, and then operates as though those values, judgments and dreams were real.

THE MACBETH ILLUSTRATION

Imagine yourself playing the role of Macbeth, so intrigued by the excitement and thunderous events on the stage that you believe everything happening there is exactly as it appears, the obvious and factual truth. Imagine that you have become so absorbed in the play, particularly your own part, as to forget it is only a play, a fictitious, intellectually created drama.

From this incorrect standpoint, you find yourself accepting and believing the identity the play gives you. You find yourself literally being Macbeth, living the burdens of Macbeth and suffering the agony heaped on his shoulders. Macduff's threats to your life seem terribly real; the blood on Lady Macbeth's hands seems fixed and permanent; her fears add mightily to your own. Believing yourself to be Macbeth, you find yourself worried, frightened and bent to the ground beneath the weight of your machinations. Even though Macbeth is not your actual identity, never was and never could be *really*, you believe it is—and act it.

When the torment of the misidentification finally becomes too great to bear, perhaps in a moment of agony and wonderment about the "why" of it all, you ask someone who is attempting to tell you the Truth, "Why do you keep saying there is nothing to worry about? Why do you tell me I am suffering *needlessly?* What do you mean, I do not need to 'take thought'? What do you mean, 'things are not as they appear' and 'my kingdom is not of this world'? What about those horsemen thundering across the stage? What about the soldiers I see hiding behind the trees? How in the world can I keep from worrying about them? Your talk is pure gobbledygook, completely beyond my comprehension." Inevitably, your questions stem from the belief the play is true and real. Questions will continue to arise until the play is seen to be the fiction it is.

This illustration makes clear that the actors have no problems outside the play. It shows that their genuine identity is of "another world." However, the actors, ever asking questions from the standpoint of the play-as-real, appear to understand only those answers given them in the play's terms—that is, using the language of the play. To answer Macbeth's questions in the terms of "reality" (the play-as-fiction) seems absolute nonsense (non-play-sense) to Macbeth. Hence, we find that answers completely truthful in their statement, come from an area judged to be too far out, terribly removed from the world-play and its immediacy. They are dubbed contrary to common sense or too absolute to be practical. "Common sense" of course, is the misidentification's stage-educated view of things.

The honest answer to every question lies in the fact that Macbeth is not our real identity. Only the fictitious identity, Macbeth-man, is beleagured, frustrated and suffering. In this illustration, we see the genuine identity is a happy citizen of another world, not being threatened by real soldiers, or by anything that can upset him. *Our "salvation" is in coming to discover this, letting go the belief that the Macbeth-identity is the real self!*

While our statements of Truth are beyond Macbeth's proud intellectuality, they are never too far out to be understood by his heart! Even though the actor is completely lost in the play, his real identity has never changed; consequently, deep within the crust of the false identification, within his heart, the *not-Macbeth-identity* hears and recognizes the words that tell him of himself and tell him that the play is not actually what it appears to be—and that there is another set of values transcending those of the play.

Looking on these events as they appear to transpire on the stage of the world, we can see that the misidentified actor, having forgotten his true identity, must discover it for *himself*. Nothing less suffices to convince him. We know he must listen to his own heart, which he isn't likely to feel or hear until he lets go some of his horror of the stage and learns to "listen." Furthermore, we know he must believe the heart when it speaks, else he will continue believing the delusion.

"RELIGION" IN LIGHT OF THE MACBETH ILLUSTRATION

The only place "religion" is applicable in all of this is on the stage where the actors have apparently not yet awakened to their real identity. We perceive that an honest religion is one that speaks of the *rightful* identity, successfully soothes the fears concerning the misvalued events on the stage, and ultimately shows the actor how to stop believing and playing the distasteful role of sinning, suffering Macbeth.

The visible "proof" of an honest religion is the *Peace* that allows the actor to watch the events on the stage in unwavering equanimity, knowing full well that Reality *transcends* the appearance of *human* values and that Power is vested in the Transcendent, not in the "things" of the world, no matter what they are or how powerful the world claims they are!

THE MACBETH ILLUSTRATION CONTINUED

Looking around the stage, judging by appearances alone, the intellectual misidentification shouts in terror, "Macduff has a great sword and he intends to kill me."

But the Heart, ever in touch with Reality, declares, "There is no power on this earth-stage that can do aught to the Identity being I! This is so! This is true! Peace, Peace I give unto you! Be of good cheer for even the place whereon thou standest is holy ground!"

While concerned with the declarations of the arrogant ego-intellect, one does not hear the still, small voice that says, "Peace, be still. Everything is all right!"—despite the appearances!

WHO CAN GIVE THE TRUTH TO MANKIND?

Who can tell *man* that he is not man? Who can tell Macbeth that he is not Macbeth? Who can tell him that his identity is infinitely greater than the limits set forth by the play? Who can prevail upon Macbeth's "common sense" and convince him that the horsemen thundering across the stage are not going to do him bodily harm?

To Macbeth, you see, everything seen by the eyes and heard with the ears testifies otherwise. His common sense makes a convincing argument that he, and everything else, is real. Macbeth's intellect will never allow him to consider Macduff's

The Real Identity

sword as anything but a threat to his life. Common sense and intellect tell him he had *better* do such and so or perish. In the face of the world's tumult, mankind, like Macbeth, says, "I do not have the faith to believe in another Identity, against which nothing in this experience can prevail. I would like to believe such a thing, but I just cannot."

So it is, our words must be spoken *to the Heart,* where they are recognized and acknowledged.

THE NON-VALUE OF THINGS

The Macbeth illustration allows us to understand that the sights and sounds on the world stage are not necessarily as they appear. Next, consider the *value* of those sights and sounds. Surely the world places some value in everything; everything, it believes, has its positive or negative worth. The whole activity of humanity is to work for the acquisition of "things" deemed valuable, and to exchange or destroy things with negative value.

Using our illustration, we see that everything (every "thing") on the stage is equally "The Tragedy of Macbeth." Not a single thing has more (or less) value than another. Macduff's sword has no more power than the prop tree in the corner or the candlestick on the table in the banquet hall. However, we see that if the actor playing the role of Macbeth forgets his true identity, for him the situation becomes a complicated and frustrating enigma. *He* attaches value to all he sees, according to *his* determination of their importance in his experience. For him the sword becomes a very real and terrible threat. The tree is a place for a soldier to hide behind. The golden candlestick is worth so much money and it is "mine" and not "yours." Yet, no matter how much value Macbeth attaches to the sights and sounds of the play, the fact remains that the play itself is the only value of the "things."

The *play* is *being* all the things. In and of themselves, the props on the stage are nothing more than vehicles by which the play is expressed, much as numerals are vehicles by which the principle of arithmetic is shown forth.

Reader, look outside at the trees, the bees, the garden filled with new green leaves. Look across the way at the buildings and the people there. See the simple sparrow on the sidewalk; the soaring swallow in the sky. There is no value there either, no matter how much you believe otherwise. There is no power or importance *there,* even though common sense and individual intellect scream otherwise.

Where is the real value? Where is the power and importance? In the ISNESS, the Reality, God, *which is being every object of perception*—in the Isness *being the Awareness* that "sees" them!

We see that as long as we believe ourselves to be the misidentification who thinks it possesses Awareness, just that long do the intellect and common sense rebel at the statement that there is no value, power or importance in "things," or that things are nothing in and of themselves. But the Heart understands! In an instant the Heart accepts these totally irrational and illogical affronts to "common sense" to which the intellect would *never* submit. Isn't this so?

A LETTER ABOUT VALUE AND IDENTITY

Dear Paul,

Mankind is preoccupied with "things." Let this be clearly comprehended: *There is no value, power or importance in any object perceived within Awareness! There is no need to fear or to be concerned about anything seen with the eye or heard by the ear!*

Understandably, humanity is reluctant to acknowledge a fact so contrary to the world's belief. "Don't tell ME the dollar

The Real Identity

bill has no value," someone says. "You can't tell ME this house isn't worth such and so; that heart trouble doesn't plague my family; that my well-being doesn't depend on the successful consummation of this contract. Don't tell ME my identity isn't Macbeth! There is my name carved in stone over the castle entrance. If that isn't sufficient to convince you, there stands the King of Scotland. Ask him!"

Man, the possessor of Awareness-in-me, no more understands the powerlessness of "things" than Macbeth himself understands that the sights and sounds on the stage are not "real" and have no value *in themselves*. What logic or reason can heal *Macbeth's* troubles?

All "things," be they objects of sight, sound, touch or smell, be they thoughts, ideas, intuitions or dreams, *are within THIS Awareness that is aware of these printed words*. Value and importance are not "out there" with the "thing," but here where Awareness itself is being aware. The value and importance are That (the Deific Isness, the Godhead) which is being Awareness *itself*, and not the sparrow, the automobile, the lover, the bank account, the beetles or the bed bugs which are included as images *within* Awareness.

The one who identifies himself as an ego containing life—the great walking, talking human Macbeth called mankind—will never be convinced of the truth of these words by using his intellect. Only the HEART recognizes the Truth. Only the Heart can convince him.

Paul, do you choose to be Life-Awareness, or do you simply want to use it; to have it show *you* what *you* want to see? The temptation is to use it. Our words, it seems, are addressed primarily to a user-Macbeth who wants very much to have his trials and tribulations ended. He wants his Lady Macbeth to stop worrying about the blood on her hands; he wants his calculations to go according to plan; he wants the threatening soldiers to melt away into the sunshine—*but he wants to be Macbeth still!* He wants to be a happy *man*, a happy *container* of Life, with no problems. He only wants the unhappy things in his personal experience healed, changed, rectified or overcome. He wants to continue as a healthy, happy, prosperous and acclaimed *human* being. He says, "I do not understand the 'real Identity' business. It is too absolute for me, too difficult to understand."

We can see that his problems are entirely the result of having two identities ("dualism") and believing himself to be the wrong one. He cannot be *both!* He cannot hang onto the "good" aspects of Macbeth's life and carry them with him into the proper Identity. He cannot worship two masters.

We must let go the old man, all of him. The intellect will never let us do this. Macbeth himself will never let us do it, for the moment we consider the possibility, Macbeth's intellect tells us that this will be the end of Macbeth. "I will lose my identity!" the old man screams. "I will be *nothing!*"

True! The old man and all his problems will be gone. He will have been relegated to the position he rightfully holds, that of a valueless, powerless image, just a part in a play. Ah, but *Awareness* will be here yet! Unconfined Awareness, beholding things as they are, *will be here yet.* Awareness *itself* will still be the Identity that I am! Unencumbered now! Free now! Not limited to the dark-glass perview of an ailing, aching ass named Macbeth.

While we may speak of a tree and state that Reality is being all there is to it, the Reality we are talking about is not multiple, not divided into many things into which it pours a bit of itself. The Isness being the tree is the same single Isness being *every* object of perception.

This is not to say that all images are *alike.* Single Isness is infinite in nature. This infinity is apparent TO ISNESS as the universe.

Awareness is the action of Isness apprehending its own nature. Just as Isness (Reality) is being the object of percep-

The Real Identity

tion—the tree, the house, the leaf, the little girl—even so, Isness is the *apprehension* of the tree, the house, the leaf, the little girl with big freckles. The Identity "we" are, reader, is *apprehending* in action, Awareness being aware. Aware of what? Of that which Reality knows ITSELF to be—the leaf, the tree, the little girl and the freckles.

THERE IS NO VALUE IN "THINGS"

Dear Mr. Samuel,
 The intellectual wants proof that there is no value in images. If man would (or could) really *believe* this, he would stop paying so much attention to "things," stop honoring them above all else; stop hoarding them; stop planning and calculating to acquire them; he would stop even fighting and contending for them.
 SHOW ME there is no value in things.
Sincerely yours,

 I attempted to make this point clear in the little book *two plus two equals reality* with the "Lump of Gold" illustration. It has proven effective.
 It shows that Awareness beholds only "qualities" and "attributes." Our eyes "see" these qualities and attributes and nothing else. For instance, we see "yellow," but there is no *gold* in yellow. We see the form and feel the weight of the lump of gold, but there is no gold *itself* in "form" or "weight." With the senses we are able to measure malleability and ductility, but there is no gold itself in either of these qualities. In this illustration, however, "gold" *is being* the yellow we see, the form we feel, the ductility we can measure. These are all perceived qualities and attributes, but none of them individually, nor all of them together, is gold *itself*. All we ever "see" are groupings of qualities and attributes which have been

given names: gold, tree, bear, bumble bee, flower or Nelly's hat.

Ah, but certainly *something* is being the "things" we perceive! Yes; this "something" is called Deity, Isness, Reality! Furthermore, this something is the value—*not the grouping of qualities and attributes!* The value is not in the thing; it is in Deity! Deific Isness is being all there is to the perceived universe of people, places and things. This universe is every bit *within* the Awareness that sees these words!

NOTHING CAN HARM US

What can "yellow" do to harm gold? What can "form" do to Isness? No matter what we do to "yellow," basic, primordial Isness goes right on being Isness, doesn't it? "The power belongs to God," not to the qualities and attributes, not to "things."

As long as Reality exists, there will continue to be every object of perception Reality is being. Similarly, scientists, whose chief concern is with the study of things, have shown that matter cannot be destroyed. The basic Isness of Being remains unchanged. Furthermore, science now agrees that the basic building block of the universe is a single "mysterious energy." Reader, you and I know that the primordial Isness being this mysterious energy is God.

Let us give to Caesar (things) that which is Caesar's, and to Truth that which is Truth's. Things are simply things, but *they* are not the value or power. They have no authority in themselves. They are the props on the stage.

As soon as one comes to understand and acknowledge (sometimes acknowledge, then understand) that there is no power vested in things, he has done much to eliminate his fear of them. How can one fear a bullet, a bomb or a business gone berserk when it has no authority of its own, and which Perfection is being, if it has any being at all? Since Isness is all, only

The Real Identity

what Isness *is* has being—and God is in no way Self-destructive.

THERE IS NO PERSONAL RESPONSIBILITY

Now we are able to perceive another vista. We have come to understand that God, Isness, is being the "form" called "mountain" or "tree." The time has come to acknowledge that God is being *this very Awareness;* that God is being this Awareness that "beholds" the trees, mountains and all other "objects of perception." God is being Awareness *itself.* The Awareness that views these words is being all it is because Isness is being It. This means that the Awareness-I-am, right here, right now, is the activity of God! *God* is the value and importance of Awareness-I. Awareness-I can do nothing on its own. Awareness-I has no power of its own. It has no responsibility of its own. *God* is being all there is to this consciousness of existence. The value is *God's.* The responsibility is *God's.* All this Awareness-I-am, which is self-evidently *all* I am, is the function and activity of God. "I" have no personal responsibility at all!

"Things" seen "out there" are not separate or apart from Awareness itself; neither is Awareness separate or apart from God who is being this Awareness. The objects perceived, the perceiving, and the *perceiver* are all the triune Reality called God.

Consider the television illustration again. Images are not separate or apart from the screen; neither is the screen anything *of itself!* The screen exists because there is a television set. The images on the screen, the screen, and the functioning (activity) of the television set are all *one television set.* It is a perfectly functioning oneness. The activity "on" the screen is the functioning itself! The screen has no personal responsibility to picture this or that image. The screen has no duty but to be the screen, and this is effortless because it is a fact already.

All the responsibility belongs to the total *television set!* As Jesus said, "I and my Father are One. The burden is His. The responsibility is His." Exactly so, this conscious Awareness I am (and you are, reader) is the effortless *functioning* of harmonious Isness, for it is a total perfection *already*. You and I have nothing to do but *be* the Awareness which *God* is being! This is the "faithful witness." This is the effortless and instantaneous "return" to the Father's house, from which Life-Awareness has never departed. The instant that big bag of wind (the pseudo-person and its personal responsibility for Awareness) is *let go*, that instant comes conscious knowledge of Identity as Tranquillity. It is a Tranquillity that does not "ebb and flow, come and go, between serenity and sadness." It is permanently established and undisturbable!

From this moment on, one is never long tempted to play the role of liar. We choose to be Awareness only!

IDENTITY AS AWARENESS

It is not possible for the Infinite to be enclosed. Who can enclose it? It is not possible for the limitless universe to be possessed. Who can possess it? It is not possible for Omnipotence to be beholden to another. Who can make demands of it? Who can insist that conscious Awareness show them this or that? Who can say to Awareness, "You are my most prized servant and I order you to show me a bank full of money or a house full of happiness?" However, there is a presumptuous tendency to do this, and it has been given ten thousand names. It has been called Bill and Mary, John and Paul; it has been called "me" and "I"; it has been called *man*.

Dear one who reads these words, you are properly identified as Awareness; improperly identified as an ego who possesses Awareness. It is the same awareness. There is not a consciousness that belongs to man and another that belongs to God.

The Real Identity

The Awareness that beholds this page is the only consciousness of being you will ever be, and it "belongs" to God! It is God's activity; it is God's awareness. It is not the servant of an ego or a personality. It is not the possession of Bill or Mary or whatever name you go by.

It seems (but only seems) that we have the choice to believe ourselves an identity, a "man" to whom consciousness (life) has been *given,* or to identify as consciousness *itself,* the Awareness which God is *being.* If we believe ourselves to be the possessor and act accordingly, we must have all the distortions that go with such an acted upon belief. If we relinquish the assumptive possessor to become aware of the *real* identity—unjudging Awareness itself—and then act as this simple Identity demands, we find the fabled Peace beyond human comprehension.

We are this Awareness anyway, whether we claim it or not. God is being this Life we are, whether we admit it or not, whether we acknowledge it or not, whether we even care or not. We are what we are, regardless of our personal wishes in the matter. One may continue to believe himself a judge who possesses Awareness if he likes, but in so doing he lives a lie, an unhappy Macbethian intrigue, and delays the discovery of the peace of mind so very close to him.

Reader, if the selections seem to have become excessively repetitious to you, proceed at once to Chapter XI, page 87. Save the remainder of this chapter for a later reading. I assure you that as your knowledge of Awareness expands, and as you practice the art of Being, the differences between selections will seem less subtle, and the redundancy so maddening to the intellectual nature will vanish.

A LETTER ABOUT IDENTITY

Dear Anne,

 This instant you are Awareness itself. This second you can stop trying to be the imposter. This moment you can let go the liar, the father of lies, the old man, and the veil will be rent from top to bottom; the mist that covers the entire face of the land will be gone! There will be no more scales on your eyes; there will be no more tears. You will see as you are seen, because Seer, seeing the seen (scene), is all there is to you!
 This second you may stop identifying yourself as the one who possesses your very Being. This second you can stop making demands of yourself. This instant you can stop attempting to enslave God, to make a servant of God, to have God show you this "good" thing or eliminate that "bad" thing. Consciousness is *who you are*, not a personal possession.
 Awareness is simply and effortlessly aware. It does not judge. It does not desire to see what it wants to see. It does not attempt to change the world. It does not dominate, criticize, cajole or demand. It does not *want* at all. It is simply beholding and being.
 Anne, you are Seeing itself, constantly about the Seer's business. You are not the one who thinks she has a lease on seeing for a few years, during which time she wants it to show her that she possesses health, wealth and fame. You are Awareness ITSELF and ONLY. This is the most infinite "only" you can imagine, because it includes the *infinity* of Reality, the *infinity* of Love, and the *infinity* of Health and Wealth—not a mere part of it, but *all* of it! Why? Because Awareness is God's consciousness of Himself! It is our good pleasure to be the witness of all God is! It is our good pleasure to be what God is being! It is our good fortune to be Infinity *itself*, and consciously so. When? As quickly as the liar is loosed and let go!

The Real Identity

Who is the liar? The personal ego who says Conscious Awareness belongs to me!

Sincerely,

The liar's elimination comes with the realization of his nothingness. His vacuous nothingness is declared to the pure in heart, to those who love God, to those willing to let God be all, to those willing to give up their egotistical, personal sense of self, to those willing to behold without judgment.

ABOUT RESPONSIBILITY

Return to simplicity. Return to the closet, to the temple, to the Holy of Holies, to the Father's house wherein there is nothing that "maketh a lie."

How does one go about returning? Simply by being Awareness *only*.

What is Awareness? It is the action of Mind. Whose mind? The Mind that Reality is—the Deific Mind—the one and only Mind.

Do you realize what this means? The Awareness aware of these words is *God's*. It does not belong to "you" or "me." It does not belong to Bill or Mary. It does not belong to man. It is not a mortal mind. It is in no way connected to a temporal experience. This Awareness is God's awareness!

As Awareness, we are not responsible *to* Awareness or *for* it in any way. We do not have to "see" certain things. We do not have to experience healings, improvements or changes in any way. We have no responsibility because God is the fullness of this consciousness we are. This is God's consciousness of being. This is God's action. This is God's kingdom, God's knowledge,

God's awareness of *Himself*—not Anne's, not Bill's, not mine, not man's.

Can you feel the rest, the relaxing and peaceful tranquillity in this fact? This Awareness, right here and now, is the Deific Mind in action. There is no way for a personal you or me to get into the act and be the actor. Awareness is the deathless action of God! We have naught to do but to be!

VIGNETTES OF IDENTITY

Dear Mary,

Understand this: if you can see so much as a grain of sand, a fleck of dust or a blade of grass, if you can hear a sound or feel the form of any conceivable thing, then the totality, the *totality* of the Ineffable Godhead is present, at hand, here and nigh, the only fact of being!

Why are we so quick to acknowledge that "God is all" and that God is being every "thing," but so hesitant to act as if that which is being every "thing" is *present?* If God is being all Awareness beholds, is not God precisely where things are? Certainly! And, since God is all, is not God being this Awareness that perceives things? Of course! Then why deny it and why *act* differently?

The simple fact is, when one acts as if God is present, the Godhead makes itself apparent in our every thought and action.

Mary, do not take my word for this. Be kind to yourself and try it. You will see.

       Sincerely yours,

II

This conscious life we are is not at the mercy of the possessor of life. It is not in the clutches of the one who is seeking wisdom—or Wisdom. *Consciousness and all it contains is to be acknowledged as Spirit's own Self-acknowledgement of all that Spirit is!* That means *this* consciousness reading these words, and not the one supposedly belonging to an image "over there" called wife or son or something else.

Because this consciousness *is* Spirit's Self-acknowledgement, our acknowledgement of it is effortless to do, and lies within the capability of anyone willing to give up the ghost of personal possessorship—the intellect, the ego. The "reward" awaiting those who do is beyond belief!

III

It is not enough to proclaim that there is no human identification while one continues to identify himself *as one;* nor is it enough to attempt to enjoy the benefits of two identities, one considered "real" and the other "unreal." Most especially, it is futile to work one against the other so that a human sense of self will fare better because of a knowledge of a "higher" order of being.

Listen to the simplicity of the New Idea: Spirit is being this Awareness of being. The function of Awareness is *Spirit's* responsibility, and it does not belong to another called you, me, he, she or it. We are not concerned about he, she or it, however; we are concerned with the only one we can be concerned about—*this* Awareness being I.

What must we do in order to let Spirit—Infinite Intelligence, Power, Authority and Being—be all in all? We simply let go the futile notion there is a "me" or a "you" *using* this consciousness. It is as simple as that.

If one thinks this is to be languid and lazy or to languish in an ivory tower of mental escapism (as intellectualism—and Macbeth—inevitably charges), *let him try it!* Just let him try it! Very quickly he finds it far removed from "doing nothing."

To those bold enough to offer up the old ego in honest

sacrifice, this "world experience" breaks forth into astonishing, joy-filled, "busy" adventures.

IV

There is but one course open to the one who wishes to discern Reality: to identify as the One who Spirit is, and not to consider it robbery to make this acknowledgment of Spirit's onlyness.

This is not to make "me" equal to God. This is to acknowledge that "me" is God's awareness of God and nothing else. It is to let go the presumptuous one who has been attempting to make himself greater than God, who has been attempting to make the already finished Perfection of Being into something more perfect. It is to begin with the Perfect Principle of all Being and therein to recognize that the one to "let go" is an impossible imposter, a fatherless bastard, a nonexistent phantom, for which there is no accounting.

Who can let go the illusion but "me"? By letting go the phantom, one simultaneously lets go the "me," because illusion and "me" are the same. The letting go is easily accomplished in the honest acknowledgement of its utter impossibility; but never on a bit by bit program, or by wrestling and contending with it. Again: only by the completely honest acknowledgement that a little "me" *is impossible* can the sputtering spook be forgotten. This is honesty with God—just simple honesty. This is the honesty that present day theology appears to know nothing about!

How long are we going to keep up the old habit of looking *at* the Kingdom, declaring the qualities and attributes of the Kingdom, proclaiming the *affluence* of the Kingdom, the presence and power of the Kingdom, *while we continue to identify ourselves as a speck-spectator IN the Kingdom?* How long before we reckon from the standpoint that That which is being the Kingdom is That which *is this Identity we are?* How long before we acknowledge that looking at the Kingdom is

The Real Identity

looking at the Holy Self we are? God, the Kingdom and the Awareness of Being are all ONE, TOTAL, SINGLE AND ONLY PERFECTION—called God.

V

This that you must be, dear reader, *is not in your hands!* It is the perfect *action* of Transcendental Isness being ALL as all! How presumptuous to think oneself an independent actor able to improve on simple Perfection; and how rewarding to stand persistently on the High Ground that dares let God be responsible, and dares to let this present consciousness be the unjudging witness (Awareness) of God's responsible action.

QUESTION: How easy is this to do?

ANSWER: How easy is it for Macbeth to stop worrying about the soldiers converging on his castle? How much courage will it take to allow him to fight Macduff without fear? Macbeth will never have enough such courage because such courage is not inherent in his role; therefore, it is not only not "easy" for *him* to be free of fear, it is impossible. But can the *real* identity, playing the role of Macbeth, be intimidated by the actions on the stage? Not after he has seen them for what they are and has challenged them with simple, unswerving honesty.

VI

QUESTION: What are my obligations to other people? That is, as Awareness, what are my obligations to images and objects of perception?

ANSWER: From this standpoint, we have no obligations to other people. We simply do all that seems to be the sensible, honest thing to do. We do this while aware that the Identity "they" are is That which is being this Self-same Awareness. What "they" call miracles appear everywhere for everyone to see.

Isness is being all there is to every object seen, heard and felt. Their "use" or "purpose" has already been established by virtue of Isness, Perfect Being, which is being all there is to them. The "obligation" and "responsibility" belongs to Isness, not to this Awareness.

As long as we simply be what we be, conscious that unfolding events (which include people) are the harmonious activity of the Principle being all we are, then we know—simply know—all that we need "do." Inner Light directs the way for every step, every word and every action, and the *means* to do all that appears necessary will be available. If we appear to need dollars, we will have enough. If we seem to need energy or anything else, it will be available!

VII

No one will deny that total and absolute intelligence would know what to do in any event, under any circumstance. Who will deny that the ultimate in intelligence is the Deific Mind's knowledge of Deity, God's knowledge of God, Isness's knowledge of itself? God's knowledge of Himself is precisely what this Awareness is! This consciousness of being, right here and now beholding these words, is Deific Self-comprehension; hence, it is "total and absolute intelligence" IN ACTION!

Consequently, no matter what seems to transpire and no matter how terrible its augury, there is nothing we must labor to do concerning images and events; rather, there is ever what we are *to be*—consciously!

SECTION TWO

Tranquillity

CHAPTER XI

Judgment—A Key to Tranquillity

THE KOREAN WAR ILLUSTRATION

All we have to do is open our eyes to see people everywhere allowing themselves to be upset by every untoward event that comes along. Truly, it is amazing how little it takes to upset humanity at large. The wrong tone of voice, the wrong look, the slightest twitch in the corner of the mouth, even the word that isn't spoken at all when we think something should be said, is enough to set off a quarrel. We read an "I don't like" into ten times ten thousand sights and sounds. The event that vexes, of course, is the event that is disliked and not wanted; so, when it happens (or appears to) people quickly become irritated, frustrated, and angered.

Reader, it does not have to be this way for you; *and it will NOT be, just as quickly as you come to comprehend what is said here.* I tell you, this very instant it is within our capability to stand unmoved and unaffected by appearances, like a rock of stability in the face of circumstances we would have allowed to tear us apart before! It is our effortless capability—no, more than that—it is our divine *heritage* to stand and see beauty, gentleness and perfection everywhere, without end, even in the world's fiery furnaces and lion's dens where it may seem to others the universe is tumbling around their feet.

The mark of a "successful" philosophy and way of life is just this ability! We may eat education's meager crumbs of comfort until we starve to death, but there is meat on the table, spread out before us, already served and waiting! When we sit down

TRANQUILLITY

(get down) to Reality ITSELF, Peace is *tangibly* present—*Peace*, not a promise of it; not a transitory, drug-induced, medicine-abetted, ecstatic, orgiastic, fast-talking *sample* of it; not crumbs from the table, but the pure Peace spoken of by the Saints and Sages; the Christ's *guarantee* to those who "come." This Peace is the Sabbath, the Shekinah, the Mantel. This is the Rest. "Come . . . and when you have found . . . *then* you will rest!" said (says) the One.

When we begin to *experience* the permanent Peace beyond comprehension, it is a sure sign that Reality is our Foundation and we are beginning to know what it is about. It is our intention during the following pages (as in our talks) to persist in this matter of Tranquillity until it becomes plain to the reader as his own experience. Let me begin by telling you an enlightening, door-opening experience of the Korean War.

I was commanding a rifle company in the mountains, in close contact with the enemy. Late one afternoon, a machine gun began to fire directly over my command post bunker where I, and several others, lived. Every few minutes it fired another burst of bullets a few scant feet over our heads. Those who have heard such sounds are likely to remember the sharp cracks, their resounding echos from the mist-enshrouded peaks, accentuated by the crisp mountain air. It is a sound and a feeling quite unlike any other.

The bullets weren't doing a bit of actual harm, sailing overhead as they were and falling into an empty green-brown valley below; but the shooting of that single gun went on interminably, day after day, night after night, burst after burst, in exactly the same place, over the command post. We paid little attention for a day or so, but as might be expected, it fast became a source of annoyance, especially after several attempts to silence the gun had failed.

By the end of the week it had become sport to gamble a dollar or two on the exact time and number of rounds (bullets) in the next burst, but, despite the diversionary tactics to

Judgment—A Key to Tranquillity 89

make light of it, our annoyance was growing into monumental proportions. Soon we could tell when the enemy gunners changed, having learned the rhythm of their shooting; and when a firefight developed, I could easily distinguish that one gun cracking away, no matter where I happened to be along the line. It stood out above all the rest. Those of us who lived in the bunker, over which that gun fired without ceasing, gave way (to say the very least) to unrestrained irritability and frustration.

During this time, my affairs as a commander did not prosper. I spent every available minute attempting to eliminate the source of that disturbing sound, but the Chinese had dug the gun into the rocks of the mountain in such a way that it seemed no power on earth could dislodge and silence it. My anger and frustration went from blue to black.

One morning after a particularly anguishing night that had seen every attempt to rest shattered, I decided the machine gun would have to go or I would surely come apart at the seams. I called for the artillery liaison officer attached to my command; from him, I summarily demanded and received the fires of an entire battalion of artillery poured onto the offending gun emplacement. Oh, it was an awesome, thunderous event! As tons of shells crashed into the mountain top, I gleefully imagined my nemesis hanging on for dear life, choking amidst the dust and debris of my revenge.

The thunder of our exploding salvos was followed by a tingling silence—a beautiful, golden silence that lasted for about ten seconds; then, another strident, excruciating and particularly long, nose-thumbing burst of bullets cracked over our heads from that damnable gun! It was still in action and my spirit was crushed! Surely, I thought, the gunner on that hilltop must be a nine-lived cat, laughing, no doubt, and, though his bullets touched no one, they were more effective than if they had.

There was no question about it; agony, despair, frustration and pure misery had taken me over completely and grown out of all proportion. I remember trying and failing to write a letter to my family that morning. Then, in quiet agony, my world came to an end and I gave up—simply gave up. In utter dejection, thinking I could not bare the grind in my stomach another instant, I surrendered within, not caring what happened. I was helpless. I wanted an end to the death and destruction and the end to my agony, but more than anything, I wanted inner peace; or, if not that, at least the "sleep that knits the revell'd sleeve of care."

This is when it happened, Reader; this is when the illuminative "lesson" came, when I had given up, completely, utterly, in hopelessness and helplessness. In an instant, the Light came with healing on its wings! As is always the case, it seems, help appears when the intellect surrenders, when the intellect gives up the ghost, when our concern for the Real is greater than our love for the old man. While no words were involved in this "Light," and though it seemed to arrive as an instantaneous "block of knowing" already finished, I can now only try to put it into the words which, in effect, it communicated.

It was as if an inner and outer Presence absorbed me suddenly and violently to force my attention. It seemed to ask, "What is bothering you so much?"

"The bullets from that ungodly gun," I answered.

"But, those bullets didn't hit you or anyone else," the Voice within spoke. "Thousands of them have passed overhead, and not a one has touched you. They are falling harmlessly into the valley below."

"It's the sound!" I almost shouted. "The incessant sound is cutting through me like a knife!"

"Listen to me carefully," said the Light. "A sound is just a sound. What is the difference between the sound of thunder and the soft sound of rain? What is the difference between the sound of the gun and the sound of music? Aren't all of them simply sounds within the Consciousness you are?"

"One is *good* and one is *bad!*" I answered vehemently.

Judgment—A Key to Tranquillity 91

"The sound that has you at your wit's end is a bad sound?" the Light asked me.

"Yes! My God, yes!"

"Has the sound a power of its own?"

For an instant I seemed supra-conscious of sounds of every tone and intensity. Then the Light asked again, "Has the sound a power of its own to make you call it good or bad? Tell me, has the *sound* the ability to make you detest it?—or love it?"

"No," I nearly whispered.

"Has someone twisted your arm and forced you to call that particular sound bad?"

"No."

"Then tell me," the Voice asked, "if the sound has no power of its own and nothing external has forced you to make a judgment, *who* determines that what you hear within yourself—within consciousness—is good or bad to you, tranquilizing or upsetting to you? *Who is the sole judge who has decided the sound of the gun is bad?*"

"I am," I answered.

"Yes, but *Awareness* is your Identity; the Awareness-you-are simply 'hears' the sound, and *Awareness* is not a judge! Judgments are made by judges, and judges suffer from their likes and dislikes, from their 'good' and their 'bad.' *That* is the one who suffers, at his own hands from his own foolishness, but *Awareness* does not suffer. Dear Bill, you are Awareness *voluntarily playing the role of judge,* reaping all he has sown."

After a time—I don't know how long—I admitted that this was so. "Why, this is true," I said. "Yes, this is a fact! Who says the sound has power to make me call it good or bad? Who says so if it is not me alone? A sound is only a sound! Who is causing me to feel so miserable if it isn't me myself?"

Suddenly I knew! I alone make the decisions I like or dislike; I alone am the master of such notions of the sights and the sounds. The bond making me so miserable was my own judgment that powerless sounds were bad and I didn't like them!

Here was a pearl of great price, revealed such that I heard, I saw, I knew! The Heart had spoken! For an instant I had entered my own Holy of Holies wherein "nothing maketh a lie"; I had entered the Secret Place, the Shekinah! The truth I discovered there was enough to solve the immediate problem and infinitely more beside. Vividly, I remember feeling as though a physical water of warm comfort poured over my head, washing away every vestige of tension. I remember the smiles of release, the laughter of peace. I recall telling myself that the pesky sound was certainly serving to show all of us how well we could hear.

From that day, nothing about the war—sight, sound or feeling—bothered me again. No one was more amazed than I at the unshakable equanimity I carried with me up and down those mountains. Here, in an instant, the Heart taught me a lesson in tranquillity that has stood me in good stead countless times since.

Reader, now listen closely, listen carefully, for I tell you a fact: Just as a "sound" has no power of its own to *make* you worry, neither has a "sight" any ability to cause you grief, lest *you* give it that ability! I tell you, no image, no picture, no "thing" within Awareness—be it sight, sound or feeling—has any power *of its own!*

Has it? Who says so if it isn't "you" yourself acting as a judge of the images within yourself? Even according to the allegory, there was no grief in the garden, until the forbidden fruit yielding "good" and "evil" judgment had been eaten. Reader, your Identity is Beholding-Awareness itself, not the *judge* of it who says this is good and that is bad. *That* is the one to "let go."

Judgment—A Key to Tranquillity

If we continue the foolishness of making evaluations, we will continue to act in accord with those evaluations. Things "out there" are not really out there at all, but "here," included within and as the perceiving Awareness itself. Consequently, human judgment is *self*-judgment, and in whatever measure one judges, he but unwittingly judges himself.

"Why doest thou judge thy brother?" "Judge not and ye shall not be judged; condemn not and ye shall not be condemned; forgive (previous judgments) and ye shall be forgiven. Give and it shall be given unto you; good measure, pressed down, shaken together and running over shall men give into your bosom. With the same measure ye mete withal it shall be measured to you again." "I came not to judge the world . . ."

The declaration that anything is "good" is dualism creating self-judgment; the declaration that anything is "bad" is needless Self-condemnation.

A DIALOGUE ABOUT JUDGMENT

"Humanly speaking, when we say something is bad, what happens?"

"We don't like it."

"What then?"

"We attempt to get away from it, change it, heal it or destroy it. If these fail, we may attempt to get over our dislike of it."

"How?"

"Perhaps by attempting to understand it, to see the 'good' in it or alter our actions such that the threat will no longer be a threat."

"Isn't it because it appears to be a threat that humanity decides it doesn't like it in the first place?"

"Yes. If it appears that something is likely to upset our pattern of comfort, we establish an immediate dislike for it. The unknown is particularly feared, and, ordinarily, if we conquer our fear we conquer our dislike. Our judgments of bad stem from the belief that what has been called bad possesses the power to disturb our tranquillity. How inane and foolish every bit of this appears when the Messianic Light blooms within, revealing *Tranquillity itself* to be our unchanging Identity; revealing, in effect, that the very *name* 'Tranquillity' is our well-being! What power on earth can change the *name* I am?"

"Isn't what we call 'good' that which we believe will fortify our sense of well-being and make us happier?"

"Absolutely, and this human determination of 'good' is no better than its opposite. Human good is only the other end of the judgmental scale established by the judgment that something is bad. You can't have one without the other. The instant we cut a circular rope it has two ends. There can't be a personal determination of 'I like' without having 'I don't like.' Identity itself—the 'real' Identity—is infinitely above and beyond either of these determinations. Since neither 'good' nor 'bad' has the power to exist outside judgment, they have no authority outside personal judgment. There is no power in their seeming *when we end the judgment.*"

ABOUT FEAR

Personal fear and consternation are invariably wrapped around "things." Fear has to do with what we believe the objects of perception can do *to* us, or what their absence can withhold from us. Man's constant quest for "things" (and his accumulation of them) is proof of the value he has assigned them and of the power he credits them with having.

When one awakens to the truth that there is neither power

nor value in *any* image of perception (thought, feeling or thing), he has made a major step in the elimination of fear.

QUESTION: How does one learn to view things as having no value or power?

ANSWER: Commencing with the alone and only Awareness (*this* one, right here), we find "things" included *within* Awareness *as* Awareness. We give "value" to the Isness being Awareness, not to the multitude of images included therein.

To use the television set illustration, the "value" is the television set that *includes* the shadows and images "within" its functioning screen. No power is given to the images. The television set doesn't hold itself in horror of the images the screen includes. Neither does this Identity I am (you are) quake before the picture that appears as a personal experience. Why? Because no image "out there" can do aught to this Identity I am.

Sooner or later we must stop paying lip service to this fact and, like Macbeth facing Macduff, *test it!* To "test it" is simply to *stop* assigning value, either good or bad, to that which has no value, either good or bad.

Things, images, objects of perception, reflections, etc., are *perfect* things, images, objects of perceptions, reflections. They are being just what they are being, but the power is not them; the power and importance is That which is being them—and the "That" is God.

HAPPINESS AND "THINGS"

To the old nature, happiness hinges on an external world of things, and especially on the possession and manipulation of them.

"How are *things* going? How is every*thing*? Is every*thing* all right?" surely implies the belief that happiness has to do with the proper alignment of the images within Awareness. Would we make happiness, joy and completeness dependent on a state of "things"? This appears to place the television set at the mercy of the images on the screen.

Externals are not the creators of Peace, Tranquillity or Serenity; *neither are they empowered to alter or remove them.* Indeed, externals are subservient, so to speak, to Tranquillity (Identity). For example, a tranquil view of the panorama yields infinitely more detail and beauty than a fearful view of it, or an angry view, or one that is "blind with rage."

How things seem, therefore, hinges on the view of things. In and of themselves, "things" are not capable of influencing the beholder, who *is* the "viewing."

WE LEAVE "THINGS"

Images are best seen in a "state of tranquillity." If they are to be seen correctly in one's experience, therefore, it should be obvious that the natural place to turn is within oneself, where tranquillity is felt and experienced. Through the eyes of Absolute Tranquillity, "health" and "wealth" are seen as they are.

To feel peace within when everything outside is awry demands that we leave "things." It requires that we let go all desire to correct, manipulate or change the troubling images of perception. It requires that we divest ourselves of the incorrect notion that happiness can be experienced only if "things" get straightened out or the mess is cleaned up—or "healed."

Tranquillity is ever present as our very Identity. It is always "here," but we cannot be very well aware of it while battling the external picture, and we cannot be aware of it at all while believing that Identity is dependent upon, and dictated to, by a world of "things."

Letting the world of things go, with the knowledge that Peace is right here, right now, closer than breathing, we feel the baptism of Peace descend like a river of water. Then, AS Peace, we "look out" and see images as they are and for *what* they are. Inevitably, this view of the world reveals that no matter how ominous the appearance of a particular situation, no matter how dire and foreboding, there is no Power *there*. No condition or circumstance is capable of altering the Peace, the Identity, that one *is!*

TO MAKE A POINT CLEARER

Take a vicarious walk into the early morning. Smell the air's freshness. Look at the wet leaves along the pathway, the damp stones covered with new moss and Spring. Listen to the crisp sounds of rock and sand under foot, the brush of twigs against the clothing. How clear and sharp come the bird's songs, how soft the rustle of the green leaves. The sun is warm; the sky is blue. A clean, beautiful, unhurried day is at hand. There are new blossoms everywhere, unselfishly giving beauty to any-one—or no one.

Now, consider another scene. A dusty room, a disordered desk covered with the accumulation of months: a rubber stamp and pad, a wrinkled and torn paper bag, a sharpened-away pencil with worn eraser. A book is open to a reading of some past time; in a disarranged pile is a carbon paper, a tissue, a jumble of arrowheads gathered from a not-so-distant walk into one of yesterday's mornings.

Who is to say that either of these scenes is to be preferred over the other? Who is to say that one is better than the other? They are both within the Awareness of the Identity being I. *To say that one scene is good and the other not so good is to* give them a power they didn't have before the judgment—the power to alter *feeling*.

II
MORE SELECTIONS ON JUDGMENT AND WHAT IT APPEARS TO DO TO THE OBJECTS OF PERCEPTION

CRITICISM

Criticism is judgment, Webster tells us, usually an unfavorable censure following a critical observation.

Those who criticize most make the most judgments. Those who make the most judgments find the most to be unhappy about.

"Yes," someone writes, "but those who are intellectually able to make the most judgments also find more to be happy about."

Not so! The happiness this refers to is only *the other end* of unhappiness, the joy that is *opposite* misery, gladness that is the dualistic partner of sadness. The one who makes *no* judgments, either good or bad, is never moved from the Tranquillity and Peace which resides in the Heart *at the very center* of Being. This is the Tranquillity that is self-evident only to those who take *no* sides, to those who prefer to judge not, even as they have been admonished.

Backbiting and criticism are merely the negative aspects of judgment. Is a positive judgment any better? It has been written, "When beauty came into being, ugliness arose." A judgment is merely a comparison of one human evaluation to another.

Critics are great peak-of-elation and valley-of-depression sufferers, plunging from the ecstatic height of happiness into the abyss of the soul's dark night.

LETTER SERIES

LETTER I

Dear Mr. Samuel:

You make me very angry! You have led me to my intellectual wit's end. Through your writings I have attained the view that appearances really have no value, that the true value is the Isness which is *being* appearances. I have put this to the test and found it to be true.

This is all well and good. I'll have to allow that it has given me a much greater tolerance of my personal experience—*but this is only an expanded ability to endure punishment.* Even though I'm not so bothered by bad sights, I'm still *seeing* just as many as ever. I feel like a gladiator who has discovered that his armor is impervious—for which I'm thankful; but I'm awfully tired of having to rely on my armor to parry lion after lion!

What I really mean is that I'd like to *have done* with these incessant onslaughts of bad experiences. I'm tired of contending. I feel like the very words you wrote for your woodcutter in *The Melody of the Woodcutter and the King:*

"How long must I labor?
How long must I contend?
How long, Father, before I rest?
Before I see Thee face to face?
Before I lay aside this axe
And take Thy scepter in its place?"

Sincerely,

Dear Dr. Wainwright,

One cannot "have done" with "bad" sights and sounds without also having done with the "good." The determination that a certain set of circumstances is "good," and hence desirable, automatically creates the opposing category, "not good." Granted, it is easier to let go the bad than the good; but why waste time making *any* classification of the Indivisible? Who can be free from *half* his own judgment?

With kindest regards,

LETTER II

Dear Mr. Samuel:

Now I see! Judgment is the culprit! The reason judgment seems possible is because there is something to judge, but this "something" (absolutely *everything*) is that which God is being. Isn't it simple? I have been wasting my time dividing Perfection into a good and bad, perfect and imperfect; into an I-like and I-don't-like. Now it is evident that I have even been attempting to divide God into a reality and an unreality.

But, why in the world have I been guilty of making judgments? If there is only the One who is incapable of making ignorant self-judgments, why have I been doing it?

Yours truly,

Dear Dr. Wainwright,

When the mighty oak is an acorn, it includes within itself all it is. When standing full grown on the hillside, it includes within itself all the acorn is, but the view is loftier. If the oak "sees," I'm sure it simply sees from whatever position it appears to itself to be.

So with us, once we've grown to the loftiness that is above and beyond judging and evaluating everything, we must *act* from this position. We must put action where the intellectual mouth once was and simply stop making judgments like an acorn.

How? First, by acknowledging that images, appearances, and things have no power to harm the Identity being this consciousness of them. Then, to perceive and admit that they are *neither* good nor bad. If they are judged either, they will be experienced as both.

It seemed for me, upon entry into the loftier view, that there was a brief but intense period when I was forced to be just as conscious of my old "good" *as not-good* as I had been in an earlier awakening of "bad" as not-bad.

When I was an acorn I thought as an acorn, so to speak; and "to put off" the acorn's ways appears to require an intense period of personal *de*valuation, "good" as well as "bad."

With kindest regards,

The judgment of images is relative; being relative, must be seen in degrees by the judge. Because the Isness being the image is infinite, not relative, the judge perceives *many* images of varying, fluctuating, wavering "values." These are the out-of-round appearances that constitute the judge's world full of trouble. These are the appearances of a personal experience of frustration, fear and foolishness.

AN EXAMPLE

The "procedure" I follow is to bring myself as Awareness back to the Father's house of Tranquillity and *here* consider the magnificence of the Deific Isness, the Divine Principle Being "I." Only then am I able to look fearlessly, unwaveringly on specific things as *God* being "thing."

Consider Mary, for instance. She is "specific," an image included within this Awareness I am. Her "being" is GOD-being-Mary. The one who recognizes this fact is God, not a personal identity called Bill or Mary. The one who acknowledges this fact of Identity is the only one who exists to acknowledge everything—God. God does not render an out-of-round judgment of Himself, does not see or hear Himself imperfectly; therefore, right here and now, I must not waste time playing the role of a judge passing a judgment of guilty upon Mary. She is not guilty of being out of round! The one "out there" is NOT GUILTY, is not in debt to health nor to the lack of health, is not a trespasser against Tranquillity! Mary is just what Mary is, and that is wholly (holy) perfect! No object of perception is indebted to Awareness, the Identity-I-am; neither does Awareness owe aught to any thing!

THE BASIS FOR ACTION

Most people base their actions primarily on what others may think about them if they do thus and so. If this is our practice we may just as well call ourselves marionettes, since marionettes have no life of their own—no identity, one might say. They are controlled by the strings *others* pull.

Is it not foolish to attempt to identify as one so bound and so lifeless?

Dear Mary Ann,

We do not hold an "out there" in bondage. We do not make an external appearance responsible to us or for us. We do not give it the power to make us happy or unhappy. We stand as immutable Perfection *itself,* against which nothing can prevail; and by so doing, we exercise the power *WE* are.

To give power to an out there is to be a slave to it. To pronounce a verdict of guilty on someone else is to be self-indicted. To free others of such an indebtedness to us is to release ourselves and exercise the freedom we *are.*

Jesus put this very well. Said He, "Forgive us our debts as we forgive our debtors."

Judgment—A Key to Tranquillity

III

JUDGMENT AND THE APPEARANCE OF "THINGS" AND EVENTS

QUESTION: I've never understood the statement inherent within so many philosophies that there is no matter. Will you explain this?

ANSWER: The statement "there is no matter" does not mean there are no mountains or flowers. It simply means that mountains and flowers are not outside consciousness, are not "external." Indeed, there *are* mountains, and little boys climbing them; there *are* flowers, and little girls picking them; but they are not apart from the Awareness that perceives them. They are not "out there." They are not one thing and Awareness another, just as the images on the television picture tube are not one thing and the picture tube another. Images, picture tube and television set are one.

How things appear to us depends on the degree to which we consider ourself a *possessor* of the viewing. To the extent we cease playing the possessor of Awareness—letting that one go—and consciously are Awareness alone, "things" appear the beautiful, flawless and harmonious aspects of Deific Isness they are. It is not that images change, or that Awareness changes; it is that the no-identity, the dark glass, is let go and cast aside. The veil is rent. The mist lifts.

Because Isness, Deity, is all, Conscious Awareness is Deity's own knowledge of Deity. Images (things) are the qualities and attributes that *Deity* knows Deity to be. This Awareness that reads these words is this knowing going on, and the objects of perception are the specific *"what"* Deity knows itself to be! If there is anything to be done, it is to see the absurdity of a "me" getting into the act, who *judges* the things seen and then makes demands of Awareness to coincide with those judgments.

God, God's Awareness of Himself, and all God knows Himself to be are all one God—being, and in action! This is the "mystery" of the Trinity.

We know the images on the television screen, the screen itself, and the television set are all one functioning *television set;* exactly so, Knower, knowing and known are one. Here and now, the reader, reading and read is the One in action, effortlessly beholding another aspect of the infinite Selfhood.

Awareness is an obvious fact because we are aware. All that "needs be done" is to acknowledge *this* Awareness, here and now, to be God's alone. It is our good pleasure to be the Deific Awareness of Deity! This is true! It is a fact! We do not have to do anything to make it so; we do not even *have* to acknowledge it and act it; but when we do, we behold wonder after wonder everywhere and see the ills of the old vision vanish.

WE MAKE NO DEMANDS

End the attempt to make experience (Awareness in action) conform to the demands of the "Bill" or "Elizabeth"-container-of-Awareness we have believed our Identity to be. There is neither "Bill" nor "Elizabeth" identity outside the

Judgment—A Key to Tranquillity

belief that they, as the possessors of Life, are who we are. Letting go that belief (to be the Identity we are instead), "things" appear beautifully, perfectly, gloriously! How else should Isness see Isness? How else should perfection appear to Perfection? How else can Health, Sufficiency, Tranquillity and Peace appear to the Deific Godhead, "Father" of this very consciousness-I-am?

You see, only the pseudo-identity, the "Bill" or "Elizabeth," sees "things" as fouled up, messed up, mangled and mashed. Only "Bill" and "Elizabeth" see images as separate and apart from themselves, "out there." They live a lonely, limited, lackluster life of lack because they hold themselves in another world, unreal from beginning to end. Holding themselves separate from "things," they hold themselves separate from *Reality,* which is *being* "things," and, for them, "religion" is just what the word means—a binding back to God, a prodigal's return from the land of Nod.

Religion seeks to return the *possessor* of Awareness to that place from which Awareness itself has never departed. By now, we understand that God's own Self-knowledge has never gone awandering, and we are that Self-knowledge! We are God's awareness of Himself. Could anything be more wonderful than to be the *knowing* of everything Infinity determines to know of Itself?

Listen carefully: If this very instant we completely let go the idea of "me" as image, thing, idea, man, possessor, etc., *awareness is still here* and being very much aware; consciousness is still going on, right here, right now. We still see mountains and trees. No "thing" has changed. Seeing is still seeing, but it is *God's* seeing, *God's* Consciousness of being, *God's* own Self-knowledge.

Reader, you and I are that Deific awareness itself; God's consciousness of existence is this reader-consciousness of events. God is being this Identity-we-are and is responsible for it. God is being the trees, mountains, rivers, oceans, stars and galaxies. God is being every*thing* this Awareness "sees" and is conscious of in any way whatever.

WE STOP CRINGING BEFORE APPEARANCES

Just because there is no ISNESS *in* the image does not mean the objects of everyday perception do not exist or are "just a dream going on"; it means there is no value, power or importance in them, no matter what they are, or what they appear to be doing or not doing. It means the bird, the bee, the tree, flower, son and daughter are being just what they are—bird, bee, tree, flower, son and daughter—but there is no power *there*. The Eternal Value is the basic, primordial ISNESS being those objects of perception. Isness is the power and importance, forever maintaining, sustaining every "thing" as Itself.

This means we can stop the foolish business of attaching values to qualities and attributes that have no value. We can stop worshipping dollar bills and automobiles and making graven images of personal possessions. Furthermore, we can stop cringing before appearances; then, when we're not wasting our time cringing, we know what to do about them!

Chief among the valueless images to which the greatest value is given is the me-judge opinion holder who is the one who attaches the values and worships the valueless. We cease playing the part of that ridiculous identity the instant we stop making judgments, the process by which we arrive at opinions and attach values to the valueless.

Judgment—A Key to Tranquillity 107

Isness is being this Awareness-I-am as surely as it is being the bee, the tree and the thundering sea. This is why "the things I see are the Self I be" and why judgment is always *self*-judgment. "By what measure ye judge . . ." says the One.

ABOUT DEATH

Note this carefully: We do not have to determine what is to be seen, or how it is to be seen, because Awareness has no responsibility in the matter and does not have to go anywhere to see certain sights or hear certain sounds or feel certain feelings. Isness is completely self-sustaining, effortlessly "caring for" this Awareness we are.

This is certain: The Awareness beholding these words will never stop, will never "die," but will continue beholding the glories of Infinite Being forever, plumbing the depths of God from joy to joy, laughter to laughter, flower to flower, little boy to little boy and little girl to little girl, from evening star to morning star. There is no death of Identity, no end of the Awareness God is being. That Awareness is *this* eternal Awareness-I-am. Dear Reader, this is the Identity you are, and it is forever!

How do I know? I know because it has been shown to me.

IV
WE DO NOT DENY THE APPARENT

It is a waste of time to deny the testimony of the senses, to proclaim the unreality of "the seeing of the eye and the hearing of the ear," as many metaphysical schools would have us do. We do not deny, "let go," or proclaim the *unreality* of the seen. Listen carefully: *We let go the one who claims to be the personal "me" who is supposed to be doing the seeing!* We let go identification with the one presumptuous enough to say "Awareness is *mine*" and who desires to have "my" vision include what "I" judge to be "good." No, we do not deny the testimony of the senses; we deny the *possessor's evaluation and judgment* of the testimony!

We continue to see children, trees, flowers and everything that goes with being aware, but it is Deific Awareness doing the "seeing"—unpossessed, uncontaminated and free. We are this Awareness itself; this Awareness is our Identity. Identity is not the physical body or the human ego that Awareness is supposed to be *in!*

Recently, I had a conversation along these lines with a well-known philosopher. In the middle of our talk, the doctor realized that even though Awareness beholds, *it* has no need of making judgments. "Awareness doesn't decide if things are good or evil," he said with new-found awe. "Awareness just beholds! It is the old ego-me who is constantly making judgments."

A bit later, the doctor ran outside into a driving rainstorm to get something from his automobile. When he returned, he observed that he was aware of rain but, as Awareness itself, he certainly didn't have to decide whether it was good rain or bad rain. "Making no such judgment," he said, "I wasn't burdened with having to like or dislike the rain, or what appeared to be its effects. This is a new freedom for me—a new experience."

There is no question about it. This *is* a new freedom. It is a new joy to be unencumbered and unaffected by the objects of perception. This is the undeniable (and effortless) ability to be "in the world but not of it." Here is the ability to be the power of Tranquillity, even when everything in the world appears to be in terrible turmoil. Reader, I tell you this is the ability to experience Peace, not just to theorize about it and wonder about it and talk about it!

Judgment—A Key to Tranquillity

Dear Nancy,

Just as quickly as we stop acting the judge—the pronouncer of "I like this and dislike that"—and start acting as the uncomplicated and unjudging Awareness of Reality that we already are, there will be no more argument with the seen; there will be no more contention with things.

If what is seen is beheld as *neither* good nor bad, we will not attempt to change it from one category to another. Then, you will find yourself with nothing to argue about. Furthermore, when you understand that your "activity" is simply to be aware, to behold without judgment, you will find yourself free of all desire to experience fulfillment!

I assure you, when you stop contending with things (and contention always stems from your own like-dislike evaluation of them), immediately everything begins to be seen as the Perfection and Beauty it is already, despite whatever appearing it may have to you during the passion of your intellectual evaluations, your likes and dislikes.

Why is this so? (1) Because Reality (Wisdom, Beauty, Deity, Isness) is being all there is to images, if there is anything to them at all; (2) because Reality is being the Awareness that *perceives* them; and, finally, (3) because this same Reality is the real *interpreter* of the perception. If it could be that Reality *is not* being images, then they are not real. If they are not real, they need not be feared!

A very practical Truth lies hidden within these faltering words. Open your Heart and discover it, Nancy. Who can do this for you? Truth is not outside your own Being. I cannot convince you of the Truth that is here; you can only *test it out* and be convinced yourself.

Sincerely,

Dear Nancy,

The great judge, caught up in the agony of his own evaluations would like to be free of the "bad"; yet, how mightily he desires to hang onto the "good"! More than that, he wants to change bad appearances into good appearances and spends every moment trying to do it. Now, various metaphysical philosophies would have us reverse our judgments to see a specific error as the supposititious opposite of Truth; and they would have us call "bad" "good" or be wary lest "good" become reversed.

This is an "improvement" of sorts because the re-evaluation of a "don't like" into a "like" appears to create *its* opposite, manifest as a "demonstration"; but what is all of this but more monkeying around with duality? The Reality being the entire universe has nothing to do with *either* end of a judgment, good or bad, and it is infinitely *"more* than" the personal evaluator's highest concept of "good."

Let us stop liking or disliking the sights, sounds and feelings of Awareness. Reality is being the Awareness that includes every sight, sound and feeling. Reality is not divisible into a good or bad sound, liked or disliked sight, sick or well feeling; therefore, it is pure foolishness to attempt to divide the Indivisible in such a manner. This is to judge the injudicable. Human activity is just so engaged, and for this reason has often been called a dream. We stop dreaming when we stop placing our own evaluations on everything and when we stop acting as if the world's evaluations were correct.

The single Awareness of Immaculate Oneness is not divisible into a good and bad, perfect and imperfect, real and unreal; however, mankind *acts* as though a division were possible and spends all its time classifying every object of perception—good, bad, valuable, invaluable, enlightened, unenlightened, and particularly, "I like" and "I don't like." This is the very purpose of the supposed ego-intellect.

Judgment—A Key to Tranquillity

Is it any wonder that intellectual humanity appears to be stumbling from ditch to ditch, war to war, agony to agony?

The misidentification to come out and be separate from is the one we work at being when we say "I like this and dislike that," therefore, "I desire this and must get rid of that."

Reader, this is the practice that has fathered the age-old enigma called dualism. One wrestles with twoness just so long as he plays the role of judge. The judge stands self-judged, buffeted by every word he utters and every move he makes. The old-man-judge is like one caught up in a dream of dreaming, like one trapped in quicksand where every effort is self-defeating.

ABOUT OUR FORMER OPINIONS

QUESTION: Are we to get rid of our former judgments and evaluations one by one?

ANSWER: Utterly impossible! Even if all our "former judgments" were finally rooted out on a one-by-one basis, such an accomplishment would yet leave the *judge* untouched! An inactive judge he would be, perhaps, and a very righteous one, undoubtedly; but the judge *himself* would still be present, claiming to be the self-purified, self-righteous identity doing the beholding.

No, we do not undertake the endless task of ferreting out judgments and eliminating opinions. There is none of that hopeless and bewildering bunk of having to determine specific causes for specific sights, sounds or feelings, as education and metaphysics would have us do—no blaming tapeworm on bitterness or liver trouble on bad living or feebleness on age or anger on a husband or euphoria on a pill. It is easier than that. There is no labor at all! There is simply to be unjudgingly aware; to be Awareness which is *not* a judge, which is not concerned with judgments or with making them; and we do this beginning right NOW. It is this simple! This is the "new birth"! This is to "become as a single one, as a solitary"; as Awareness unpossessed; as Awareness alone!

LISTEN!

Awareness does not judge. Awareness is just aware. Awareness does not say this is good and that is bad. Awareness is just aware. Awareness doesn't say I like this and I don't like that. Awareness is simply aware. Awareness doesn't desire this or attempt to rid itself of that. Awareness is simply being aware. All the while, Awareness *itself* goes right on with the business of being effortlessly aware. Isn't this true?

Ask yourself: Isn't the Awareness-I-am *being aware,* even this instant? Yes! Is it making judgments? Is it calling something good or something else bad? Is it desiring, hungering, lusting after certain things, eschewing, abhoring, changing others? No! Awareness is beholding, only! Right NOW it reads these words.

Simple, unjudging, effortless Awareness is being this Identity you are and I am. Awareness *only* is the Identity we consciously bring ourselves back to and consciously identify ourselves as—*as!* Awareness is Life!

Anything more than this simple, beholding Consciousness itself is the false ego a-building. Anything that would look upon the objects of perception and call them good or bad is the old personality whose part we have been playing like a role on the stage but who is not, and never has been, our *real* Identity.

V

Let me share this revealing letter with you:

Dear Mr. Samuel:

I have just had the shock of my life: I have put one of your precepts to the test and have been dumbfounded. Really!

My drive to and from work takes me through a congested area at the peak of traffic. I can't tell you how many times things have happened along the way that have upset me terribly, especially in the afternoons when I'm in a hurry to get home.

Recently on one of these trips, a lady driver behind me began to blow her horn. At every intersection, just as the light changed, she blew again. I couldn't go any faster than the car in front of me; I couldn't pull over and let her pass, and she couldn't have passed me anyway. In short, there wasn't anything I could do about it, but at every light change she sat down on her horn as if that would help matters.

I noticed that the driver in front of me had become furious. He was turning around, glowering, waving his arms, apparently beside himself in rage. It appeared that the driver two cars up was angry also. To put it mildly, I found myself thinking thoughts that were thoroughly unpleasant, and I nearly wanted to punch the lady in the nose.

Then, something you said the other evening at your talk came to mind, and it dawned on me I ought to try it out. "A sound is just a sound," you said. I thought that this must mean the sound the lady is making doesn't have the power to do anything, much less spoil my drive home. The sound is merely proving that I have very good ears, and this is nothing to be angry about. Mr. Samuel, this is all I remember thinking; in fact, this is all I thought when instantly, and I do mean instantly, all my anger left me! Every bit of it! More than that, I became amused by the lady's antics. The more she blew, the more calm and collected I became about it all, and the more I was able to see how others were letting a harmless sound have a power it really didn't have. I saw how all my life I had been *giving* power to things that had no power. I saw, too, how insidious the habit of *reacting* to things had become with me and how rewarding the practice of *not* reacting promised to be.

I must write and tell you that this very simple thing has opened a new world to me. Thank you for saying it all in such a way that I finally climbed down off my theoretical stool in the clouds, made the decision to *practice* being judgeless awareness, and then *did* it. In the instant I did it, just as you said it would, the Light came quickly.

Now, I have expanded this practice to include sights as well as sounds—in my family affairs, business and everywhere I go. I am practicing being Awareness *only,* and am slowly, but surely, letting go the old habit of acting like a reactionary judge of Awareness. All you said about the wonder of it is true. I have never known such peace of mind.

I will be forever grateful.

Sincerely yours,

P. S. I didn't realize how hard I had been working to like or dislike everything.

The "old man" is the one who plays at judgment making, making his own hell thereby; but that is not the real identity of you or me. That is the one to cease identifying ourselves *as.*

How do we do this? In the easiest way imaginable: by being this already-Identity as unjudging Beholding; by making no more judgments.

QUESTION: What is our personal responsibility in this matter?

ANSWER: God is the one who is being all that is. God's Awareness of all is this Consciousness-I-am, therefore, God has the "responsibility" to be This that I am and to sustain me. There is no demand upon me to do a thing. (This doesn't mean that I don't appear to do things!) There is no need on my part to worry, fret, fume, fuss or fear. There is only to go about the Father's business of *being* the Father's business—Awareness, witness of Infinity. This is my very own Identity.

EGO

The ego is an elaboration of Consciousness, a dream extension of Awareness, a phantom addition to the Single One. *That* is the one who would say, "God—Isness—*and me too;* God and something besides God; All and a little bit more; Isness and a little bit of ain't." That one is the liar from the beginning, the father of lies. That one is the devil who suffers from his own judgments, wandering to and fro among the objects of perception, calling them good and evil and attempting to devour them all.

NOTE THIS!

Dear Paul,

We are prone to be over-concerned about the people in our experience, forever worried about what they are doing or not doing. Re-Identifying as Unjudging Awareness, we stop *our own* judgment making; we do not lose ourselves in concern about others who appear to go on making judgments and who seem so unaware of the True Identity. We are ever concerned with *this* Consciousness, here and now. *This* one only!

Undeniably, we are forever alone as this Single Consciousness—and it includes the images of "others"—but in this matter we cannot be bothered with what appears to be the incomprehension of our viewpoint, nor with the apparent reluctance of others to do as we do. *First,* let us see the beam out of *this* eye, and not worry about the speck we believe exists in husband's, sister's, mother's, daughter's or friend's eye.

Then, as we persistently *be* the Identity *we* be, we appear to see the mote removed from the eyes of everyone we love. We are able to do this effortlessly, without preaching, indoctrinating or "praying." "Mankind" has never been outside (or other than) *this* Conscious Identity God is being. "As *I* be lifted up," the Christ declares, "I shall see all mankind *drawn unto me*." And you will!

Whom do we tell of the One Identity? Those who are "drawn unto me."

Dear Mary,

The principle of arithmetic is the fact of true calculation, despite the numerical mistakes that may appear on the printed page; exactly so, Established Perfection is the fact of existence, *despite all apparent conditions,* even those you say are so horrible.

If one is bugged by a mistake on his arithmetic paper, he will never get back to the principle while lingering with the error. He "returns" to the basic principle of arithmetic which *precludes* all error, in which no error has ever or could ever exist.

Similarly, if conditions seem disturbing in our experience, we "return" attention (affection) to the basic fact of Established, Perfect Isness, in which there is not the least possibility of a circumstance capable of producing upset, concern, unhappiness or dis-ease.

This is not a head-in-the-sand attitude. This is not to ignore trouble, hoping it will go away. Neither is this a process of correction, healing or demonstration. Contemplating the attributes of perfect Isness, one is not long disposed to continue his sojourn in the far country of dualistic distortions. We *leave* the far country rather than continue the attempt to correct the distortions within it.

Therefore, Mary, regardless of the "chilling situation," we

Judgment—A Key to Tranquillity

return again and again to the Established Perfection which is the fact! We return to the Heaven *at hand!* We acknowledge the Kingdom that is even now "spread over the whole face of the land" but overlooked in the disproportionate concern with the minutiae. We let go the infinitesimal fiction for the Infinite Fact which is here, right now.

We have only to keep doing this "over and over" as long as we continue in the belief that images (the "things of the world") have the authority to make us healthy, wealthy, happy or sad. When Established Perfection, the allness of Isness, becomes one's unwavering conviction *acted upon,* that very instant, experience (including all "things") becomes an unending, unshakable Tranquillity!

There is no truth in the notion that the objects of perception—people, places and things of awareness—can dominate us or influence us. There is no hypnotic power over Awareness vested in the perceived. *Nothing* can make Awareness sick, sad, sour, sanguine or supine. Just who or what says such a thing?

That which is being I, could never be on guard against anything because no thing exists outside Perfection, Completeness, ALL—and *This* is being who *I* am! It is insanity to act as if one were another who *is* influenced by images.

A LETTER ABOUT IMPENDING DOOM

Dear Bill,

You write that your experience "appears terribly dark and foreboding." Well, so what? It doesn't make a bit of difference what the objects of perception appear to be doing, or not doing or threatening to do!

You write, "Everything portends great coming woe and tribulation. The painful lessons of the past make me absolutely certain that a personal disaster is inevitable." Again, so what? What if everyTHING in the universe appears arrayed against you, your business and your bank account? Ask yourself aloud, *which* is the value and the power, "things" or God? Images or God? Objects of perception or God? Choose ye this day! You will appear to serve and be the servant of whichever one you choose.

Listen carefully: If God is being the images, things, objects of perception, then no matter how you personally judge their appearing, they are not harmful and cannot do one thing *to* you or *for* you. If Reality, God, is *not* being "the ominous sights and sounds," you assuredly do not have to fear them. In either event, there is no need to stand in fear of "things," of objects of perception! There is no need to be afraid of what appears to be going on! Therefore, go ahead and look at them if it appears you must. Who needs to fear either what God is being or what God is not being? Like Daniel, you are now enabled to look the lion in the eye!

Does it take courage to do this? It does. It requires the same courage it takes to stand up to a paper tiger when one is not yet convinced it is made of paper. *But can one ever be absolutely convinced until he has made his stand?* Of course not!

"Misery" concerning events and circumstances "lasts" only until one pops the bubble to discover that images of awareness have no power, no value or authority, no matter what other *images* claim to the contrary. The longer one postpones this devaluing action, the greater becomes the seeming, until such time as the dark dream of desperation leaves no alternative but to awaken from it and be convinced that God really is ALL—*that there is no personal experience contrary to Perfection.*

Sincerely yours,

Dear Bill,
    Consider Macbeth about to be put to the sword by Macduff.

Judgment—A Key to Tranquillity

If the actor believes the action is real, he surely suffers from that belief. Now, suppose someone off stage, perceiving the actor's fright, whispers to him that Macduff isn't actually going to kill him; that it only appears so. Can the actor playing Macbeth really *know* this until he faces up to Macduff and *experiences* the fact of truth? His courage to face Macduff fearlessly is in proportion to his trust in the "someone off stage"—the Heart.

Dear Margaret,

I have discovered that, when I bring myself to stop stating judgments aloud, I save myself the ordeal of listening to the same judgments made of me. When I bring myself to stop thinking judgments, *I save myself from every untoward event!*

If you would have a better experience, end judgment making; stop believing that sights and sounds have the power to force you to make qualitative judgments about them. In the instant you acknowledge there is no value, good or bad, in any of the objects of perception (including "feeling"), in that very instant you will discover what a perfect universe this is! You will leave the minutiae, the multitude of things, to discover the *wholeness* of Awareness which is always quite perfect. This "whole awareness" is your Identity in action.

The misidentification's manipulation, or "healing" of the misidentification's illusions, is no accomplishment or mark of attainment; *but the unshakable presence of felt Tranquillity is.*

CHAPTER XII

About Experience and Our Daily Affairs

A TALE ABOUT WHO SAYS WHAT'S EVIL

Once upon a cold January day, a story goes, the village preacher named D. Thomas (he was also the village judge) went fishing and found a rock with a note attached. The note read: THIS IS A MAGIC STONE. LET THE ONE WHO FINDS IT GO OUT INTO THE COLD NIGHT OF A JANUARY FULL MOON, THERE REMOVE HIS CLOTHES, TURN HIMSELF UPSIDE DOWN, STAND UPON HIS HEAD NAKED EXCEPT FOR HIS SHOES; THEN, AT PRECISELY MIDNIGHT, RUB HIS SHIVERING, QUIVERING NAVEL WITH THIS COLD STONE. IF THESE INSTRUCTIONS ARE FOLLOWED IN THE PROPER SPIRIT, THE SHOES WAVING ABOVE HIS HEAD *WILL TURN TO GOLD!*

The preacher read the note, shook his head and wondered who among his flock would perpetrate such a lewd, cruel and evil hoax. Imagine his embarrassment, he thought, if the village judge and preacher were caught standing on his head, naked except for his shoes, rubbing his shivering navel with a cold stone—at midnight. This was the work of a dirty minded prankster, he thought; "A fool in my congregation is trying to provoke my downfall."

Then, musing that a talk about this shameless vulgarity would make a properly jolting topic at the next prayer meet-

About Experience and Our Daily Affairs

ing, the preacher sat down on the spot and prepared a firey sermon about Evil and Deceitfulness (to be aimed at the obscene prankster in his congregation) to which he attached the vile note of instructions as evidence. Then he tucked the papers into his trousers and threw the stone in the lake.

That night, in the light of the full moon (and precisely at midnight) every fish in the lake turned to gold, and the sermon about Good and Evil in the preacher's pocket turned to horse-feathers!

Could this be, the story wonders, where goldfish came from?—and why, to this day, the difference between Good and Evil is the rather ticklish matter of a judge's personal opinion?

Experience and Awareness are one and the same Identity-I. I cannot look at a single, unified Perfection, divide it into pieces, then call some of them good and some of them bad; consequently, I have no right to act as a judge. If I do, I must surely appear to suffer the consequences of one who pretends to sit in judgment of God; and if I'm stupid enough to do this, who would I be fooling but myself?

QUESTION: Exactly what is this daily coming and going of the images of awareness we see? What is this "daily experience"?

ANSWER: It is the eternal nature of Awareness; the continuity of Mind *being aware*. Because there is no end to Mind's action, "experience" appears to NOW as an ever new "unfolding." We refer to this unfolding as *newness,* and this is what "experience" is—*the ever newness of Now*. This very instant Now is brand new, isn't it? Isn't it always?

QUESTION: Yes, but what is *change?*

ANSWER: It is the old man's *judgmental opinion* of Newness. When the intellect is let go, all that has ever been called change (for the better or worse) is seen as sparkling Newness, unbeholden to a past of accumulated causes.

When one unbinds his Now from the belief that all he sees is bound to a passel of prior causes, "miracles," "instantaneous healings" and all kinds of bright experiences are the usual.

IDENTITY = AWARENESS = NOWNESS = EXPERIENCE

Listen carefully: Nowness is not a framework within which Awareness operates. Awareness *is* nowness. Nowness is Awareness. This Now-am-I is my very being and Identity.

Listen again: The combination of awareness and nowness has been called (by philosophy) "experience." Inasmuch as experience is this now-awareness and since this now-awareness is my Identity, *this* Identity I am is being all there is to *this* experience!

We do not *have* experiences. We do not suffer through one experience after another. *We are no longer acted upon by events after we recognize that experience is the perusal of Identity!* Experience is Isness being Self-aware! The experienced is the image of the Self!

Do you see what this means? We need quake no longer at that which turns out to be the mere shadow of our Self! Eternity is but the ever newness of Now. Pristine Now is "my" Identity. Nothing can happen to "me" unless it can happen to Eternity.

It is not that Now is tributary to "I" or that I am tributary to Now; rather, it is that Now and I are one Identity, the same Being.

About Experience and Our Daily Affairs 123

Re-identification is instant release from the misidentification's self-stultifying pronouncements and from the effects they appear (to the misidentification) to have.

WE EQUATE SELF AND EXPERIENCE AS ONE HARMONY

Since we do not have experiences, and experience is being who and what we are, experience is the action of Isness being Self-aware. Our daily experience is greater than could ever be imagined by the one who judges. It is above all comparison . . . no matter how it seems!

QUESTION: How is this applicable in a practical way?

ANSWER: I can only tell you to go about your daily affairs actually mindful that perfect Experience is the very Identity you are. Then just watch how practical it is!

Even by ordinary standards, Identity is established quite beyond the power of anything to disrupt. The force of an atomic blast can do nothing to Identity.

Tranquillity is Tranquillity. Love is what Love is. Spirit is Spirit and nothing inserts itself to make it something else. Perfect "Experience" is what it is—perfect experience. It includes all that is called "the power of the atom," yet there is no force within it harmful to itself.

Experience is my Identity. Identity, like a name, is untouched by tribulation!

We equate Self and Experience as one Harmony!

QUESTION: What do we see?

ANSWER: What Awareness "sees" is our own heart-felt Self-Identification. If one has been looking on a personal poverty, misery and fear, he is assuredly mistaking his Identity and viewing the evidence of that mis-identification.

Inevitably, the mis-identifier's view of a Perfection considered outside himself must appear to him as a universe "out there," as a world divided into two camps and those camps subdivided at every point to their mutual distrust and ultimate neutralization, as a good versus evil, white-black, hot-cold, materialistic-idealistic orgy of opposing judgments, ending only with the "new birth"—reidentification—and with the end of personal judgment such reidentification brings.

HOW TO VIEW THE WORLD

Experience appears as however I view my own Identity. Considering myself limited, frustrated, bound-to-a-body man (manifestation), I appear to myself as I believe I am. Contrariwise, knowing Identity to be that which is being the universe and all in it, I must commence to view Now (and all that appears as the "things-experience" within Awareness) as the *actual*-I that I am, as the Holy Perfection of the One perfect Being. I see every petal of every flower, every twig, every leaf, every rock, every mountain, every star and galaxy that thunders through the heavens and constitutes the universe, as one of the infinite qualities and attributes of my perfect Father, the ineffable Godhead itself; Single Identity perceiving Itself and being "I."

Reader, read this selection again!

The day one is enabled simply to let experience be what it is—that is, to let Awareness be unjudgingly, motivelessly aware—is the day one takes tangible hold of the mantel.

How to "let" is the question of the day. It is not done with effort. It is not done with much grinding of the teeth. It is not done by ignoring appearances. It is done by grace and motivelessness. It is done as love, as gentleness, as tenderness and forgiving. It is not done by the old nature at all, but by letting the old nature go with re-identification. It is done by Identity come to bloom—and the nourishment for the new bloom is the insistent acknowledgment that Isness, Self-Identified, is even now the only one I am. This is God's grace! This is Light and Love!

The flower blooms when it blooms.

CHAPTER XIII

Practicality

MISIDENTIFICATION IS THE "ORIGINAL SIN"

Mankind thinks consciousness is the activity of his personal mind. He thinks of "images" or "things" as external objects upon which his personal mind places its attention.

Well, this is a lot of applesauce. The *belief* that this is true is all there is to "original sin." The belief that one is the possessor of Awareness creates the personality, the ego, that poor, miserable misidentification. The *pseudo-possessor* of Life is the misidentification, the identity we are not, the "old man"; and when we operate from that idiotic viewpoint we must appear to suffer all the distortions of its perspective. Some of them are corkers!

In order to see Truth as Truth is, it is only necessary to be the Truth one already is—*and cease from the false identification,* from the one who uses, manipulates and "possesses" Truth. *Letting go* the identification as a personal ego, that is, as the one who contains this Now-Awareness within himself, we comprehend as the proper Identity, immediately and effortlessly.

This statement is often followed with the question, "But how do I do this?" The answer is simple and easy to understand; we do this by simply being motiveless Awareness *only*—which, among other things, is to perceive *without* opinions (judgments), without saying "this is good" and "that is evil," "I like" and "I don't like." Inevitably, the first step is to end judgment, then to perceive that our real Identity is Aware-

Practicality 127

ness itself, not the ego-container. It is as simple as this. Words cannot tell of the wonders that become apparent when this effortlessness *is put into practice!*

CONVERSATION ABOUT PERFECTION AND IMPERFECTION

STATEMENT: There are not two selves—God and me. Or, we could say, there is not God and humanity. There is God and God being Self-aware. God's Self-awareness is this Self-being-reader, aware of these words. There is no other "you" or "me."

God (Perfection) is being this Self, which is Self-aware. Because God is *all,* Awareness is seeing what God is and this Awareness is perfection-aware—Perfection aware of Perfection. No matter *what* is seen and no matter what terrible label has been put on it by the entire world even one second ago, the scene remains Perfection's view of itself. We cannot be aware of *real* imperfection! The one who says the scene is "bad" is that idiotic, dream-liar who exists with the same authority as Cinderella, a figment of the imagination.

LISTENER: Well, it certainly seems I can be aware of imperfection, Mr. Samuel.

ANSWER: Listen closely: God does not see what *God* calls "bad"—yet THAT "seeing" is THIS seeing going on right here and now. An appearance *humanly* judged "bad" has no actual power to upset the Awareness-I, within which *all* images are appearing.

LISTENER: So, what do we *do* about threatening appearances?

ANSWER: What do we *have* to do about them? We need only see them as the "faithful witness" we are—as motiveless, judgeless, opinionless AWARENESS.

LISTENER: Tell me precisely HOW to do that when I'm suffering the agony of a mortgage about to be foreclosed.

ANSWER: We perceive the powerlessness of the old man's "bad" picture by the knowledge that ISNESS is being *every* picture, including the one presently being called "bad." A very *perfect* Isness is being pictures *perfectly*. Then, with this "in mind," we *respond* to the "appearing" *as a picture that does not have the authority it professes to have to alter* this Tranquillity-Identity-I-am; that is, we respond to the appearing *as an appearing*.

We do not merely *profess* this while we continue to react to the appearing as something to be feared, as something to be healed, as something to be changed or overcome. And, most especially, (listen, listen!) we do not *ignore* the picture as a "nothing claiming to be something"!

LISTENER: But, *what physical action* do we take?

ANSWER: We do whatever comes as the simple thing to do, but in so doing, we observe the "mal-appearing" itself as a guiltless, *powerless* myth. We do all that appears to us to be the sensible thing to do (if it is to breathe, we breathe; to eat, we eat), and we do it knowing that the judged picture of imperfection has no more power to alter Perfection-being-this-Tranquillity-I than any other picture within Consciousness. We react to the images *as images*—as images—not as a "nothing," or as a something to be feared or seen in another way; NOR DO WE *REFUSE TO ACT, fearing such action indicates we are "making a reality of error"*!

When we *actually respond to the myth* as a powerless picture, the human judgment of power-in-it very quickly goes out of it. It cannot seem upsetting to the Identity-I-am. What metaphysics terms a healing is instantaneously perceived.

LISTENER: What do we see?

ANSWER: Not necessarily a *change;* we find the "seeming" *itself* is neither the good nor the bad it was personally judged to be. In fact, using those particular terms, it will appear to be a big fat blessing!

Practicality

The Deific Self-being-I sees nothing that could or would deprive Self of joy; consequently, it is a foolish waste of time, an affront to Serenity, to decide that something is about to, can, or has deprived us of Joy.

The Single Self-being-I is very consistent in this stand because it is the only honest position to take. Every ill "appearing," every threatening situation, is a judgmental *opinion* of good or evil never made by the Single Self of Serenity; it is an opinion of the imposter, the liar, the phantom-judge-of-what-is-good-and-what-is-evil. The Holy One being this Awareness-I-am is not *that* one; the Selfhood of *God* is being me—never less than unchallenged Joy, Supernal Serenity!

This is the "reidentification" one comes home to in the presence of trouble. THIS is the Identity to re-mind ourselves we are. As surely as we do—and act it—we come to discover that there is no power (to do aught to Awareness) vested in the images included within Awareness, no matter what portentous power the entire world of human judgment insists they have. We stop reacting to the rope across the trail as though it were a snake, or to the whirlwind as if it were a bull.

ABOUT GRIEF

Dear Janet,

You write that you have just seen something that induces terrible grief.

Look away for a moment. Look up. The sun is shining; the December wind blows cold across the field; the birds seek out and find their winter sustenance; the forest sends its sap into the roots. With all your apparent grief, nothing has been altered. Neither sight nor sound nor emotion can change the perfect Isness being the apparent universe. The earth isn't spinning off course because of the appearance of a pseudo-ego who lies and labels the Superlative and claims to judge the Unjudgeable! Janet, the world isn't wobbling the least, least bit—much less the Universe! Perfection REMAINS Perfection. Look away for a moment, Janet; look up, and joy in this knowledge.

Dear Janet:

It seems we must be firmly convinced that the power is the Ineffable Reality which is being this Identity-I and that power *is not in the multitude of images seen "out there,"* or even in the thoughts and feelings "within."

This does not mean that feelings and images are the detail of a *dream*. They are "real" enough, *but they are not Reality*. Rather, Reality is being images. It has been argued that this difference is merely academic, and very small at that, but it is this "difference" that allows us to understand, and test ourselves in this understanding, that the images within Awareness (including "feelings") do not have the values and the powers we have been accustomed to giving them for so long.

The old nature of us has many arguments to the contrary, and they are every one supported by a mistrust of the Transcendent Reality being this Identity. To "gird up the loins" is to be mind-full of this Reality again, despite the appearance of an "external" trying to prevent it. Our ability to do this lies in the surrender of the old nature—which is simply the gentle admission that *Reality* enjoys the "mind-full"—and not in an impossible "old nature." We recognize that Reality is not distrustful of Itself.

Dear Janet,

Of course it "works"! And I understand your joy; but we joy in the BEING and not in the "works." Now that we have *found out* that appearances do NOT have the power to upset

Practicality

Tranquillity, we do not succumb to the desire to rearrange appearances to fit a personal idea of how they should appear. This was one of the early temptations Jesus battled with. We *rest* and let the Supernal Godhead be this Awareness-we-are, assuming no responsibility whatever for the what, why and how "we" (Awareness) see.

IMAGES ARE EQUAL

Reality is exactly "where" the pebble, the trees and the mountains are, but the *authority* is in the Reality-being-images and is not fragmented within the multitude of forms. Images are equal in no-authority; everyone is a perfect monument to Reality—a monument with which Reality attests Its nature to Itself.

Reader, we are that attesting going on!

If we are agreed that no appearing can upset Deity and that no other actual Identity exists, why should we react to appearances as though we were a mortal identity which certain appearances upset? As some folks I know who live in the Alabama hills say, "That's just chittlin' choppin' crazy."

How *do* we respond to images? As images simply being images within this Awareness-I-am!

ABOUT THE JUDGMENT AND CLASSIFICATION OF PEOPLE: ABOUT COLOR, NATIONALITY AND RELIGION

Ultimately everything boils down to the fact that Reality is all and that personality, racial identification, body-ego and the like *are nothing*.

Wherever awareness is going on, LIFE is the common denominator. The place of Awareness for me is perpetually *here* as *this* single and only consciousness I am. All other life is seen within *this* perview. All that is perceived as the conscious awareness of "other people" (and all living things) is an extension (or an inclusion) of *this* Identity-I-am. The life that is the actual value is THIS life which *Isness* is being as *this* Awareness, here and now conscious.

Any classification, judgment and breakdown of "people" into races or ethnic groups, into inferior and superior nationalities, liberal-conservative, smart-stupid categories, is a complete waste of time and effort, even though the *judge* claims justification for making his judgmental divisions. More than a waste, it is self-stifling activity that hides, nay, prevents, the realization that God, Reality, Isness is the Supernal Value "in" the universe, and that images, things, people, are tributary, not primary, to God!

None of us would consider the color, size and shape of a bottle of greater importance than the contents and purpose of the bottle. While "people" are not *containers* of life (even though this is the classic philosophy of all education and religion), whether they are or not does not gainsay the fact that the characteristics of the body-form—color, religion, ethnic origin, nationality and all else—pale into insignificance alongside the conscious awareness, the life, that animates the body. (In turn, consciousness itself is less than nothing outside Deity who is the One *being* all life.)

Coupling this Self-evident fact to the equally obvious truth that "people" are but image-extensions within *this* consciousness-being-Identity-I-here-and-now, we see that the racial classifications we make of people, and any judgment of them whatever, is *self*-judgment and *self*-classification, very foolish, inane and useless. "Putting off" the old man puts an end to this farcical foolishness.

The pity is that even those pompous institutions that preach that life has been given to man by God have failed utterly to

Practicality 133

comprehend and teach that God-Life is the common denominator and the value, not the pulpy organism which purportedly contains it. With unbelievable hypocrisy, the followers of our august institutions almost to a man still judge their fellow man (Life) by the color of his skin, by the jut of his jaw, by his church affiliation or lack of it, by the size of his bankroll and the quantity of his material possessions; all this judging, classifying and condemning, mind you, *contrary to their own creeds, dogmas and holy books!*

Such is the flagrant, senseless, monumental hypocrisy of man whose breath is in his nostrils: the old man of few days and full of trouble, *trouble self-imposed by self-judgment!* More than this, the great prevalence of man's judgment of man is positive proof of the ineffectuality and vapidity of his so-called religious institutions which are supposed to lift him out of his excesses and give some degree of peace from his passions.

What is the solution to this human balderdash? Why, *to come out and be separate from all of it immediately!* How? By identifying oneself as Deity's life, and not as the human-personality who supposedly *contains* life. How else? By identifying Deity as life *itself,* not theology's *bestower* of it! How else? By simply being God's unjudging, motiveless, already complete and whole (Holy) *Life-Awareness* here and now. By acknowledging God as all of all, the only presence, the only power, the totality of wisdom. It is this simple! But it takes more than the professing; it takes the doing.

ABOUT FRIENDS AND ENEMIES

Dear Mr. Samuel,

As it is said in the Bible, "I have opened the door and let in a viper."

I have had a close friend for many years who has suddenly

turned on me like a snake. Now, the very sight of him upsets me terribly. Will you help me in this painful situation?

Dear Mr. Scott,
The presence of an image judged to be an "enemy" is only the opposing end of an image judged to be a friend. Both are judgmental opinions of images appearing within consciousness. But who is the judge that looks at their actions and makes a determination? Who is the one that calls one a good man, another a bad man? Who says one image is happy and healthy, the other diseased, fearful and miserable?

Awareness merely beholds images, knowing full well that Isness is being them all. Awareness simply beholds, knowing Isness is pure and perfect, not a house divided against itself into positive, negative, good, bad, sick or well. Awareness beholds the indivisible perfection of Isness (appearing as the universe in its infinity).

What of feelings? Tranquillity is the only legitimate feeling to be felt. Isness IS Tranquillity (itself); hence, Isness "feels" Tranqullity only. Tranquillity is the balanced, wholesome, withiness called Love. Tranquillity is the felt sense of Self-satisfaction which looks at everything and sees a quality of the Ineffable right here!

Therefore, to consider certain events "bad" is to dishonor Isness and place qualifications on "that which God hath made." Well, Awareness has called nothing bad. Awareness is no judge. There is no house divided and nothing to war against, *really*—so our task is to *act* in accord with this Fact. With girded loins and gritted teeth, we step over the rope that appears to be a snake. Within the arena of images, how else can we be certain it isn't really a "bad" image! In what other way can we be sure that judgments are invalid?

With Tranquillity as the Identity, and with Omniscience, Omnipotence and Omnipresence being this Awareness *functioning*, Awareness-I is the power to remain unscathed, "to

Practicality

tread on serpents and scorpions, and over all the power of the enemy; and nothing shall by any means hurt (us)."

ABOUT FEAR

One more thing about fearful and foreboding experiences: there is no ability in any object of perception to do aught malicious to this one I am for the simple reason that an un-self-destructive Isness is the basis for the existence of images, their apparent activity, and this Awareness of them.

Who can steal from me? No wealth or value can be taken from the Identity-I-am. The Identity which is Sufficiency itself cannot be made to contend with chicanery or made aware of malicious actions with nefarious intent. The Identity being Tranquillity cannot be made into *another* identity called distrustful, disgusted, fearful or angry, whether it appears as this body-image or that one.

Furthermore, no image "out there" is empowered with such an ability. Wisdom does not delegate its authority, and consequently, no *image* called by any name has power to do aught to God's own consciousness of being—*this* Awareness I am!

Images have no capacity to be aught but images, and thus we cannot *actually* contend with malicious, conniving, dishonest activity from them.

A LOLLYGOG DISCUSSION ABOUT PAIN

Feeling that is not a balanced equanimity (tranquillity) is not a legitimate sensation. (The subject of "feeling" is discussed in more detail in following chapters.) It is a judgmentally produced liar, powerless to move immovable Tranquillity (Identity) from its center. Tranquillity is Deity's Self-satisfaction—the only feeling capable of being "felt." This very consciousness-"we"-are is Deity's Self-awareness and Self-satisfaction in the process of BEING.

QUESTION: What about pain?

ANSWER: Let me use an analogy. The ringing dinner bell indicates a meal is ready to be eaten. The sound is not the dinner, only an indication of it. The sound is *neither* good nor bad. It has no power of its own.

Similarly, "pain" is a powerless indication; no more than a sight or sound. Pain is neither good nor bad, and, most especially, not evil. What does it indicate? The only thing that exists—Deific Identity, in which there is no painful dis-ease possible, no weakness, no aging, no atrophying, neither birth nor death.

QUESTION: But I want to get rid of the pain. How am I to do this?

ANSWER: To silence the dinner bell, one goes to the table and eats. To have done with pain, one goes to the Identity he is. To attack the pain is akin to attacking the bell ringer. It may produce silence for a time, but the bell will be heard again if the meal remains uneaten.

Usually, the bell ringer hushes *when we go to the table to eat*—an action quite different from an attack on the sound. We "silence" pain by doing something equally "different": we return to the real Identity, to the Fountainhead, to the firm foundation of Existence, to our already established, painless Identity! There is no more pain in Identity than bell-sound in the dinner!

But it takes the trip! It takes the conscious acknowledgement that there is but one Self-Identification, THIS Awareness-I that Deity (Spirit) is being; and that this Awareness is not the possession of some sort of personal "me."

It appears to take this conscious position resolutely enacted. Only from this fully honest stand can one "have done" with the apparent presence of a lingering lie—should the lie seem to persist. After all, when we are seated at the table enjoying the feast, we may tell the bell-ringer to stop sounding the call

Practicality

to dinner, if it appears this is what it takes to silence him; and we can do this with absolute authority, *knowing* we are seated at the table.

Pain is utterly without real power or capability of any kind. Long ago we stopped denying the senses to discover that the ideas-things-images of awareness were without the value, power and authority human judgment had given them. Now, let us stop *denying* the reality of pain to see that it is neither real nor *UNreal*, but is simply being what it is, without the ability to hamper Awareness; unable to keep Tranquillity from being tranquil, and apparent only to call our attention to the transcendent Peace ever residing as the Center-I-am.

Reader, from this moment on, *end all argument with pain, weakness, consternation and the rest.* You have seen the wonders of viewing images without attaching values to them—so now end your judgment of feelings; go ahead and feel whatever feelings come to be felt, but without fear for every twinge that is not (or was not) judged "good." We do this and thereby end the desire to change one feeling into another. A sensation has no more ability to alter Identity than the sight of yon field of violets to rearrange the alphabet! And here is the secret: an *unjudged* sensation will not appear to try to!

CHAPTER XIV

A Lollygog Lecture on Thinking, Thought, Meditation and Miracles

Very often one wonders how he managed to get into the mess he appears to be in at the moment. He looks about himself and sees a faltering business here; a quarrelsome home there; a philandering husband or a nagging wife; a monotonous, humdrum, lackluster life of limitation. "If only I had done such-and-so," he berates himself, "this trouble would not have occurred."

Reader, if such a thing appears to be our experience, rest assured we are attempting to hold this Now-awareness in bondage to a long history of causes. This Now-awareness-I-am (and you are) is not so bound! Mankind believes he sees the accumulative results of an infinite number of prior events. To such a belief the future must appear to depend on present action, so the believer battles constantly with his own "cause and effect." He creates an experience governed by self-made karmaic law. "Success" to him is merely the adroitness with which he and others are able to think, plan and calculate their way through this self-imposed, self-binding jungle, and come out smelling like a rose. Saddest of all, the greater the attempt to *think* oneself out of trouble, the greater the bondage appears.

"Who by taking thought . . . ?" the Christ asks. "In such an hour as ye *think not,* the Son of Man cometh."

Thinking, Thought, Meditation and Miracles 139

Few have discovered that we are able to "think" or to listen and see without an individual intellect. Mankind, mighty container of awareness, is proud of that great possession of *his*. He prides himself in his ability to analyze every sight and sound within it and react accordingly. All education has trained him this way. Indeed, the mark of the ego's intelligence, it is said, is its ability to (1) *comprehend* with alacrity, (2) *compare* situations in a flash to past experiences stored away in memory, (3) *judge* righteously, (4) *plan* a personal action accordingly, and then (5) *execute* that plan.

Without doubt, the primary "action" of humanity is "thinking"—thinking construed to be evaluating, analyzing, reasoning, calculating, planning and judgment making, not to mention the worry that ordinarily accompanies all its decisions.

Well! This is the very business that has gotten the world into its apparent trouble! This is the activity that produces the intellect's trials and tribulations—just plain, everyday "thinking."

For generations, the slogan has been "THINK! PLAN AHEAD! CALCULATE!" Cocktail lounges, psychiatrists' couches and hospitals are filled with those who have had their fill of such thinking—without success, without finding happiness, and without discovering the first thing about their Identity.

The time has come to *stop* thinking, planning and evaluating. The time has come to stop the incessant judgment of every sight and sound. Why? So we may go about our daily activities with unencumbered vision and unabated enthusiasm and see everything as it is: beautiful and perfect. I tell you, when we end this personal, intellectual evaluation habit, our desert, seemingly barren of health, wealth, companionship, love or happiness, will run with rivers again! When we stop all this "I like-I want; I dislike-I don't want" nonsense, our desert will blossom as a rose! Sorrow and sighing shall flee away! When worried thinking ends, we find that Perfection is already established and at hand!

Extravagant statements? Don't take my word for it; listen to your Heart and your own experience will be the proof!

Personal evaluation and judgment require the memory of past events and experiences. Such thinking is the activity of the ego, the personal intellect. Men determine the intelligence of others (or their lack of it) by how adroitly they "reason" and make use of "logic." When does such "thinking" take place? In the NOW. What is its purpose? Supposedly, to usher in a better experience or to hold on to one that is thought to be more desirable. Often, thinking is a woeful rehash of the past or a fearful mental rehearsal of an anticipated event.

Consider what happens to the NOW while one is doing this thinking. It is covered over with a veil, as the rose illustration has already pointed out. It is viewed "as through a glass darkly." In fact, when thinking is ponderous enough, the right-here-right-now appears to be lost to vision completely. Isn't this so?

Awareness *itself* is our Identity. Awareness is being aware. Awareness is beholding. We are this Awareness aware whether we take thought or not. As Awareness *only* (not the possessor of it), we simply view things without judgment; without planning and calculating; without comparison and criticism; without dividing and subdividing and without making a critical analysis of everything. As Awareness we behold! We muse wholeheartedly. We enjoy color and form. We examine the infinite detail of Deity. Effortlessly, we see the precision and perfection of the ALL that NOW is!

In so acting, I assure you we are not worrying about the blunders of yesterday or of what might happen tomorrow. As Awareness, one is active *NOW*, and—listen carefully—NOW is all right! NOW is always all right!

Life is unencumbered NOW. Awareness is free NOW; but the very minute one starts labored thinking, the instant he

Thinking, Thought, Meditation and Miracles 141

begins planning, calculating, reasoning, judging, criticizing, condemning and worrying, the NOW *seems* covered with a veil, and we have plunked ourselves right back into the middle of the cause-effect area of human activity called "the seeming dream." The start of that dream is *personal* thinking, thinking that is not the great necessity the world makes of it. The time for thinkers is coming to an end.

NOW is now already. It needs nothing to help it along. "The world is a perfect vessel," wrote the sage. "Perfection is spread over the whole face of the land," says the Christ.

TAKE NO THOUGHT: BE STILL AND KNOW—ABOUT MEDITATION

QUESTION: What is meant by meditation, "practicing the silence," and what is its importance?

ANSWER: Many things we read and study, many philosophies and the teachers of them, tell of the wonders of meditation and of the benefits to be reaped from "practicing the silence." Throughout history we have heard the many admonitions to "take no thought," to enter into the silence, to meditate in quietness and to "be still and know." Judging from the letters I receive and from the comments of those with whom I talk about this matter, many feel that they have failed and feel guilty because they find themselves unable to "exclude thoughts from consciousness." Many say to me, "To take no thought means that I am to become a mindless blank—a vacuum! How in the world can I stop thinking?"

Understand this: Even though to *"stop thinking as a personal thinker"* (as a possessor of Life) appears mandatory, nonetheless *it is effortless!* And it does not mean that we must become a mental blank. Not at all!

A story has been written that will make this clear. It is about a prince who was raised as a poor woodcutter, unmindful of his kingly identity. For many years, the prince labored and toiled, felling the huge oaks of the forest one after another, cutting them ino kindling to sell at the market place. Despite the magnitude of the toil, he was barely able to provide for his family. The fervent prayers that came forth from his agony went unanswered. Then one day, in the midst of a great despair over his hopeless situation, the lost prince was found by his father, the king, who told him of his royal identity and kingly heritage. At first, the prince didn't believe it; it was simply beyond his comprehension. But then he was taken up into a high mountain by the king and shown the entire kingdom *that was his very own.* There, on the mountain top, his heart whispered, "It is so!" and finally the prince believed. With this, he received the mantle and scepter and was told to commence his reign. Then, in great relief, he threw down the heavy axe and shouted aloud:

"I have sought Truth all my life, but lo . . .
That that I seek, I am!
Every tree in the forest is mine!
And every forest in the land is Thine, oh Mind that is Me!
The borrowed axe was borrowed from Myself;
The acres leased were rented from Myself;
The wood was cut for Me alone."

With some reflection, this story should serve to make clear that one does not have to stop thinking and "empty out his thoughts" before he is enabled to assume the rightful identity. Just as quickly as the prince recognized his honest identity *and accepted it as his own,* he instantly and effortlessly stopped thinking as a woodcutter. *But he did not stop having thoughts!* He did not become a blank! He thought consciously *as the king,* not as the woodcutter. His thoughts were effortlessly kingly. He stopped thinking limitedly, narrowly, impoverishedly, hungrily, greedily, angrily and desirously. Such woodcutter-thinking was let go without hesitation. Why? Because he was the prince and always had been, not a woodcut-

Thinking, Thought, Meditation and Miracles

ter. Furthermore, it was immediately apparent to the prince that thinking and acting *as the misidentification* had resulted in the *misidentification's* trials and tribulations!

So what do we do? We accept and assume our rightful heritage, our proper Identity. This is an effortless task because Identity is an already-fact. But we can assume this heritage only as we stop playing the role of the woodcutter. We cannot continue to keep consciousness full of *woodcutter* plans and calculations, *woodcutter* fears and phobias, *woodcutter* judgments and thoughts. How can we do *that* and simultaneously be the New Identity? We cannot serve both. We must "choose this day" one or the other. Really, there is no choice in the matter; Identity is established. It exists outside the influence of a phantom's personal choice.

So, the "silence" we practice is the silence of the *woodcutter's* thinking; a silence of worry and concern for what appears to be going on in the woodcutter's affairs; a silence from the plans and calculations the misidentification makes in order to establish peace where peace already exists. We practice silence from fault finding and *judgment*.

This is not to become a mental blank. This is not to sit in a chair and attempt to push out every thought, erase every image, silence every sound, negate every emotion. Not at all! Our silence is to sit loose and simply be the *thoughts* of Deity, the *thinking* of the One Mind, the Awareness of beauty and harmony, which assuredly includes more wonderful thoughts, ideas, sounds, images and emotions than the world has dreamed of!

ABOUT POSITIVE AND NEGATIVE THINKING

It is a well-known worldly fact that man sees what he looks for and confidently expects to see, whether it be "good" or "bad," "success" or "failure." We have seen the results of "positive" expectations and have watched the apparent failures that negativity brings. Within the human picture of things, those who look for certain "effects," confidently expecting to see them, generally get to see what they are looking for. From out of this phenomenon has grown the cause-effect metaphysics of the Western world, generally an expansion of the Eastern idea of "karma." It teaches, in part, that one's personal experience will be greatly improved if he will turn his thinking from the negative into the more positive expectation of "good." There is an expanding assortment of books along this line of "positive thinking," as the Eastern idea gains in popularity around the world.

But, reader, listen carefully. Is this expectation and realization of "positive good" what one really wants? Undoubtedly, for a time it seems so to us all, but is there any *lasting* freedom in such action? *None at all!* On the contrary, this "positive thinking" is to take the weight of the entire world on one's shoulders, endlessly having to determine what is positive and what is negative, what is "good" and what is "evil," and then to make positive calculations and eliminate negative thoughts, expecting positive results and refusing to anticipate negative effects. This has us attempting to judge, heal and make over the universe to fit a *personal judgment* of positiveness.

This, of course, is what the world is doing, but such action is widening, not lessening the apparent dualisms of "good and evil," "real and unreal," "truth and error," etc.

"Positive thinking" is only the humanly judged "good" aspect of thinking, planning, calculating and evaluating. *All* personal thinking, every bit of it, positive or negative, glosses over the transcendent NOW and leaves us trying to manufacture a personal idea of another perfection; it places this Now-awareness in another time and in another place.

"Who by taking thought can add one inch to his stature?" Jesus asked. "Take *no* thought . . ." said He. We have done with *all* personal thinking, positive and negative alike!

How? The big question, *how? Of himself,* the personal thinker can never stop thinking. Thinking is his entire activ-

Thinking, Thought, Meditation and Miracles 145

ity, his happiness and sadness from birth 'til death. Like Macbeth, thinking is his role on the stage and is all there is to him. "I can't stop thinking," says he. "Neither can you," he adds. "Thought goes on even while we are sleeping."

This is true; the personal thinker, the great *possessor* of mind, cannot concentrate himself out of thinking, cannot meditate or ponder himself out of thinking. Then how? Listen softly: One ceases thinking as a personal thinker just as quickly—and only—*as he stops believing himself to BE a personal thinker*. At that instant, in the twinkling of an eye, he is the *thinking* of the Divine Mind; he is Awareness itself, filled with joy-full thoughts—not the plans and calculations of the manipulator, but wonderful thoughts of a beautiful and complete NOW! Indeed, as thought-full Awareness itself, he becomes aware of thoughts that are a continuous surprise and delight, thoughts that are spontaneous, automatic, effortless—so wide, so all-inclusive as to astound the old judgmental sense of self. *This* is "the Mind by which the prophets spoke"; this is "the Mind which is in Christ"; this is the Mind being the Awareness I am—this Awareness right here, right now.

CHAPTER XV

The Way to *Experience* the Miraculous

To the unregenerate *thinker,* a miracle is "the unexpected; the unanticipated"; a miracle is that which is considered least likely to happen. To the thinker, what appears as his own experience is primarily the expected, anticipated, planned for, calculated and worked for event.

As mankind becomes more scholarly and sophisticated, he devotes ever more time to thinking, planning, calculating, and anticipating the fruits of his personal, intellectual endeavor. Then is it any wonder that the miraculous appears to be gone from his experience?; is it any wonder, when he leaves no place for the unexpected, no time for the unanticipated?

When does the "healing," the "demonstration," the "miracle," the "wonderous event" take place for us? In the NOW, the only time we are ever concerned with. The daily experience is a continuing unfoldment of NOW, an eternal newness of NOW.

Reader, if you should hope to have a special event happen in your life—if this is the reason you are reading this book—the time such an event will happen for you is sure and certain! Your miracle is within the Awareness of this NOW, this very instant! There is no other place for it to exist, no other time for it to happen. How close can you get?

The Tranquillity, the peace and perfection of this NOW, including the sights, sounds, images and all we experience, is

The Way to Experience *the Miraculous* 147

bound (tied) to a long string of past causes *in personal judgment only!* But, oh how tenaciously we clutch this personal judgment-making to our hearts, constantly looking for the *causes* of everything we see.

Reader, this moment we are consciously able to free our NOW from the past to which we have bound it with the simple recognition that this NOW is NOW, the Deific time of perfection—immaculate, free, untarnished, untouched, pristine and pure!

Envision what this means! There does not *have* to be the appearance of an aging body breaking down under the accumulation of effects! Chains that seemed to bind us even moments ago are not required to appear NOW! *No external circumstance or image has the authority to put us in bondage or appear to keep us there.* We experience freedom from every untoward event NOW, simply by freeing our concept of this NOW.

Who can do this for you, but you yourself?

HOW TO EXPERIENCE THE MIRACULOUS

The old man, the liar, the possessor—the THINKER—would have us believe that now, this instant of experience, is the result of countless past causes. "I am in this room," says he, "because I brought myself into it. I am holding a book in my hands because I picked it up. I am old because so many years have passed. I am lonely because my companion has departed. I am poor because of economic conditions."

The personal thinker's experience is based entirely on causes and effects; but what *kind* of effects? Effects that are *expected, anticipated* and *looked for!* Drop a glass (cause) and what does he expect (looked for effect)? He expects gravity to pull the glass to the floor. If he closes his eyes and opens them again (cause), what does he expect to see? Why, absolutely and positively, with no doubt at all, with no mental reservation in the matter and without thought taking, he expects to see about what he saw before he closed his eyes. In addition, he *expects* to see what he looks for.

So, what does he usually see? What he expects and believes to be possible. Mankind sees, experiences, and works to experience what he expects to, what he considers possible or likely.

Now, listen carefully with your Heart: all we see and experience is seen and experienced as this Now-Awareness. If we are to experience the fulfillment of a dream, if we are to experience a "healing" or a "miracle," it must be in this self-same NOW. *Here we come to the crux of the "miraculous."* Ask this question and answer it for yourself: "Can I feel and experience the Perfection *this NOW already is* if I keep it cluttered up looking for the *anticipated* effects of my own personal thinking?" Can you? One doesn't see his completeness, the miraculous perfection of NOW while, out of long habit, continually looking for the effects of prior causes—human causes built upon a personal judgment of limitation, lack, dis-ease and imperfection. The universe appears to him as it does as the result of his clutter of judgments, evaluations and anticipated desires.

NOW is perfect. NOW is new. NOW is clean, fresh and immaculate. Nothing about this very present NOW of Awareness exists because of human history. NOW is what it is because ISNESS is being this NOW. ISNESS!

Reader, when you discern the wisdom of ending the age-old habit of unconsciously expecting good or evil "effects" from good or evil "causes," you will have the conscious experience of the uncaused, uneffected NOWNESS that God is. When we stop anticipating and expecting the small, ordinary effects from prior causes, we experience the magnificent, monumental, miraculous already-perfection of NOW.

MORE ABOUT THINKING

Again we are asked, "How does one stop thinking?"

We don't; *we stop being a personal thinker,* to be Awareness itself. Awareness is the thinking of Deity. We can only stop trying to be a thinker *on our own* and acknowledge Isness as the all of Consciousness; hence, the all of thinking and thought.

We "stop all thinking" as though we were an identity who possesses Awareness. We stop all thinking as if we were a personal *judge* of the images contained within Awareness. We stop planning and calculating as a personal thinker to *be Awareness alone* and *only.*

Awareness is the "witnessing." "Be a faithful witness," says the Christ. Be this alone! How? Become mindful of the Heart, the only place any of this makes sense. From out of the Heart comes the first beam of light to penetrate the dark personality's nothingness. Shortly, we find our entire experience to be Awareness in action. *Then* we see whatever is seen, without judgment and without fear—because Awareness need not (cannot) fear what Awareness is.

Only Isness presents itself to be witnessed, and only Isness is present to witness itself. The beholding, the witnessing, is *this* Awareness I am! (And you are, reader.) Deity *witnessing* is being this Identity!

Thoughts continue to come to us concerning everything, but they are happy thoughts and complete. They are no longer involved in ponderous planning and calculating nor with human reason and logic. They are God's thoughts, not "ours"; yet "we" are the happy *Awareness* of an infinitude of thoughts and ideas as surely as we are the awareness of the qualities and attributes ("things") which transcendent Being is being.

NOW is untouched and unbound by "positive" or "negative," good or evil, cause or effect! NOW is brand-new! NOW is ever unfolding and renewing itself from glory to glory!

Let us get this straight: NOW is in no way beholden to humanity's "time." NOW has nothing to do with cause or effect. NOW is above them, beyond them. NOW is miraculous!

THE HEIGHTENED SENSE OF ALIVENESS

QUESTION: Mr. Samuel, now that I am engaged in this study I seem to be more acutely aware than I have ever been. Why?

ANSWER: The rose illustration spoken of earlier shows that as one commences and sticks to the NOW, *conscious* Awareness is less cluttered with the fears and frustrations of personal thinking. Consciousness (Awareness) is the activity of Isness, the Divine Mind, whereas personal thought taking is the action of the intellect, the would-be *possessor* of consciousness. As long as we consider ourselves to be the intellect, we are not identifying ourselves as Awareness and are not as acutely aware of that which Awareness includes. Sticking to the NOW we are consciously *being* Awareness, letting the intellect go hang. This is one of the "reasons" everyone engaged in this activity enjoys a heightened sense of aliveness—Awareness and Life being synonymous terms.

Even though it seems otherwise, Awareness has never been less than perfectly aware, because it is the activity of Isness itself. These apparent differences of degree are mere intellectual opinions of the personality-me. Nothing more. Isness does not begin to see itself *more* clearly!

QUESTION: Why am I enjoying so many more *thoughts* now than ever before?

ANSWER: This is like asking, "Why do I hear so much

The Way to Experience *the Miraculous*

more music now that I've stopped eating potato chips?" God is being "thoughts" as well as "things." The Awareness Isness entertains of itself includes these thoughts. Letting go the intellect, the possessor-ego we are *not,* the Awareness we *are* is found overflowing with thoughts that come from (and are) the Deific Mind. These thoughts appear to rush in and take the place of the great glut of comparative judgments and evaluations which were the fearful *thinking* of the intellect.

What wonder and awe is ours when we find Deific thoughts—angels, as some call them—effortlessly included within the very Identity we are: *perfect* thoughts, serene and peaceful thoughts, "arriving" to maintain the integrity of the NOW-"moment," arriving that we may know whatever appears necessary at the moment.

Now you see, "taking no thought" is not to stop thinking or to empty consciousness. The cluttering thinking to "stop" is the foolish business of *judging* sights and sounds, of *giving values* to the images and thoughts of Awareness, of planning and calculating to bring about a more perfect perfection. Those are the foolish things we do when identified as the personality-ego-intellect who believes he is the possessor of Awareness. Identified as Awareness, we find the Identity-we-are *filled* with every tangible and intangible thing that ever appears necessary.

ISNESS is the thinker, the thinking and the thought. What has this Thinking-I-am to do but sit back and enjoy the Thought of the Thinker? . . . like a mighty mountain watching the wonders of the seasons as they paint their pictures of perfection on my face!

"The time for thinkers has come." Bosh! The time has come to reckon God to be the only mind in all existence, and *God,* the only thinker. The time has come to stop playing at being an opinion-thinker, to be the *listening* for a change! Awareness listens; it doesn't think! Awareness hears the incomparable music of Supernal Being which personal thinking only covers over with a veneer of erudite sheep dip.

We do not stop thinking, as such—we stop thinking *ourselves,* to become consciously aware of the Godhead thinking *as this identity*—as "us."

EFFORTLESS THOUGHTS

"Splendor beyond words!
   . . . sweet sounds bathed in gossamer beams from an expanded heaven . . .
The immaculately conceived now so effortlessly perceived;
Incommunicable language of gentle words;
Intimate symphony without sound.
"Questions no longer!
   . . . a simple basking in the soft new sound of the NOW that ALL is . . .
The 'has been' and 'shall be' are passed away."
        From The Melody of the Woodcutter and the King

CHAPTER XVI

Boundless Energy, Effortlessness and the Rediscovery of Youth

> One of the many amazements of this philosophy *lived* is the unexpected discovery of boundless energy, a sense of effortless activity and the truly astounding rediscovery of youth in all its aspects.
>
> The following selections pertain to the why and how of these phenomena.

I see a grain of sand on the ground. How much effort must it expend to be there? How much work must it do to be just what it is? And over there is a pebble. How much labored activity must the pebble engage in to be a pebble? There is a tree, effortlessly being just what it is, reflecting every law of life and grace that is being the tree.

The mountain there—must it do anything to be a mountain? The rivers? The lakes? Must the ocean muster its own energy to pound the shore, or is a greater law being the power of the tide? How much effort must this earth expend to turn on its axis and wheel in its great circle about the sun? Consider the sun in its galaxy of countless stars; how much power must it expend to maintain its place in the spiraling nebula? None at all. None at all.

In the infinite universe where Reality so orders everything from the wheeling galaxies in the heavens to the little pebbles at the edge of the brook, why must man, of all the images within consciousness, struggle and strive so, stretch and strain so, to *reach* the Order, the Harmony, the Power, that is inescapably here and all already?

Everything is Harmony, present as a perfect universe. Reader, look at the sunshine. See the blue sky. Behold the bird soaring there while the earth turns so silently. Look at the effortlessness of yon flower just being a flower.

All this serene effortlessness am I!

A LOLLYGOG DISCUSSION OF ENERGY

Reader, for you the unpleasant aspects of physical labor can become a thing of the past! It is possible to discover "the power within" that actually makes physical labor effortless! This is not to say we won't puff and blow when we carry the piano upstairs, but we can find ourselves fresh and full of enthusiasm after the job, such that everyone wonders where the strength comes from. We will know!

The "life cycle" as perceived by the world is an energy consuming activity, alternating between periods of work and periods of revitalizing rest, until finally the old machine appears to wear out, rust, decay and dissolve in death.

Among mankind's many myths is the entrenched belief that action *must* consume energy. Though this appears to be the case, enlightenment reveals it is not an inviolate rule. Man is constantly being confounded by those who appear at every scene to do most of the work, who "run without being weary" and possess an inexhaustable supply of energy. Let me tell you their secret.

They have discovered that there is no struggle involved in consciously being the Identity one is. Many have come to see that "Being is effortless," as Laotse, among others, has written.

"Being" is Isness—God. Its activity is inescapable awareness, *the only activity going on.* (This is why Awareness is total, alone and all to each of us, why we live alone *as* Awareness, why we have never seen a sight nor heard a sound but our own. Isn't this so?)

Awareness is the sum total of all the activity that is ever going on. For this reason, activity is effortless, no matter what it appears to be, and could not possibly be the cause of fatigue. The consciousness of this fact, acted upon as the only reality, appears as work done without effort!

QUESTION: Does this mean that my body does not have to age and wear out?

ANSWER: Awareness includes *all* body-images. Letting go the finite view of images, we also let go the limiting opinions of the image we have been calling "my" body-image. It too is included within Awareness.

Awareness is no more concerned with individual images (as more important than others) than the television screen is concerned with individual cowboys. It doesn't consider "mine" any nearer and dearer than "yours," or the good guys better than the bad guys. If the screen could be concerned at all, it would be concerned with its business of being a faithful screen, reflecting the perfect images of the television set.

This knowledge surely appears as bodies remaining youthful beyond human standards; as strength, unabated and sufficient for every situation, irrespective of years. Furthermore, this appears inevitably as a zestful spirit, filled with wonderment about all things and enthusiastically beholding Love in (as) everything.

ENERGY

Functioning Awareness is obviously "who" and "what" I am. This Awareness, and the goings on within it, have nothing to do with the personal determinations of a human being called Samuel. Awareness is the activity of the Deific Mind. Therefore, the responsibility for Awareness' experience is entirely up to Isness, the only Mind. There is no personal responsibility, no Samuel responsibility, no Jane, Mary or John responsibility at all. There is nothing to do; nothing that needs to be done; nothing that must be left undone, learned to unlearn. There is just to be what one is already—Beholding Awareness. *This is effortless because Deific Isness is doing the beholding.*

This is the knowledge one stands pat on: knowledge that one's Identity is "energy" itself, not an organism that energy passes through, not a body-form that alternately accumulates and discharges energy. This is the "practical" knowledge that is demonstrably anathema to fatigue, weakness and debility.

I would like to share another letter with you:

Dear Mr. Samuel,

The events of the past weeks have been wonderous beyond measure. Where are the words to tell it? How can the effortlessness of so great an effort be told? So much appears to have transpired in so many areas and so much has been accomplished. Where are the words to tell how serenely, how effortlessly, it has taken place?

My business was a vast production, a prodigious effort that had snarled. Worse than that, it had bogged. Every appearance shouted for labored management, careful manipulation, dexterous control with awesome responsibilities and awful consequences at the least mistake.

Somehow that vast mess responded exactly as you said it would. The unsnarling took place in direct proportion to the absence of management and manipulation. The less personal control exerted, the less intellectual planning and calculating, the more speedily the machinery operated, the more unbinding was accomplished, the more corrective events whirred and purred, pouring a healing balm into and over the apparent picture.

Surely, during these days, my wife and I have been the witness of a miracle, so called; *witnesses*, not participants, not manipulators. All we have said we have been led to say. All we have done we have been told to do, while the saying and the doing were without effort or strife. We faced every harrasment as a nothing, incapable of upsetting the tranquillity of Witnessing. Every obstacle vanished as the nothing it was. Every stumbling block has been seen as the blessing it always was in reality.

Even to this moment the wonder of it all has not stopped. There will never be words to picture it in the detail a telling demands. For my wife and me there is just the looking out upon a prodigious "accomplishment" that appears as a monumental turn of events, the undeniable work of God. What is the quotation? "Acknowledge God in all thy ways and He will direct thy paths."

As you wrote me, "Perfection is directing this experience-being-I by being the Experience I am."

This is so. This is true. This is a fact!

ENERGY II

I am activity *itself*, not one who is being active!

As a personality, I consider myself an identity who can be active or inactive; as that ego, I consider myself one who *uses* action. This requires strength which ebbs and flows and must be stored like energy in a battery.

Letting go the personality and assuming conscious command of the Identity being I, I am activity *itself*, not one who acts; I am action itself, not one who engages in constructive and destructive action; I am nothing as an ego, but am the functioning of Mind, because it is Mind (God) and none else who is being aware.

Awareness is MIND'S responsibility. That means that this very existence I am is God's responsibility and there is nothing I must do—or can do—to help Reality be more real, to help Perfection be more perfect, to add to the Isness of Am.

Identity-I is not Mind, as alleged by many. Rather, Mind is I; Mind is being all I am; the Deific Mind is being this Identity I am. What care, worry, fear or frustration have I? None at all! None at all! Here is where I—Identity—stand!

QUESTION: You say there is nothing to do, there is just the Identity to be, and that is "effortless." How in the world can you stand up there with your bare face hanging out and say such a thing when there are *obviously* many things to do? I have to walk, talk, breathe, eat and care for a home, don't I? Aren't these things *to do,* and don't they require energy?

ANSWER: The human (limited) view of a "job" (say, taking care of a home) is (1) work, (2) energy expended, and (3) eventual physical fatigue. On the other hand, the view of the same "job" (as the Identity-being-I) is "Energy *itself* am I, *functioning* as a home being cared for."

Note the difference between these outlooks. Ponder the second one. To perform an activity as *Inexhaustable Energy-being-itself* is far different than a personal concept of self *doing* something that requires energy; yet, in both instances, it appears as the same job being done.

Energy-I, self-Consciously being energy-in-action, is to go about "doing" whatever appears the thing to do, either working or playing, *but to do it all with a grace and ease that is a marvel beyond words.*

If you don't believe it, try it! Often, it is to look up and find the job over, everything done; or to find tasks performed for us in an amazing manner even before we've asked.

EXAMPLE

Here I sit at a typewriter, answering your letter. The "normal" view of this activity is that of a man working and spending energy which must eventually end in fatigue. But the fact is, I cannot identify as man-expending-energy because that is not the Identity who "sees" the words written here! Since God, Mind, is *all* that *is* present here, this very Awareness is the activity of *God,* not that of a powerless, valueless image seated at a typewriter. Obviously, this Awareness "includes" a "body" pounding away at the keys. The typewriter, paper, keys, letters, ink, thoughts, ideas and evidences of "work" going on, are *all* included within (and as) this Awareness being I. Awareness, as stated before, is the action, the functioning, of MIND. Now, I ask you, can I identify as ACTION, ENERGY, FUNCTIONING itself, and at the same time identify as a body seated before a typewriter expending energy? I cannot! I am not two. The one Mind being aware am I. Action itself cannot become tired action, limited action or non-action. Action is action. The Identity being I is unchanging forevermore!

As Energy itself, it is honestly stated, there is nothing to be done—there is only Energy (Identity) to be. This is accomplished without labor because it is already a fact.

Then, what is "fatigue"? What is the dragging spirit that thirsts for sleep? What is the aching muscle, the flagging step, the drooping shoulder, bent back and bowed head? What is the "toll of time?"

They are the frustrations a misidentified Macbeth suffers from attempting to rewrite Shakespeare's play to suit himself;

they are the *expected* dissolution and death of the pseudo-ego who first dares to co-exist with God, the Alone One, and then *to be* God.

Fatigue stems from the judge's attempt to put the galaxies into an orbit more perfect than Perfect.

CHAPTER XVII

More Selections on Effortlessness and Energy

Science will agree that little energy is expended in the process of being aware, but great effort is spent in the action of placing the sensing organism (believed to be the identity) where it wants to be aware; i.e., in placing the body in a position to see, hear and feel what it has deemed good to perceive. Furthermore, the sensing organism spends incalculable energy attempting to change, heal or get rid of everything it considers "bad." For this one, daily activity is a constant expenditure of energy, an unending labor until its death.

Ah, but listen closely, those of you who have ears to hear: the energy, the power, the strength of "daily affairs" becomes consciously boundless to those who acknowledge (act) their discovery that ISNESS is the Identity being consciously aware, *not the body-identity!* ISNESS is the strength of this Awareness-I-am! GOD is the one aware, not a personal "you" or "me."

Energy is spent in action. The only action is THIS Awareness, here and now aware of these words, paper, ink and the sound of birds in yon field. THIS action is the effortless action of Isness. *Being* expends no more energy than is expended by the principle of arithmetic being the principle of arithmetic.

One of the many wonders of this work is the "discovery" of new youth and boundless energy. We literally find ourselves doing ten-fold the work of before. Furthermore, we find ourselves with the necessary strength for every job, whatever the occasion. We find ourselves with "wings on the feet," weariness of body and spirit a thing of the past. Ultimately, you will not find it unusual to sleep only minutes each evening, needing no more rest than that.

I could tell you much more along these lines, but I hesitate.

THE ETERNAL FLOW OF AWARENESS

Awareness is Self-discernment in action. All action, be it the lifting of the finger or a great weight, walking, talking or picking periwinkles, is effortless Self-discernment, Self-discovery.

When we discover this, we discover simultaneously that nothing being done is empowered to cause fatigue. We find ourselves being boundless energy itself.

How much energy is expended by Infinite Intelligence in the process of being Infinite Intelligence?—by Wisdom in being Wisdom?—by a pebble in simply being a pebble?

Is it possible for action to be something besides Self-discernment? Only if it is the futile action of a would-be ego-self attempting to rejoin God; only if it is the peregrination of the prodigal striving to return home.

Energy is the expenditure of the "old man," the *identity* of the new. Consciously to be energy itself is never again to be the fatigued, worn out, aging prodigal "too pooped to pop."

QUESTION: What is "power"?

ANSWER: Contrary to popular belief, power is not the ability to *do* something. It is the ability of the Identity *to continue being what it is*—undisturbable Tranquillity, the Center of Being, the Awareness of Deity. Identity is immutable Center-of-Being-Tranquillity which cannot be disturbed. *This* immutability is the "power" of being, not, as humanity judges, the ability to work great works. The capacity to continue being the Identity one is, is effortless and inescapable.

The only power ever "necessary" is a power completely unavoidable: the power one already is, the ability to be and remain the Self-awareness of Deity. We stop thinking of it as the capacity to work, accomplish and experience.

The more conscious one becomes of the attributes of Identity, the "closer" he approaches to power. The actual exercise of Omnipotence is steadfastly living as the simple, unjudging Awareness of the universe.

ACTIVITY IS SELF-PERCEPTION

Human opinion divides "action" just as it divides nearly everything else. It construes activity to be creative at one extreme, destructive at the other. Isn't all human action intended to be one or the other?

For man, that big, personal, intellectual ego, activity is far from effortless; rather, it is the "punishment of Adam," who with the sweat of his face must "till the soil outside Eden." For man, action is inevitable fatigue and death, forestalled only for a time by recuperation and recreation. "Rest" is the hue and cry of the struggling *creator* who would attempt to make himself equal to God, who would attempt to reconstruct and recreate the universe. It makes no difference whether one plays the part of constructive creator or destructive devil, the end of that one is the same: deterioration, death and decay.

Listen again: activity is *neither* creative nor destructive. Never! The reality of action—any action—is *Self-perception,* and Self-perception is effortless. Come to recognize this! Acknowledge that every step one takes, every finger moved, is the natural activity of Self-discovery, the holy discernment of already established Identity, not of creative or destructive action. Discern that Self-discernment in action is all there is to *every* action. This is effortless, natural, inescapable—even as is this Awareness being I.

How is this applicable to daily affairs? This is to pass through the "chores" of home, business and recreation discovering wonder after wonder everywhere. This is to do all that ever appears necessary to do with power unabated, strength undiminished, youth eternal, and fatigue a nothing of the past! This is to be a "passerby."

This is also to rediscover the *eternal* nature of youth! In this work, I tell you I have seen backs bent with age become straight again, the wrinkles of years vanish before the eyes and the strength and zest of youth return in the twinkling of an eye!

Reader, search yourself right now; see if you *feel* a sense of enthusiasm within. You do! You do! Strength is the Identity you be! I *know*, for it is here to see!

CHAPTER XVIII

The Return of Youth, Expanding Awareness, and Death's Death

THE PICTURE ILLUSTRATION

Consider a painting on the wall of your room. Do you see it as you did years ago or did you see it more clearly as a child because you were not viewing it through the eyes of worry, grief, fear, boredom and all else that goes with sophisticated adulthood? Would you say the present state of your academic knowledge of color and composition allows you to see the picture more nearly as the artist intended?

One thing is certain: The picture remains the same. The *viewing* appears changed by the thickening lens of intellectuality.

Suppose an angry man stands before our painting. How well does he see it? We know from our own angry moments of the past that a preoccupation with anger thoroughly limits our view of things. This is why rage is called blind.

Suppose two lovers enter our room. How will they see the picture? "Love is blind" the saying goes, so they may not be conscious of our painting at all.

Surely, passion tends to limit the viewing. The judge's awareness of everything is limited by the judge's opinions of everything.

It is interesting to note, psychologists point out, that even though our angry man and lovers may be unconscious of it, they have very likely seen the picture in perfect detail, which they can recall under certain circumstances. Awareness, we find, is not limited. What seems limited, and is, is the possessor's *grip* on awareness, the prodigal's *knowledge* of awareness—limited by the passions that grow out of personal evaluations. Awareness *itself* simply goes on functioning.

As the possessor subdues his passions (and religion fails in the attempt to show him how), "his" possessive *hold* on conscious awareness weakens and appears (*to him*) as a broadening, expanding consciousness which includes an ever greater portion of Wisdom's infinity.

Now hear this carefully: when at last the so-called pseudo-possessor HIMSELF is let go (and no external thing—not even drugs—can do this for us!), Awareness ALONE is left on the field, entirely unencumbered by personality! Identified as Awareness *itself*—unlimited, unbound by the phantom liar who would hold Identity to a place in space and a bind in time—we soar with the freedom of Omnipresence! And why not? Omnipresence is being the Awareness I am!

IDENTITY DOES NOT DIE

Awareness will never experience non-awareness, death. The one who is already dead (not the one who appears to die) is the one who says, "Life is *mine*. God is MY life."

The "my" who says "mine" is the possessor, the liar from the beginning. This one can be loosed and let go here and now if one will simply, consciously, be what he is already. What is that? Unencumbered, unjudging, unpossessed, motiveless, opinionless Awareness ITSELF. No *effort* is necessary.

What is the activity of Awareness? To BEHOLD, WITNESS, SEE—ACKNOWLEDGE, LOVE and BE!

Does Awareness have authority to judge? Awareness is awareness, not an evaluator. It makes distinctions, not judgments. "This is a hickory tree," it says. "That is a mountain." It is the poor judge who agonizes over *bad* hickory trees.

THE CONDITIONS FOR "DEATH" ARE IMPOSSIBLE

"Death" is supposed to be the absence of Life. The dictionary says Life is "conscious existence . . . the vital force" of being. Death, then, is the absence of conscious existence, the absence of the vital force.

Well now! The vital force is a term denoting Isness being self-conscious; there is no other vital force in all existence. Before it could be absent, Reality would have to be absent. If "death" is intended to mean that this vital force has gone out of a body, we would have to picture a universe having areas (within inanimate bodies) where Reality is absent. Foolishness! "Lift a stone and I am there," said the Christ. "Cleve a piece of wood and I am there!" He stated, referring to Identity. There is no spot where Isness is not, no place from which the vital force has or can exit. The conditions for death as "real" are impossible. Obviously, then, death is not what it is generally believed to be.

The "vital force" has never stopped being the Awareness reading these words, nor can it. Does this mean "I" will never appear to experience a funeral? *It means Awareness will never be buried!*

Does this mean the one I see buried has awakened from the misidentification? It means *that* appearing is included within *this* Awareness *I* am! This seeing is not "their" seeing. There is no seeing going on *out there*. What "this seeing I am" is ever experiencing is an event, divinely correct, pure and perfect in every respect, but in which there is neither good nor bad! And, because no value is there, no power is there.

One is tempted to be grieved at the "loss" of a loved one, but grief is the old man's self-pity, directly proportionate to the value he has given the image. Where *is* the value? In the Godhead, Isness, *being all images.* Tangible images are the infinite appearing of all-comprehensive Awareness in action.

"Tell us how our end will be," has been asked so often. "Then you have found the beginning that you should wonder about the end?" Jesus asked in reply. *This* Awareness, right here, right now, is deathless. It never had a beginning. It is for us to identify as God's *function,* Life, and no longer to identify as a potty piece of poppycock that claims to contain Life within it, and then worries for fear it will lose it.

Awareness is embodied *as* the entire universe of "things," seen and unseen. It is not *in* anything, even the body that professes to have the eyes that do the seeing and the ears that do the hearing.

ABOUT BODY

The image that has been called this flesh and blood body is nothing *of itself.* This is not to say it is nothing, but to think as though this mere speck in the universe is "my" body is the most limited and limiting view I could have. The *unlimited* view of body is the view which admits that *Godhead is being body.* The body-I-am is UNIVERSE, not speck.

Should you shoot this particular body-form and grind it up in a meat grinder, you have not altered the Isness Identity being UNIVERSE-BODY. Awareness is not limited to the purview of the speck-body. If you think it is, close your eyes and see the ocean, the distant mountains, the stars—see for yourself if Awareness is contained, imprisoned or limited!

What appears as the physical dissolution of this or that form does not alter the Godhead, Absolute Reality, which includes the universe as that-which-the-Godhead-knows-itself-to-be; and it includes the *knowing*, the "awareness of," which is THIS present conscious Identity being "you" and "me."

So, you can beat "me" to death if you like; all that will appear to suffer is a personal view of an ego-I-am-not; all that will appear to writh in pain will be the most limited aspect of ego-identification which includes killer as well as killed. Awareness *itself* will be totally unaffected, unaltered, and still aware of an ever newer view of Isness.

THE BODY IN THE MIRROR

Without question, the one "thing" which man gives the greatest value, out of all proportion, is the "thing" he sees when he looks in the mirror.

The body in the mirror is not our Identity, any more than Macbeth is the identity of the actor playing that role. The one and only Identity is That *which is being* the consciousness that *perceives* the body in the mirror. Awareness is the action-activity of That which is being the body in the mirror, the mirror itself, the door frame, the house, the world and the entire universe, every bit included in (as) the Awareness that looks in the mirror.

Identity, then, is infinitely more than a single outline in the consciousness of images and things. As a matter of fact, Identity has no more to do with a particular body-outline than the picture hanging on the wall. The Identity-being-I is being *every* object of perception.

It is well we say again that the images in the mirror (and all other objects of perception) are *neither* real nor unreal; they are nothing in themselves. The "value," the "something," is That which is being images! The "That" is Reality, Supernal Isness, God.

WHERE? HERE!

An image of perception is what Isness knows Isness to be. The perception of images is *God's* awareness of being, not the personal action of another identity called Bill or Mary.

All that appears to die is an "image of perception" which "was" that which God knew Himself to be. However, God still *is* what He knew Himself to be—*and still knows it;* therefore, the "departed" is not a "was," but an "IS." John IS; Mary IS; husband IS; mother IS; son IS: right NOW, this instant!

People are perceived in one "place": Awareness, the action of God knowing God. Therefore, the place where the departed are is where they have always been—where the Awareness of Being is being aware. Awareness is HERE forevermore! Isn't it? John is HERE; Mary is HERE; husband is HERE; mother, son and daughter are here. NOW!

"But they are not *tangibly* here," someone says. "I cannot see them or hear them."

Let the pendulum stop swinging between life and death, past and future, value and non-value, let opinion and judgment end; then, in the still Center of Being, we find everything anew.

Tangibility is a "here and now" experience. To the personality-possessor of Life, "here" and "now" are the most limiting aspects of Infinity and Eternity. Both are included within the consciousness of being called Awareness. Awareness is our Identity, inclusive of all that is called "here" and "now." **We** *include* all there is to tangibility itself.

As we cease to think from the standpoint of our *own* identity as the possessor of Deity's Self-awareness (Life), and begin simply to *be* Deity's Self-awareness itself, we find the here-

and-now experience of tangibility "expanding." It expands to RE-veal aspects of Infinity and Eternity that the limiting liar, the possessor, excluded via a process appearing *to him* as birth and death, beginning and end, tangible and intangible, animate and inanimate, male and female.

Not only are images that which Deity knows Deity to be, but they are the eternal *KNOWING*. Obviously, this knowing is going on here and now as awareness. Because we *are* it, there is no personal responsibility *for* it, nor dictatorial control over it.

Dear Dr. Lee,

No, Awareness does not actually "expand." It only appears to, just as it sometimes appears to contract, wither, become narrow and limited with the years and struggle of the possessor.

The longer we misidentify as the accumulator of experience, the more layers of lack and limitation the *misidentity* has to contend with, and the more foolish fears it fancies and fights.

Modern psychiatry is busy digging under those layers in order to readjust some aspect of the misidentification's affairs. There is no question but what psychiatry is capable of making many changes in *that* one's experience, but it does nothing for the actual Identity that exists instead.

If present day psychiatry wants to render a real service, let it call attention to the pre-existing, perfect Being being this Awareness called "you" and "me." It goes without saying that the only "psychiatrist" who can do this with honesty is the one who has discovered it for himself and operates as the re-identification.

Sincerely,

THE ACCUMULATOR

Why identify as the gatherer of wisdom? Why consider oneself the collector of experience and memories? This is to look out at a universe through an ever grimier window; this is to bury the unencumbered brightness of youth; this is to forget the feel of earth underfoot, the crispness of morning air, the smell of green fields and the wonderment of distant sounds.

As we disassociate ourselves from the "accumulator" to recondition ourselves again as pure and simple Awareness, isn't it reasonable that we should be aware as we once were without the insulating blanket of age and debility?

Identifying oneself as an accumulator of flotsam and jetsam, it is only natural to experience taking aboard an ever-increasing load of stulifying anchors, chains, nuts and bolts until they sink the misidentification to the bottom.

WE STOP PLAYING THE ROLE OF A DYING MAN

So long as one acts as the recipient of Life, then just that long he must take aboard the accumulations of a personal experience. This ever growing conglomeration of bunk is like the grime that darkens the attic window, ultimately shutting out the light. Is it any wonder age weighs so heavily on this stockpiler of experience? Is it any wonder he eventually bends and breaks under the weight of his accumulation? He never *lets go* anything, but tucks every tidbit into a corner marked "memory" or "experience" and has the effrontery to call it wisdom.

Am I suggesting that this process be reversed? No. It would be futile to reverse the old man's actions and still have him aboard to work more mischief.

What is required? The answer is simplicity itself: RE-

IDENTIFICATION, simple, unadorned and effortless re-identification. All that is ever "necessary" is to reconsider oneself from the enlightened standpoint of *unpossessed* Awareness itself, not as an ego, attempting to stuff itself into a pulpy, aging body and then have images do all sorts of tricks for it.

This is not the endless task of reversing the old man's "effects," dropping his burdens one by one, as religion teaches. This is not to wash clean the window of perception. (Yet, re-identification surely appears to render these results.) This is to *end the agony*, by identifying as the sunshine, not as the attic window through which it shone dimly. *This annuls the relentless march of time's accumulation.* The sunshine is not concerned with a silly spook who was never real.

So, reader, stop being a rag collector, a junk man, an accumulator of flotsam and jetsam. Stop considering yourself as one who goes *through* life amassing as much experience as possible. Stop pigeon-holing memories. Stop your incessant planning of what to do in order that tomorrow's events will be more to your liking.

"But what will happen to my affairs if I make no plans?" asks the business man. "Re-identification does not allow for the terrible things that will happen when 'the human experience' is let go," he says.

"What about my school work?" asks the student.

"Or my home and family?" wonders the mother.

Re-identification is like switching primary attention from the shadows on the television screen to the complete and beautifully functioning television set itself, the basis for all the images in the first place. Activity among the spots on the screen does not go to pot when we concern ourselves with the television set. We do not lose our footing when we lift our view from the moonlight shadows along the walkway to behold the majesty of the heavens. Re-identification is *living* the Identity that is the fact anyway.

There is little we can say to the business man, the student or the mother that will convince them of this. *There is but to do this ourselves; to show forth the happiness that "results," and then speak as best we can to those who ask about it.* In effect, that is what this book is—a statement concerning things it has been my good pleasure to find; what I have seen and heard and done that you may also discover if you choose to. Our words mean nothing to those who have not grown weary of beachcombing or of the great pile of junk they carry along with them.

I have been asked, "How do we go about *not* accumulating memories? How do we *keep* from pigeon-holing all that transpires within one's daily activity? Are we supposed to forget?"

Infinite intelligence does not forget what it knows itself to be, and it does not acquire more than it already is.

Somewhere along the line we are required to make the break with the old identification. It is not enough to know that the old man is a fiction. It becomes necessary to think and act from the position that we *are,* rather than from the one we *are not.* In the determination of one's honest Identity, we find tranquillity, thereby letting go that which we ignorantly believed ourselves to be and the misery attendant to such a belief.

Dear reader, let me tell you this: UNENCUMBERED AWARENESS ITSELF AM I. This is the Identity I am. This is the "who" and "what" I am. This was my Identity before I seemed to recognize it and it will be my Identity should it appear I forget it. This is likewise YOUR Identity. This is the ageless Identity. This is the undying and eternal Identity. This is the Whole and Perfect Identity which was and is and forever shall be!

A SELECTION ABOUT "YOUTH," "DEATH" AND "EXPANDING" AWARENESS

It may be said that the vistas of Awareness widen and widen until such time as they include again the pure sights and sounds we experienced as children.

Do you remember the tender thrills of childhood—the smell of freshly cut grass, how clean the air after a rain, how little things were so exciting, how small surprises were such breathtaking, joyfilled moments? Do you remember how very blue the sky and how white the clouds within it, how rich green the fields, how unfettered and free the feeling of the first day of vacation? Do you remember the joy of experiencing no care, no responsibility, no worry, no fear of health or wealth? Can you remember how wonderful was your father's praise, and how comforting your mother's touch? Can you recall the time when there was no consciousness of age, debility, sorrow and death?

Reader, I tell you that in this work *all these things will be your happy experience again! Every bit of this is "regained" as we become non-evaluating Awareness, as we let go the judge, as we drop the accumulation of judgments and opinions.*

When can we do this? Today! Right now! We do not have to die first. There is nothing to die but the belief in a possessor called "me" who is capable of enslaving God's own Awareness of Himself, the veritable I that I am! As we let go the age-old liar, we return to honesty, "born again" to "become as a little child."

And this is only the beginning. Just as Awareness consciously appears to regain the uninhibited enthusiasm of youth, so it appears that the *body* you call yours regains its agility, poise, grace and strength.

Even more astounding, *"expanding" Awareness consciously perceives that the loved ones of old are yet within its Vision,* loved ones that the narrower sense of a possessed and opinionated Awareness exclude in a process called death!

EXPANDING AWARENESS PERCEIVES THE "DEPARTED"

Judgment narrows the conscious vista of vision exactly as anger narrows it. Who can see the beauty of a flower in the midst of a fit of rage? Judgments, the products of reasoning, planning, calculating and manipulating, would, within their chimerical province, smother Awareness completely if they could. The sooner we stop this, let all of it go, the more quickly we *consciously* joy in the regained vistas of unlimited Awareness.

Expanding Awareness regains the sense of the departed as surely as it regains the tenderness of youth, or sees the beauty of a flower again when rage subsides. Then we *know* that nothing has gone away. It has no place to go. HERE is where Awareness is; All that All is, is forever here within Awareness.

Impossible? Nothing we consider impossible ever happens. When it does, we simply exclaim, "Here it is; therefore, it is not impossible!"

Dear Nancy,

This is not difficult to understand. We know when one stops worrying he sees and hears things he was unconscious of while thundering through his worry-thicket of thought-taking. This is all we mean by Awareness "expanding."

This is a simple example of Awareness apparently "regaining" all the judge excludes for himself by his own opinions of good and evil. Invariably, his judgment of "good" constitutes the basis for his passions and appetites.

As one stops attempting to be the judge, *conscious* Awareness *"regains"* the joy, the happiness, the effervescence and sparkle of youth ever more and more, from glory to glory, until such time as the veil—the ego, the personality—is rent and "we see as we are seen."

How do I know? *Let go* the intellect; *be* Awareness, unjudging and unyielding; *joy* in the carefree, pristine world of the Heart and see for yourself what awaits you!

MORE ABOUT DEATH

Death is real only if Deity ceases to be conscious of existing. The Awareness that "sees," "feels," and does all that constitutes Self-consciousness, will never die, will never stop being aware, will never cease being conscious. Why? Because Awareness is Deity's activity, not the personal activity of an opinion-holding ego.

All that "must surely die" is the belief that such an ego exists, capable of being the custodian of Awareness. The possessor is of few days and full of trouble. It flourishes in the warmth of its own concoctions, to be cut down and cast into its own hell of values which it gives to valueless images.

Death is the appearance of the inevitable sacrifice of the possessor's values and opinions. That which man assigns the greatest value often appears to be devalued before him or taken from him, even as all he hates is usually heaped upon his shoulders, until he sees that nothing is good or bad; until he sees that nothing is to be cherished or despised; until he sees that "things" are being just what they are being—"things"—and that perfectly!

"HE SHALL RETURN TO THE DAYS OF HIS YOUTH"

Those who study this "philosophy" with us on Lollygog are always amazed to find a return of youthfulness, not only in outlook but in action and appearance. Why should there be surprise? To *be* this NOW of UNJUDGING Awareness is to *let go* the great weight of opinions, notions, prejudices, quirks and idiosyncrasies which, added to personal memory, are all there is to "age." It is the one who acts as though he *possesses* life who ages and seems to suffer the decline and death of the deceiver.

"Hast thou not known? Hast thou not heard, that the everlasting God (who is Being all there is to the Awareness reading these words) fainteth not, neither is weary? He giveth power to the faint; and to them that have no might he increaseth strength . . . but they that wait upon the Lord [they who will simply *be* the unjudging, motiveless Awareness we be] shall *renew* their strength; they shall mount up with wings as eagles; they shall run and not be weary; and they shall walk and not faint."

When one lets go the worried plans intended to improve the already perfect NOW, he discovers the Self that "turneth the shadow of death into the morning." "The former things are passed away . . . and there shall be no more death."

"If there be a messenger . . . an interpreter, one among a thousand, to shew unto man *his uprightness* . . . his flesh shall be fresher than a child's; he shall return to the days of his youth . . . and his life shall see the light!"

EXPANDING AWARENESS

I

One stays with the Now and lets go the hinterlands, past and future. Surely that one experiences an "expansion" of Now such that it is no longer a sharp edge dividing "was" from "will be." Then, to his amazement, he *knows* what was and what will be; He lets go fear and sees with new clarity!

II

One stays with Tranquillity and lets go the hinterlands of depression and ecstacy, abhorance and desire. Surely that tranquil one experiences an "expansion" of Tranquillity, so that the world is no longer divided into good and evil. Then, to his astonishment, he knows what "good" is and what "evil" is. He lets go ambition *to be* the miraculous qualities of Deity!

CHAPTER XIX

Concerning Dualism

A DISCUSSION ABOUT DUALITY

The great struggle with duality will never be ended by declaring the *impossibility* of duality or by denying the sundry appearances attributed to it and calling them unreal. It is even more unavailing to pooh-pooh every written or spoken statement that speaks of duality or appears to make use of dualistic assertions to explain something. Our denial of the reality of duality is only half enough. We do not perceive the dissolution of the appearance until we make the precise discovery of *what the appearance is and what it is not,* the root "cause" for the seeming, and *then end those of our activities that appear to produce its appearance.*

While we may pinpoint the "first and basic" dualism as the primordial misperception that has a "me" existing in *addition* to All (there are thousands of ways to depict the pseudo-"fall"), there is a way much closer to home in which we are involved. It is the apparent split of everything we see, hear, think and are concerned with; black-white, hot-cold, up-down, old-young, weakness-strength, birth-death, *real-unreal, correct-incorrect,* truth-error, tangible-intangible, to Infinity's infinity. These are the "dualities" with which metaphysicians continue to struggle even while denying the possibility of them —even while attempting to write and talk as if they were not so engaged. "This is just a seeming that isn't going on at all, *really!"* they say. How many times have we heard or said this?

Isn't it a little strange that one would take care not to do

Concerning Dualism

battle with the appearance of a "seeming" dis-ease for fear that would be indication of admitting to "duality," but would, at the same time, struggle, strive, strain and stretch to discern Truth, comprehend Reality, experience an illumination, and study for a "breakthrough," a "ray of the Light" and all the rest? Isn't there as much demonstrated "duality" in this last position as in the first?

Friends, if one finds himself facing any wayward situation to deny or "have done with," he has *already* "left the bridal chamber" and "become two." We can say that duality is a "seeming" if we like; and we can say that the *appearance* of "causes" for duality is a "seeming" and "an utter impossibility in Reality" but, I tell you this for a fact: our *seeming* duality will never *seem* to stop bothering us *until we seem to STOP executing those seeming "causes"* that have been labeled "an utter impossibility in Reality"! When the *primary root-cause* of dualism has been ended *in practice,* the seeming ends. Protestation of its unreality is a lot of hot air that tinkles the cymbal and becomes the opiate of the absolutist.

Within the intellectual struggle for the *attainment* of wisdom, there is a plateau upon which those who choose that long road to Reality are all too prone to linger. It is the platform of lovely theory upon which they sit in not very silent condemnation of those they hear talking of healings, demonstrations and "overcoming." "Healing what?" they ask. "There is nothing to heal!" Well and good; once I also thought this position had to be the end of awakening, the final position, the absolute ground, but I had another think coming! It was barely the beginning, a mere milestone, if I continued to choose the long intellectual path from the bottom of the hill, the awakening-by-degrees-path, the "absolute" path.

Ah, reader, there is an easier "path," a much simpler comprehension! IT IS TO *DISPOSSESS* THE PSEUDO-POSSESSOR OF AWARENESS AND COMMENCE IMMEDIATELY *TO LIVE AS UNJUDGING, OPINION-LESS AWARENESS.*

This one, from this actually LIVED standpoint, sees the entire intellectual pathway spread out before him from beginning to end. He sees where he entered the path and where he left it. He comprehends the why's for every position the path takes; he perceives the subtle intellectual arguments for its every twist and turn, plus those in the other paths as well. He sees, too, that even though this is spoken of as a path, it is not that at all. There may be intellectual division and subdivisions of a flower being a flower, but it is a flower being a flower nonetheless.

It is time to stop being a judge, taking sides in the dualisms between real and unreal, Spirit and matter, above and below, inside and outside, good and bad! Listen: this is not to say that we will not appear to perceive these differences; it is to say that when we stop *taking sides* we perceive with infinitely more clarity and find ourselves knowing what to do to have done with contention.

There is the story of a king who took the long lost prince to see the kingdom he would soon reign over. The prince, who was still uncertain of his identity, was asked to relate what he saw. He answered:

> I see a high mountain with many plateaus and I see a multitude walking up many paths that wind great distances toward the top. On each plateau there is a herald proclaiming his way the only way; and on the many plateaus are many ministers shouting, "Rest here! View this vista, the most beautiful of them all."
>
> Yet, there is no tranquillity there; there is no happiness there. They curse each other on the different paths and stand on their separate plateaus in silent condemnation of those above or below. On the higher plateaus, I hear judgment of those whose vision is not as wide; and from the *highest* plateaus come the sermons of those who deny the duality of things—in the *day* they deny, but in the night, as I,

Concerning Dualism

they still cut wood in their jungle; they still search the crevasses for sustenance; they still stagger through their thickets and slash.

Then the prince asked, "Which path am I to follow? On which plateau may I rest?" and the king answered:

My son, to climb o'er the ground from plateau to plateau is not the way to go. There is not a single path on the mountain that leads all the way to the top; not a solitary plateau where the woodcutter may let go his axe, nor any place along the way where one may stop contending with opposites.

"But *how*," asked the prince, "*how* do I reach the throne?"

Then, in the jargon of simple and ordinary words came the answer, most "absolute" of all, but the most difficult to be comprehended by pilgrims still plodding their precarious, intellectual paths:

Said the king, "There is no way but to *be* there."

Reader, we "BE there" when we stop playing the one who makes judgments and has opinions.

KNOWING AND DOING

If one believed a blank piece of paper to be a five dollar bill, he would treat the paper as money. But, suppose he discovered the paper were not money, but continued to treat it as though it were! Someone would take him away.

Reader, what is the difference when we discover that images, things, objects of perceptions, appearances, have no value and then go right on acting as though they did? Is this not a bit of the same foolishness? What good does it do to be mindful of the fact that images—all images—are the responsibility of Isness, and, as such, are perfect, while we go right ahead *reacting* to them as if they had the plague? What good does it do to know these things if we do not alter our actions to correspond to the facts of Reality? How can we stop seeing things through a thick lens without going through the act of *not looking* through the thick lens? *Knowing* to put away the distorting lens and *putting* it away are *both* required, it seems, before we have done with the distorted view.

"Knowing," and the actions that correspond to that knowing, are "two" to be seen as one, if the personal imbalances of separateness are to be tangibly ended.

ABOUT "EVIL," "SIN" AND EDUCATION IN THE LIGHT OF AWARENESS

Evil and sin have no reality whatever except as they pertain to a pseudo-identity, which is a phantom in the first place. With this in mind, we see that the "original evil" (Eve) is the *basic misapprehension* of Identity which creates (for itself) the inside-outside dualism that "I" (the old man) am one who *contains* Life (Awareness). From the standpoint of UNCONTAINED Life we see that "sin" is everything that same silly *misidentification* engages in (consciously or unconsciously) *to perpetuate its own belief in its personal possessorship of Awareness.*

The old man's definitions of "evil" and "sin" have no bearing on the matter whatever; as a matter of fact, they are everything the *misidentification* could judge to be detrimental to its continued pseudo-existence. This is why man reckons a knowledge of Truth as something suspiciously evil. He doesn't quite know why, but it isn't something he thinks he should be interested in, and he isn't. Ah, but it is *our own* disengagement AS this impossible-in-fact-misidentification that permits us to see the *image* of unpossessed Awareness ("others") no longer appearing to reflect *our own former* ignore-ance of the Identity-I-am. Simple Awareness is not of the opinion that its own image of awareness is attempting to maintain a state of misidentification; absolutely not! The people and living "things" we see within simple Awareness are not independent actors! THEY are the infinite appearing (and how else but in "form"?) of UNPOSSESSED, PURE AND PERFECT AWARENESS simply being very much aware. There is no SELF-awareness *out there;* the only SELF-awareness going on is THIS Awareness, right here!

We see the end of antagonistic activities "out there" as we stop playing the misidentification right *here!*

QUESTION: Considering the allness of perfect Isness, *where* does this pseudo-Identity exist?

ANSWER: Certainly not within Isness. There is no place in Reality for a personality that believes it has God acting as his servant. Such an identity is clearly impossible—an imposter—and so are his judgments of good and evil. Such evaluations are "real" only within the imposter's dream of his own existence.

QUESTION: Then who is this one I am who wonders "why" and asks questions?

ANSWER: This is the intellectual *role* we play as long as we consider ourselves an identity who possesses an awareness of existence (life). We do not possess Awareness; we *are* Awareness—and Awareness does not have to be educated. As long as we play the role of this pseudo-intellect, we are attempting to make a misidentification understand Reality; we are attempting to make a phantom personality equal to God; we are attempting to elevate a misconception of ourselves up to All; we are attempting to teach infinite wisdom to something that has no existence.

Surely there is no stupidity *within* the perfect allness of All, nor another intellect *outside* the entirety of All; therefore, is it not being silly to attempt to play the role of one who thinks he is stupid, needs education and pretends to exist in an imperfect environment?

Let us have done with the attempt to be the pseudo-intellect and then teach it something. Who can educate a ghost? It can no more comprehend Truth than darkness can comprehend light. The presence of eternal Isness precludes the possibility of an ignorant is-not. Reality, Self-identified via Self-awareness, is the *only* Identity.

Reader, the Awareness you are is this Deific Self-awareness in action. Consciousness is Deity's Self-knowledge functioning.

Awareness cannot be possessed by a personality, so why waste time trying to reunite an illegitimate identity with God? The attempt merely makes the belief of its existence fight furiously to maintain its fraudulent position within thinking.

QUESTION: How can I get rid of "that thinking personality" when it is impossible to stop thinking?

ANSWER: By living in the "here and now," *which is to stop attaching values to everything.* This does not stop *Awareness,* you see. We go right on being Awareness aware more acutely than ever. By surrendering our evaluating opinions, we are enabled to enjoy all that is to be seen, heard *and thought,* right here and now. We simply stop playing at being the thinker *to be the thinking.* Then, as we enjoy *living* opinionless Awareness, we discover it is not *necessary* to pass judgments and establish opinions on every sight, sound and feeling.

But listen to this carefully: It seems we cannot perceive the fruits of non-judgment *before* we end the *practice* of judgment. We find it is impossible to have the proof in hand *first,* as the intellectual nature insists. Judgment making (intellectual thinking) is the life's blood of the imposter-identification, and it "ends" only when we stop playing the part. By consciously *being* unjudging and opinionless Awareness, we cannot be the miserable intellectual, the confused judge, the bewildered, impoverished personality at the same moment.

Concerning Dualism 187

QUESTION: But what will happen to my business when I stop thinking about it?

ANSWER: You do not stop thinking about your business. Your only business is being the Awareness God is being. You have no business playing the role of another, and you have no business fooling with his business.

You will discover, however, all that appears to be "your" business will manifestly prosper from your new ability to do whatever comes to be done in the Now. Why? Because your actions, unworried, unhurried and fearless, will be more apparently perfect than had you spent long hours planning, calculating, making judgments, and then worrying about the wisdom of your decisions.

If it is to continue its seeming, the belief of twoness has no alternative but to *deny* the *singleness* of Being—sometimes vehemently! The more nearly words strike at the root of the ego's many dualisms, the louder the intellect screams about the insanity of Truth; ah, but the louder sings the Heart of the sincere and simple. Only the Heart convinces the actor that Reality is not as it appears on the stage. The Heart is not lost; merely the pseudo-intellect is!

CHAPTER XX

A Lollygog Class on "Feeling" and Transcendent Tranquillity

Our trials and tribulations are not so much the external problems we face as our effort to do something about the awesome feelings, fears, dreads, anxieties, tensions and frustrations that develop "within." Most people would gladly move out of their homes and take up unabashed residence in hospitals if that would free them of their inner turmoil. Whether mankind realizes it or not, the root-problem he most desires to change (and works himself to death trying) is his confounding problem of "feeling." "I don't feel good," says he, "so I must do this or that, in order to feel *better*." And then he does, but the ensuing satisfaction is all too short-lived.

HAPPINESS IS EQUANIMITY EXPERIENCED

QUESTION: Where does misery come from?

Nearly always, a "miserable experience" arises from the evaluation of "things," but the equanimity everyone wants resides *beyond* "things" with the Real—and the Real is That which is being this consciousness of things.

For a time one seems bound to the belief that his misery is "out there," even while his agony is the "awful feeling of fear and foreboding within." One may believe an errant member of the family is the cause of his agony, but it is the agony *of that belief* which is felt within as a disturbance of one's equanimity. To eliminate the agony, for the past ten thousand years we have been doing everything possible to change the suspected cause of it "out there" with the husband, daughter, business or something else. We have believed that if we could *see* an external situation changed, automatically we would feel the restoration of some degree of equanimity; and we did, perhaps, for a short time, until something else "out there" failed to gee-haw.

Now listen: This procedure puts us and leaves us at the mercy of "things"! This makes the "feeling within" *tributary* to appearances without. This is self-imposed slavery!

The presence (or absence) of something we see is good or bad only as *we* are of the opinion that it is good or bad. The *image* has no value *of its own*. We have given it value (hence, power) based on its *desirability*—"I like it; I don't like it." Yet, all enlightened instruction speaks of the joy to be experienced *when desire is overcome*. Can one conceive of a more immediate way to overcome the desire for things than to recognize their valuelessness and then to perceive the impossibility of being one who desires?

AWARENESS HAS NO DESIRE

We have been told that Heaven, Tranquillity, is within. *Heaven is opinionless, desireless Awareness.* As long as we look to people, things or conditions for happiness, we are making "heaven" tributary to the objects of perception. One who stands identified as tranquil Awareness *itself* finds people, things and conditions tributary to his harmonious Identity.

Tranquillity is our Identity. We are not *another* identity attempting to experience the absence of desire. If we believe we can *find* happiness and harmony, then we must believe we can lose them. In addition, we must believe they are absent (or can be) at the moment. We can no more be absent from Identity than light can be absent from light.

ABOUT HAPPINESS

Just as quickly as one realizes that happiness (tranquillity) is his Identity and that he doesn't have to go out and do this or that in order to "be happy," just that quickly happiness becomes a present aspect of conscious experience. Standing pat upon the acknowledgement "Happiness *itself* am I, already!" we realize that *nothing* can change the happiness that is our *felt* Identity.

Desist from the statement, "I am one who is happy." That is not the truth! State the fact as it is: "Happiness is who and what I am! Happiness is Identity-being-I. Happiness *itself* am I!" Find yourself amazed that you need nothing to *make* you happy, and more amazed, that nothing can take it from you.

The happiness we speak of here is Tranquillity.

Dear Lena Mae,

I have discovered a Transcendent Tranquillity I never dreamed existed; and now that I have found it, I live it because I am it. I cannot give it to you except to tell you it is here and yours for the taking. Better yet—it is here and yours *and you.*

I will be happy to help you because it appears I have no other purpose than to help others discover this Peace.

WHAT TO EXPECT FROM THESE STUDIES

Now, we come to the very heart of our work here at Lollygog. As you know, it appears all of us have a purpose in mind

"Feeling" and Transcendent Tranquillity 191

when we commence these studies. Some come looking for health; others want wealth; some are looking for love and companionship. Others are running away from something—maybe grief or guilt or an unhappy home. Nearly every one who comes here has studied along one of the many paths of Truth, but some have not and they are the least encumbered.

In the day I was *looking* for something specific, I regarded the metaphysical system that *gave* it to me to be a "successful" system. Then I looked over the vast field of religion, psychiatry, psychology, metaphysics and mysticism and noted, as I'm sure you have, certain "teachers" that were eminently "successful" *along specific lines.* Mr. _____'s followers were known to become leading business people; _____'s students went on to become teachers in their own right. Mrs. _____'s work was noted for its physical healings, and Mr. _____'s very large group has been particularly successful in solving matters pertaining to supply, and on and on.

Well, I don't go for such labeling of the various philosophies, but I intend to put a tag on *this* study we are engaged in here, because I want it well known what each of you may anticipate as the *inevitable consequence* of our activity here. This work, as appearances go, *uncovers our Identity as Tranquillity.* The fruits of this endeavor are Tranquillity, Serenity, pure Peace. We are not in the money demonstrating business or healing business or overcoming business, though all these things appear to become a part of our experience. We do not promise anything but peace, simple Tranquillity; and I assure you that everyone who will silence intellectuality for a time and listen to our words about Reality, Isness, God with an open Heart—and who will make the slightest effort to try them out and practice them—the *slightest* effort—will leave here with a sense of equanimity and tranquillity he has never known before! It will be like a new-found seed within the self that grows into a powerful, wonder-full Presence.

I tell you, there are no human desires or designs that any one could be seeking here that will compare to this simple, tender Peace that is already your Identity, here and now awaiting recognition.

Jesus did not promise healings or wealth or the solution to problems; neither did Buddah, Laotse, or any of the lights of the universe. They said to those grown weary of the world, "Come . . . and I will give you *peace*. I will give you Peace—not the kind of peace the world comprehends, but a Tranquillity beyond understanding."

The enlightened, since the beginning of time, have told of Peace, the *transcendent* Tranquillity. I do not hesitate at all to tell you this is the fruit that appears to come from this work, for which I take no personal credit or responsibility, because this Identity "we" are is already established forever. There is nothing new about Reality; it has been here, and very real, all the while. It is inevitable that we should now be at that place within experience wherein we find ourselves, wherein we discover this Self-being-I, and where we effortlessly let go all the silly encumbrances that have appeared to blind us from ourselves. Inasmuch as Transcendent Isness is *everything and all*, must it forever appear to remain a mystery to itself? We expect to "find it" *eventually,* don't we? Why not NOW, inasmuch as NOW is the only time?

What I am saying is that we may all expect, as the fruit of this tender work here at Lollygog, a growing serenity, a building tranquillity and peace such that it will never leave or forsake us. And I will tell you this, too: within this Peace, living it and being it, are all the things we may have come here for. Healings, supply, wisdom, love, companionship, home, family or whatever else, will be seen through new eyes, no longer as objects of desire; and when they are put into their properly disenfranchised positions of no-value, they are often looked back on and found to be fulfilled in ways more rewarding than we could have dreamed.

Now, listen closely: I want to tell you *this* about Tranquillity. Many longtime students of metaphysics have grown to love the emotional binges they derive from their study and

"Feeling" and Transcendent Tranquillity 193

their traveling over the country going from one teacher to another. Many of them (though they may not be aware of it or won't admit it) derive the same sort of pleasure from mystical experiences that the drunk gets from a bottle of liquor, or a drug addict from a shot of morphine, or an animal from an orgasm. All of us, playing the role of humanity, have gotten carried away, filled with enthusiasm in our intellectual pursuits wherein we thoroughly enjoyed the emotional enema that ensued.

Well, this was fine until we awakened to find ourselves entrapped in the search for the excitement and enthusiasm instead of the Truth. This is precisely what intellectualism leads to, until we are addicts, and our only purpose for meditation and study is to enjoy the emotional jag, or lift, it produces.

These are heartless words, friends, brutal words to the intellect, because ninety-nine percent of us are looking for just such a metaphysical shot in the arm to produce "Light"! "Illumination"! How many times all of us have seen this excitement in the imbalanced actions of busy little bodies all but fainting in ecstasy at the old church meetings and religious lectures.

If, wittingly or unwittingly, this is the sort of thing you have come here expecting *Tranquillity* to be, I must sorely disappoint you; because the Tranquillity-being-Identity is not an excitement at all—it is not an emotion—oh, not at all! If we were to attempt to use intellectual terms we would have to say that it is more nearly the absence of emotion, the absence of "feeling" *as we have been accustomed to it*. And this is precisely the reason its discovery is such an unwanted, unlooked for and *seldom* event—a one in a thousand and two in ten thousand. This is why there are hundreds of philosophies that will do millions of things, but so very few with *Peace* as its actual gift. And, of course, this is what makes talking about it nearly impossible.

Many come here thinking the discovery of Identity is to be an "illumination." Oh, how many times we have talked about that! Well, it *is* an illumination, but it has nothing to do with wild or unearthly emotions. It has to do with a joy quite beyond sensation. It is like a very small seed of brightness and cleanness that suddenly appears in the midst of an ocean of emptiness; and the seed grows slowly and becomes the focus of our interest, instead of the vast sea of nothing which tosses in turmoil all around it, threatening but unable to engulf it. This Peace is an expanding, growing Center.

Are there any questions to this point? If not, then we will proceed.

TRUTH IS NOT OPPOSITE ERROR

Even this instant, Truth is spread over the whole face of the land. Peace, affluence, wisdom and absolute perfection are as close to us as our nose. Even where an unhappy judgment persists, there—right there—is *Peace!*

The Truth spoken of by the sages is not a truth that is opposite error. The Deific Peace the world so longs to experience is not the peace opposite tribulation, war and persecution. Wealth is not those riches diametrically opposed to poverty, penury, limitation and lack; nor is it *spiritual* as opposed to *material*, as ecclesiasticism preaches. We must understand this if we are to discover Tranquillity.

Erringly, heretofore, we searched for happiness *as the opposite of unhappiness*. We looked for wealth *as the opposite of poverty*. We looked for happiness in the shadow of our agony, but the tranquillity Jesus talked about is a Peace *beyond* comprehension—beyond comparison, even in reverse: not the *opposite* of anything, real or supposititious.

We have been looking for the "highest right" precisely opposite the "greatest wrong." Metaphysics tells us the highest right is "real" and the opposing "wrong" is merely a supposititious opposite. Now, at long last, we are prepared to understand that there could not even *seem* to be a personal experi-

"Feeling" and Transcendent Tranquillity 195

ence of a "greatest wrong" had there been no judgmental determination of a "highest right"! We find the root-cause for the "seeming" in the unnecessary action of making *either* of these determinations (not in someone ELSE doing this, mind you, but this one-I-am right here!).

THE PERFECT PICTURE ILLUSTRATION

QUESTION: Mr. Samuel, You have said that those seeking Reality find themselves more entangled in *unreality* than ever. How can you make such a silly statement when "unreality" isn't even real?

ANSWER: I do not know what an artist would consider a perfect painting, but, once upon a time in fairy land, one existed. Even the ordinary people of the land said it was perfect—holy, in fact—and everyone who saw the painting was happy. Every one, that is, except the old man who owned it, one who fancied himself a judge of judges, critic of critics and artist of artists.

"It is not a perfect painting," said he. "It is not! Something about it makes me unhappy. If it were perfect, it would make me feel better."

"What is wrong with it?" he was asked.

"I don't know," he said. "I don't know. I cannot put my finger on it, but *something* is bad."

Well, thought the judge of judges, what is it? Could it be . . . could it . . . yes, that must be it! Black. The color black. Doesn't everyone know that black denotes darkness and depression, that black portrays decay, despair and death? Of course, everyone knows that. The picture is full of black. No perfect painting should contain such darkness. "Black is bad," he said. "Black is evil."

This is what he believed and this is what he said.

"What are you going to do about it?" people wanted to know.

"Plenty," the artist answered with determination. "I am going to eliminate the black. I am going to paint over the black paint with white paint; everyone knows that white portrays purity and perfection. *Then* it will be a perfect picture!"

So the old man, judge of judges, critic of critics, artist of artists, betook himself of a powerful magnifying glass with a cross on its handle and spent the rest of his life searching the perfect canvas for sinful specks to eliminate, thus binding himself to his own private hell.

THE SURRENDER OF INTELLECTUALISM

None of us is likely to give up something that works as well as metaphysics unless we have something to replace it. Yet, most of us are here because we have found that metaphysics is not the final answer. We know it appears to solve problems on a one-by-one basis, and sometimes on a ten-by-ten, but it does not stop the rise of new problems to be solved. As a matter of fact, most of us have been brought to admit that, within its absolute strata metaphysics creates more problems than it solves. We would like to have the appearance of problems over and done with. We want the seeming to stop its seeming, or no longer seem to seem. (Just such a desire is expressed in the letter on page 99). However, until we have something to replace the old magic formula that has done a good job in times past, we are not likely to make much of a change in our views; but, reader, a change is demanded if we are to experience TRANQUILLITY. I have made the change and found the Peace, consequently, I speak with authority. Eventually all of us will take the step that has us stop searching for *extremes* to discover the overlooked CENTER GROUND. We go beyond lip-service to end our battle with duality *in actuality!*

To explain what is meant by this, I will use another illustration. The swinging pendulum has long been used to picture dualism. Its simple swing is a graphic depiction of bound together opposites (good-evil, first-last, etc.). Dualism's sundry pairs (there must be a million million of them) are clearly comprehended intellectual *opposites,* one at one side of the pendulum swing, the other at the other, and they comprise the basis for mankind's unceasing struggle from birth till death (still another duality). By and large, theology unabashedly rests on a foundation of out-and-out dualism wherein it sees the universe dominated by the opposing principles of good and evil; and while certain strains of philosophy espouse the idea of an indivisible One, as yet they have failed to solve the problems of dualism *practically,* or (to my knowledge) even to explain why the world is apparently forced to wage an unending battle with it. But the day for the battle's end is at hand!

All human activity may be likened to this swinging pendulum. If you will, consider "past" on one side of the swing and "future" on the other. Humanity, going about its daily affairs, is constantly making plans for the future (one side of the swing) based on the memory of past experiences (the other side of the swing). This planning and calculating, you see, ranges from side to side, back and forth, to and fro for as long as humanity is concerned with time, and until now it has not been shown him in effective detail *how* to extricate himself from this maze.

THE PENDULUM ILLUSTRATION

Now, reader, I ask that you visualize a *special* pendulum. It is hanging very still. On the bottom of the pendulum, at the disk, shines a bright, white light. *Picture this pendulum as immovable, a pendulum that no power on earth can move, change, alter, or harm.* Now, visualize a *second* pendulum superimposed directly over the immovable pendulum—this second pendulum, however, is an *unreal, imaginary facsimile.*

The pseudo-pendulum differs from the real one in two respects; it is *not* immovable and can swing from side to side in the manner of an ordinary pendulum, and it contains no white light. Where the white light exists on the genuine pendulum, the pseudo-pendulum has a clear *prism* instead.

We have all seen sunlight shining through a prism wherein the light was sundered into the colors of the spectrum—from red at one extreme to violet at the other. In your mind's eye, give the phantom pendulum a slight swing and imagine its movement in slow motion. You will see the white light from the immovable pendulum come shining through the swinging prism broken down into the rainbow colors of the spectrum; the swinging prism changes from red at one peak of its swing to violet at the other, back and forth from red to violet to red again, changing to all the colors, back and forth, again and again, until the pendulum stops. When it has stopped, the unrefracted white light re-emerges and the phantom pendulum vanishes.

The colors are equally divided along the swing; therefore, half of them appear when the pendulum is to the right of center, the other half are to the left of center. It is paramount that we understand that the white light of the *immovable* pendulum is the "substance" (the basis in being) for all the colors seen on the prism of the imaginary pendulum's swing, and we see that the imaginary pendulum's *movement* causes it to appear as the many colors of the rainbow, its color at any particular moment depending on where it happens to be along the swing.

Reader, I haven't the slightest idea if one would actually see the pendulum change into all the colors of the spectrum if he were to swing such a prism to and fro before a bright light. I am only asking that you *picture* such an event. There is no complexity intended here; this is an uncomplicated and simple picture you are being asked to imagine in your mind's eye, but hopefully it will serve to illustrate the still center from which the age-old enigma of dualism springs. It will allow us to

"Feeling" and Transcendent Tranquillity 199

explain a number of metaphysical "mysteries" that have puzzled the world for generations.

We return to the illustration. Notice, when our attention is on the swinging disc, changing from color to color, we are but barely aware of the real white light behind it, unmoving and unchanging. We see the swinging arc grow smaller as the prism slows and the changing colors increase in intensity (because the prism is closer to the white-light-real), until finally we become fully conscious of the unchanging pendulum and its transcendent white light. Then the pseudo-pendulum vanishes into the brilliance of the white light.

Now, with this in mind, we return to the "here and now." Reader, we know this present NOW is the time of comprehension, the time of experience, the time of concrete awareness. Stretching infinitely in one direction of not-now is the "past," and in the other is the "future." How much more is this NOW than all the dreams of the future! There is no "tangibility" or "sound" or "warmth" in the future-not-now, but they are here and NOW! The past is not NOW; only the now is now—a TRANSCENDENT NOW, infinitely above and beyond the not-now, past or future.

We place this NOW into the picture of the swinging pendulum. This present, transcendent NOW corresponds to the *unchanging* white-light pendulum. In our great concern with the swings of the pseudo-pendulum between the past and future, this happy NOW is hardly noticed; even when it is fleetingly observed, the magnitude of its transcendent nature remains unnoticed. NOW is the Real, the "white light," while the not-nows are the swings of the not-real. Furthermore we see that NOW is the light which is the total light of all the colors on both sides of the spectrum! We see that the centered NOW is infinitely more than a "real" between two "unreals," for it is being all there is to the entire duality. We even see that the unreals *are not unreal,* but incomplete views, refracted views, segmented and divided views of a vacillating view of the Center-Real.

TRANQUILLITY

We find a "center" for every apparent duality. The "change" demanded of us (about which we spoke earlier) is our own individual change of interest from the extremes *to the "center."*

Heretofore, we have been attempting to go from one extreme to the other: from the bad to the good; from agony to ecstasy; from the sick to the well; from the bound to the free; from lack to affluence; from unreal to real. Now listen: the attempt to *get* "good" only pushes the phantom pendulum away from the center-real and necessitates a swing in the other direction as well. The search for one extreme makes the discovery of its opposite inevitable. The longing for wealth brings an equal and corresponding fear of poverty, without fail.

THE PENDULUM ILLUSTRATION CONTINUED

Now let us use the pendulum illustration to get down to the basic misinterpretation, that we may be able to "lay the axe to the root." None of these illustrations means anything beyond the academic unless we are able to put ourselves *into* them. If we can do this we are more likely to examine the points of the illustrations and, most important of all, *try them out.*

Listen with the Heart: the belief, the judgment, that there is an ego-identity here who *contains* Life, Consciousness, Awareness (they are all the same) is the belief that *creates, constitutes and IS* the pseudo-pendulum itself. The judge (the believer) and the *swinging* pendulum are IDENTICAL! (Reader, I do not mean a judge-container somewhere ELSE. If one exists at all, even in belief, it exists HERE where THIS consciousness is presently perceiving these words, if I—not others—if *reader*-I construe reader-self, right here, as other than simple Awareness ITSELF!)

But what makes this pendulum swing? Why is it ever swaying between mountain and valley, good and evil, life and death, male and female? Why? The answer is so simple it causes the ego to scream in contemptuous disbelief. The old man will argue with it and deny it until the cock crows thrice. The primary force that sends the old man, the phantom, the pseudo-identity, swinging its miserable, light-refracting way between its own self-created opposites is "this is good and that is bad; I like and I don't like; I want, I don't want." It is as simple as this!

Personal judgment is the action that sets the pendulum into its sundering, fatiguing, aging motion from extreme to extreme. The judge IS the swinging pendulum itself, whereas IDENTITY-BEING-I is Awareness, the immovable, unchanging Center Light! The very instant we misconstrue Identity to be a possessor of facts, a container of opinions, in lack or in wealth, in sickness or in health, we find ourselves engaged in a primary concern with the fragmented minutiae, the spectrum, while, in fact, we are ever the unchanging Awareness of Transcendent Wisdom!

We understand this, we say, but our understanding is only theory until we stop making judgments and holding opinions, until we let go our identification as anything but the Center Light!

Again, what is this Center Light? It is opinionless, motiveless, judgeless, desireless *Awareness*. It is the same consciousness that comprehends these words, *divested* of that nothing-identity who says, "This is good and that is bad." It is this Consciousness-of-Being, here and now, simply being conscious of being without condemning everything on the face of the earth, without having judgmental opinions of this or that, without desire to acquire or get rid of, without motives for every action. Primarily, it is the end of the swinging pendulum and his "I like and I hate."

POVERTY AND WEALTH IN THE LIGHT OF THE PENDULUM ILLUSTRATION

Suppose we label one swing of the pendulum "poverty" and the other "wealth." You may prefer the metaphysical terms "lack" and "affluence." When one finds himself on the negative side of the swing, suffering impoverishment of one sort or another, his desire and all his actions are directed towards pushing himself to the other side. If he should consider himself already there, he wants to stay there or go higher.

Totally *overlooked* in this transaction—*trans*-action—is the stilled, unchanging pendulum at the Center, the white light Center which is being all there is to all the colors on both sides of the swing. We choose to call this "center" SUFFICIENCY. Sufficiency is already the fact of every appearing. THIS is our identity, and THIS is where our interest (attention) stays; THIS is the REAL!

Notice that Sufficiency appears within the world of images directly between the extremes of poverty and wealth, exactly as NOW appears centered between "past" and "future." NOW is NOW and so is SUFFICIENCY! Look around reader; is there not a sufficiency for every image to appear just as it appears? How could it be appearing if this were not so? Is there not a sufficiency for this very Awareness we are to be aware this very instant? Of course there is, and there will always be this *sufficiency* of all that is necessary. SUFFICIENCY is the Identity, not wealth, not abundance, not superfluity. (What is this foolishness of trying to lay up ten thousand times as much as is *sufficient?*) It is not *poverty,* either! It is not lack! *Both* are clearly *impossible,* but not in practical experience until we stop trying to demonstrate wealth, or Wealth.

Reader, can you see that if you have been seeking wealth, health, positive, good, right, real, life, truth, wisdom, that you have merely been trying to gather in and lay claim to one half of the pendulum swing, the half judge-you has considered "good"? Now can you see that your successes in this direction only made the pendulum swing farther in the opposite direction? Now can you see that the good half of the swing is no better (or worse) than the opposing swing? Is it not apparent that both sides, the desired and the detested, are but the REAL white light being viewed from a silly swinging position by a sillier oscillating misidentification?

What to do? Rest as SUFFICIENCY. You are this NOW! There is no wait! After we take hold of it to enjoy it and be it, we find it grows into a TRANSCENDENT Sufficiency we never dreamed existed! Oh, I tell you again as you have been told before, Kings and Potentates would gladly surrender all their riches for this Truth we are perceiving here this instant! Center-Sufficiency transcends the wealth of all mankind as surely as sunlight exceeds a single color of the spectrum!

There is no effort involved in ending all this foolishness; there is only to stop the effort of taking those actions intended to fulfill the desires personal judgment creates in the first place. When we stop playing the role of judge, we stop our incessant oscillating twixt ups and downs, highs and lows; or, as my hill friends say (and much more to the point), "we stop flip-floppin' like a flappin' flock of fools!"

TRANQUILLITY IN THE LIGHT OF THE
PENDULUM ILLUSTRATON

Now we come to Tranquillity. This Deific Peace-beyond-comprehension is no more the opposite of human misery than Sufficiency is the counterpart of poverty. The Deific Peace called the Sabbath is *overlooked* in man's mad scramble to move from his blue misery to the opposite of that misery which he thinks is red-hot peace. It is red-hot, all right, but it isn't Peace.

Again, visualize the imaginary swinging pendulum and its

spectrum of color, superimposed over the Transcendent white-light. Suppose we liken the blue moods of pain, agony and depression to the blue end of the spectrum; the much desired and sought after "feelings" of elation and happiness to the red side of the spectrum. When the old judge opines as to how his identity is on the unhappy side of being, filled with agony, woe and want, what does he most desire? To move to the *other* side of the spectrum, to exchange his blues for happiness. Then, with the help of sundry processes of intellect (based on his memory of past events, his knowledge of causes and effects, and ten thousand other calculations), he performs those actions designed to move his blue concept of himself into the desirable half of the spectrum. Needless to say, his actions have him moving from one side to the other, sliding up and down, back and forth, flopping like a fat fish out of water only to discover he cannot have redhot happiness without acquiring cold blue agony in the bargain. Where is the rope with only one end?

The human desire to seek happiness, wealth, wisdom or any extreme, good or bad, is the attempt to slide from one side of the spectrum OF THE SELF to the other. Inevitably, this is to slide *past* the undivided, white-light CENTER, barely aware that it exists. Had there been no *desire,* there would have been no refracting swing of an imaginary identity. We end the desire and return to the center.

QUESTION: Mr. Samuel, I think I understand what you are saying here, but it seems to me this means that I must experience the total of the negatives before I can enjoy the total of the positives. Am I right? I base this question on the fact that my Identity is the white light which is broken down into all the colors of the spectrum.

ANSWER: This has nearly missed the point entirely. Listen again to the tender thing we are trying to say, though I know there hardly seem enough new words to say it. You are correct when you perceive that the white light (Centered-Tranquillity-as-Identity) is being all there is to "happiness" and "sadness," the positives and the negatives, *but these opposites do not even exist outside their creation by personal judgment.* They exist *in belief* only when (if) the "light" is divided into a spectrum of good and evil *by an opinion maker.* This division is the unavoidable consequence of our playing the role of a judge.

UNJUDGED, the center light (Identity) consciously remains the transcendent Identity of all the colors of the *judge's* spectrum.

So it is, we find Tranquillity infinitely more, *more* than an emotionless, desireless, blasé "midway" between the loathed and loved as the *judge* thinks of it. To our amazement, we discover the proverbial Peace beyond comprehension. We live in the Light of total Tranquillity *as* Tranquillity and step out of the judgmental spectrum, *free* of the old man's self-created world of conflicting dualisms.

THE CENTER

Tranquillity is the unchanging, white light Identity. *Judgments of Identity as other than this Unchanging Identity* yield their dualistic pairs—ecstasy, happiness, elation, joy, etc., *opposed* by agony, misery, depression, dejection, despair and disease. Our effort has been very often an unconscious effort to seek out the opposite of our judgmental misery. In so doing, we have overlooked the Peace-beyond-understanding, the Peace which *appears* to rest midway between the sundry judgments of *feeling,* but which is inescapably and unavoidably present, right here, right now, even as NOW is ever here, ever the fact of being. And we have seen that Now is ever NEW and RENEWING; exactly so, this Identity-being-us is ever

NEW and RENEWING, never aging, running down, wearing out or collapsing.

"Peace is spread over the face of the land and men perceive it not," said Jesus, and He was right. Be content with the "center" which is *neither* depression *nor* elation, yet is being all there is to whatever could be so judged. I tell you this "center" called Tranquillity is so much more than "ecstasy" and all the rest of the world's judgments of "good" rolled into one that they are not even in the same ball park. Consider how transcendent the white light is to the individual colors of the spectrum—even more than all the colors judged "good." Yea, even more than all the colors called good and evil put together!

CHAPTER XXI

Identity Is the Center of Being

Imagine the awe-struck wonder of the cicada when finally it climbs up and out of its two-dimensional, earthbound darkness where it has spent seventeen years in confinement. Fancy the marvel as it wrests itself free of its old shell, opens eyes it did not know it had, and then, in an instant, perceives a new, three-dimensional universe of color, sound, sunlight and love!

If you can imagine the miracle this would seem to the cicada, and multiply it a hundred thousand times, you may comprehend the wonder of the power of this "new" Identity come to bloom, power beyond the comprehension of an earth-bound, two-dimensional misperception of Identity. And this is only the beginning, reader, of countless wonders!

THE SEED-CENTER

As we have pointed out, there appears to be a "center" being the Reality of every intellectual dualism. The "center" is often quite different in nature from either end of the duality. For instance, NOW transcends the judge's intellectual split of it. NOW is the "beginning" from which the past and future spring and to which they return. The NOW is the "two become one"; it is the "rest," the Sabbath, after the effort of swinging back and forth like a pendulum; it is the "solitary"; it is the "tree that stands unmoved in winter and summer."

We do not find the "white-light-centers" of appearances by looking for them. They are discovered unexpectedly and effortlessly in the course of living as opinionless being. Their real import cannot be comprehended intellectually. Though I may tell you that Sufficiency is the "center" from which poverty and wealth spring by way of personal opinion and judgment, and though you may be certain you understand what is meant by this, it remains for you to feel the transcendent significance for yourself. To do this, you pay a price; you surrender the old identity that makes judgments and holds opinions.

WHAT I AM

Our Identity as Awareness is the totality of the eternal qualities and attributes of the Godhead, Isness. The Deific qualities, every one, are aspects of "our" Identity, of this Awareness, present right here, right now. When we have discovered the "center" of an apparent dualism, we have comprehended an inviolable fact of the Self-I-am. The judgmental dualisms that appear to confound the intellect are the consequences of the pseudo-ego's judgments and evaluations of the eternal Center. They are the arena within which the *judge* must operate; but the Center itself ever remains the transcendent Identity-being-I. (Much of the early Christian literature speaks of the "immovable trees" which reside "in the midst of the garden"; these are the Deific qualities and attributes we have been writing about.)

AWARENESS IS THE BALANCE THAT PERVADES
THE UNIVERSE

Is not conscious Awareness directly "between" seer and seen, as seeing in action? Who will deny it? Generally, the world is

Identity Is the Center of Being

unaware of the Balance that pervades everything, permeating the events of nature and the activities of men. Balance is more than a simple presence, however; it is the basis for the *way* images appear—animate and inanimate, tangible and intangible, etc. More than that, it is the foundation for all that is seen as movement and action.

Words are insufficient to picture this Balance adequately. The Balance, the Whole-Center, is not Isness itself, but the *totality* of that which Isness knows Itself to be; it is the Self, the Identity-I. The Balance appears to our opinion-making, "thing"-evaluating, self-misidentification as a constant contention between all the dualities judgment creates—open-closed, male-female, hot-cold, good-evil, life-death, first-last, old-young, and on to infinity.

Now listen: To experience an end to all contention with "duality" (not in lip service nor in "Absolute" theory, *but in fact*) experienced Tranquillity, the end of experienced emotional duality, *hinges on our mindfulness of Tranquillity as a balanced center between "feeling good" and "feeling bad."* If we are to enjoy the vistas of Peace lived, if we are to enjoy the Sabbatical Rest that comes from no longer swinging back and forth, *we must stop the judgmental pendulum.* The Kingdom of Identity "is a movement and a rest," exactly as the one called Jesus said!

"PROVE ME NOW HEREWITH"

When at last we find the "past" and "future" are mere judgmental divisions of NOW, and when we perceive that the transcendent NOW is inevitably appearing as the balanced center "between" them, we are enabled to let go the imbalance, or over-concern with either.

What does this do? It allows us to experience the peace of the NOW on the spot! Likewise, we are able to leave either of those restrictive, opinion-created domains called "poverty" and "wealth" when we discover the "real" of them, their "center," their Balance—SUFFICIENCY!

Reader, you have only to test this for yourself. You can let go poverty in an instant! Oh, what can I say to convince you of the here and now Sufficient Tranquillity being the Identity this unbound Awareness is!

THE MYSTERY OF THE MICROCOSM-MACROCOSM

One of the "profound enigmas" of the physicist today is the mystery of the microcosm-macrocosm. It has been discovered that the average "mass" of man exists (in size) exactly midway between the macrocosm, the largest known bodies of matter in the universe and the smallest, the microcosm. This is a strange mystery to the physical scientist, but it is no mystery here. There is no "place" wherein Awareness may judgmentally *appear* to reside but precisely "between" the Reality-being-aware and that which Reality is aware of being.

Well, so what! The "so whats" are monumental! Just as we have discovered we can make an instant "return" to the inescapable NOW and let go all fearful dreams of past and future, we find we can let go fearful and foreboding *feelings* in the twinkling of an eye and return to an equally inescapable TRANQUILLITY!

Sufficient unto Tranquillity is the NOW-Awareness thereof.

A LETTER ABOUT REAL AND UNREAL

Dear Paul,

There is no "real Spiritual universe" and an "unreal material universe"! Reality—all in all and all as all—is being everything to *this* universe, the only universe in existence!

Identity Is the Center of Being 211

The old man's action (the personality's evaluation of good and bad) gives a dualistic, real-unreal, spiritual-material, good-evil experience. Judgment has him overlook the perfection at hand to labor after knowledge of a spiritual world construed to be invisible, or somewhere else, and of course, his religion perpetuates this insanity.

As surely as one plays the personal judge, he leaves the balanced center of Identity (in his own judge-role belief), and his experience moves out of round, wobbles and swings like a pendulum between the extremes his judgment creates. Inevitably, those seeking (desiring) the "real" find themselves more entangled than ever in their own idea of "unreal." Conversely, surrendering this desire by "returning" to the unjudging "center" of Identity, there is a lessened drive to seek the real and a corresponding lessened involvement with an ailing, imperfect view of Existence, which, after all, is usually the reason for seeking the "real Spiritual universe" in the first place. (See the illustration of the perfect painting, page 195.)

As we stick to the "true" Identity, to this simple, tender Awareness, refusing to play the role of judge to the best of our ability, we discover a rapid lessening of the swing between elation and depression, between ecstasy and the dark night. Soon, we reside *"consciously"* at the solid Center *as* the Center, as Tranquillity, which, in reality, has been our Identity since "before Abraham was."

RETURN TO IDENTITY

Dear Anne,

If something in your experience appears amiss to you, return at once to Identity; return to the Center-Tranquillity, to the Center-Harmony, to the unjudged Here and Now wherein you know there is silent perfection and harmony; wherein you know "nothing worketh or maketh a lie"; wherein exists no need for judgments or opinions of good and evil, or correct and incorrect, "duality" or "absolute."

Here at the center, one *unchanging* Identity exists: Spirit, Consciousness, Awareness. This Identity is Father-being-I, being this consciousness of existence right here and now. Here it is recognized that all the action going on, including the situation you write about, is the action of God perceiving Himself. Here it is seen that all substance is Spirit being Spirit, and no other Identity *actually* exists to misperceive or be misperceived. The Identity who is present "belongs" to God!

Here at the Center of Being—simple Awareness—there is no need to judge, no need for labored thought or grinding concern for what seems necessary to correct an out-of-round appearance. Neither is there any wonder about a "cause" that makes it appear out of round. In the place of turmoil comes a simple, quiet resting in the Holy of Holies, the Secret Place of the Most High. Then, Anne, from this position of *felt* quiet, as Tranquillity itself we look at our situation without having to cringe because of it, and we find ourselves knowing precisely what should be done, or not done, about it!

Does this correct the situation "out there"? For those who have the courage *to rest as* the Heart's wholly, Holy Awareness, there come "corrections" of more than has been dreamt of!

ABOUT BETTER AND WORSE

Ah, but mankind says NOW is not good enough. So, he leaves it, he thinks, to go scampering around in the imaginary world of not-now. Exactly so, he says this Center-Peace is not good enough. Ecstasy and elation are bound to be so much better, he believes.

Don't believe it! They are not! It is the belief of a "better" and a "worse" that has humanity bouncing back and forth like a puppet on a string, swinging between valley and mountain, life and death, sickness and health, poverty and wealth.

Who can convince another to stop at the NOW? To stop at Tranquillity? To stop at the center called Sufficiency? Reader, it happens that Now-Tranquillity and Now-Sufficiency is this Identity we are. It is time to stop desiring the positive, "good" side of the old misidentity. It is not good we want, neither wealth nor health, not even illumination. Ours is the Identity that is unjudged and unjudging. This instant—this NOW—Tranquillity am I! Peace am I! Sufficiency am I! Love am I! The One Identity am I; and there is no other "I" but Isness being Itself! Here Identity stands as I!

TRANQUILLITY DEFINED

QUESTION: Mr. Samuel, will you define this word Tranquillity you use so often?

ANSWER: Tranquillity is another name for the Identity we are. We each determine its significance for ourselves. To "me" Tranquillity is an inner sense of peace, contentment and desirelessness. It stands fast before the sundry onslaughts of the world. It is a place of refuge, a peace-be-still to tribulation. It is a rock, a solid foundation to stand AS when human values crumble and fall in a sea of sand. It is the Christ-real-within that appears to rectify the misjudged-without. It is the Identity through whose eyes the universe appears the Heaven it is.

Tranquillity is found to be just that—Tranquillity, and not elation, ecstasy, or super-exhilaration; it is serenity and calm, not the mere opposites of agony or depression. It is a balanced, centered quiet which appears to the intellect as a "midway" between emotional extremes in precisely the same way that "sufficiency" has an intellectual residence between poverty and wealth.

Tranquillity is not a condition of overflowing happiness, but happiness itself; not a state of jubilation, but joy itself. Tranquillity is the *preclusion* of consternation, desire and fear. Tranquillity is Love. Tranquillity is the Secret Place, the Heart, the Christ, the Shekinah, the Holy of Holies wherein nothing enters that makes a lie. Tranquillity is being absolutely all IDENTITY is; hence, all "I" am! Tranquillity am I!

Here is where one stands! From this posture we do whatever appears necessary to do. From this *felt* standpoint we look the universe in the eye and behold all is Heaven at hand!

II

LIVING TRANQUILLITY

This leads us to another point that involves the "living" of this Truth. Once we have ascertained "felt" Tranquillity as "real" Identity, we are able to comprehend this feeling in the light of another fact already known: the fact that Identity does not change and that Identity cannot be altered. We are able to stand on *and as* a concrete, here-and-now FELT Self-knowledge with the positive knowledge that "I cannot be changed into another identity and made to feel and act a different way every time the wind blows."

If something would attempt to upset us or remove our happiness, professing the ability to change the unchangeable Tranquillity into a feeling of agony, fear or unhappiness, we know it is a boldfaced lie that cannot do what it claims; and, without hesitation or question, we know we have no business believing it! Then, reader, when we no longer *act* as if the appearing has a power to upset us, we discover the threatening sight, sound, or feeling is quite something else.

I tell you, the Identity as Tranquillity *insisted upon and lived* is powerful indeed! It is the obliteration of the old man's authority. It is an amazement awaiting everyone to discover for himself. With positive knowledge Jesus said, ". . . and after you have found you will be amazed . . ."

TO FEEL TRANQUILLITY

Become acquainted with the "feeling" of Peace. Understand that it is the only legitimate sensation. This "feeling" *itself* is one's identification, not the body-ego which appears to be experiencing it. Proclaim Tranquillity and insist on being this one only!

"Round" is "round," forever being itself. Exactly so, Identity does not change; it forever remains itself; *nothing* changes it; nothing prevails against it! If one finds himself disturbed and untranquil, suffering fear, loneliness, grief or any contrary emotion whatever, he need only make the conscious "return" to Identity to re-mind "himself" that *unchanging* Tranquillity is who he is—not grief, not loneliness, not any wayward thing! No misery can turn Perfection into imperfection; no experience can change Tranquillity-I into grief-I or loneliness-I.

WE NEED ONLY INSIST ON BEING TRANQUILLITY TO FEEL TRANQUILLITY! "Ask and it shall be answered. . . . behold, I come quickly," says the Comforter. Reader, try for yourself and discover that this is so.

PEACE IS INESCAPABLE AND EFFORTLESS

You will find you can no more escape Tranquillity than you can avoid the Now! As human judgment goes, Now appears stage center between dreams and memories, a razor's edge of non-attention; and, in the world, Tranquillity appears an elusive, undiscovered midway between ecstasy and depression.

Even as man seeks a way to escape his agony, he ever stands as Tranquillity itself. While he is reveling in what he takes to be greener pastures of "feeling good," Tranquillity seems hardly worth noticing—just as the ever-new-Now goes but barely noticed while one dreams dreams.

What joy is experienced when we let go our reluctance to accept Tranquillity as the only fact of Now! Why fight it? Why attempt to bar the door to it? Why wrestle with the Identity we are? Why attempt to hold it from ourselves?

The time has come to be and tell of the everpresence of "Peace, My Peace." This is what the world is searching for, not the surface foam called happiness, mere opposite of agony. We are here to tell of the Center Place, the Heart, wherein Tranquillity is experienced uninterruptedly.

Did we not find great joy with the light that Now is always all right? Listen carefully: there is joy unbounded in coming to discover and acknowledge the deeper wisdom that Tranquillity is *inescapable;* that It is here and now the fact which nothing can alter, nothing can destroy and nothing can take from us!

DETACHMENT FROM FEELING

We have come to see it is not the tree or mountain or dollar bill that is the real value. Instead, we perceive that "value" rests with the Primordial Isness *being* the tree, mountain, dollar bill and all else that appears as images of awareness. This is the knowledge that lets us view the world of people, places and things with such a degree of detachment. "Things" do not have the power over us they seem to have for others. Recognizing that the Reality "behind" things is their true power, we are not so likely to credit a powerless sight with an authority it does not have. This astonishes others. They refer

Identity Is the Center of Being 217

to our "mysterious ability" "to be in the world but not of it." It is more than that! It is our ability to remain untroubled by the world, neither seeking it out nor cherishing any part of it, but loving every moment! To those who honestly and actually credit Reality as the only value and authority comes a new view of images as totally powerless to upset them in any way. This is the natural way to perceive.

Now hear this: there is yet another aspect of "detachment, devaluation, and withdrawal" not so quickly perceived by those who yet identify as seekers. This is the detachment from (and devaluation of) *emotion, feeling, sensation*. It seems many times more obvious to withdraw a false value from an external object of perception than to do the same with an *inner* "feeling." An emotion is not so tangible. It is one thing to devalue an image that has been the apparent cause of frustration or fear, and quite another to "come out and be separate from" an emotion, especially a desirable one. Consider how reluctant one might be to let go the value he places on the warm inner feeling of "compassion."

The Enlightened know there is no value, good or bad, in images; yet a student is prone to hang onto the good while detaching himself from the not-good and/or to detach himself from the not-good in order to experience more "good." He does the same with emotions. It is surely more pleasant to let go fear and foreboding than to dismiss "that grand and glorious feeling of exhilaration." One is more willing to give up emotions akin to anger than those emotions and responses that have to do with sexual pleasure and excitement; yet the latter are only self-judged "good" emotions, the inner counterparts of exterior "good things." Sooner or later, we are required to devalue *all* emotions, good and bad alike. (*Devalue,* not deny, not *put off!*)

Skeptics declare the impossibility of such a requirement. "Even if such a goal were attained," they let us know in no uncertain terms, "the results would be absolutely awful! This would leave us an emotionless, passionless clod of inane nothingness," they lament. "Who wants to exist, even for a minute, as such a dead thing without life or spark?"

They have a surprise in store for them! We do not, like ascetics, attempt to end the experience of *any* emotion. When we de-value emotions and stop *searching* for them, we find that those we experience are infinitely *more* than we ever imagined.

It is the I-possess-a-feeling view that would have us constantly striving to feel the positives and eliminate the negatives, only never to feel *enough* positives, and inevitably to find the negatives hanging on like flypaper.

We come to see (contrary to the educated world's view, and the teachings of many religious bodies) that *the Deific Peace is not elation or exalted feeling; it is not ecstasy nor "Illumination."* Instead, it is the *center* of feeling that resides "between" the ecstasy of Illumination that appears on the one hand and the agony of the dark night that seems on the other. Tranquillity, Peace, is the gentle Shekinah, the promised Comforter.

TRANQUILLITY IS NOT A VOID

Because of the old long-standing desire to feel well-being and avoid dis-ease, we have come to overlook simple, unobtrusive Tranquillity, here all the while, existing "between," and in the calm of NO judgmental preferences and no abhorrences. It is in this sense that the world (our old nature) asserts that **Tranquillity is a** *void,* the *absence* of feeling and a *lack* of

Identity Is the Center of Being

emotion. It shouts to high heaven how awful (and how nothing) the state of desireless, motiveless Tranquillity would be. It relegates Peace to the same overlooked position in which it puts NOW, or SUFFICIENCY. "Why, I'd rather be dead," I've heard it said many times, usually from someone who appeared nearly that way.

Just let them discover this transcendent Tranquillity and try it! I will assure you, it has never been condemned by one who has!

Only for the shortest time Tranquillity seems to be the absence of emotion, but—LISTEN!—it is the very "absence," this seeming nothingness, as opposed to the former orgy of vascillating passions, that allows us to distinguish the wheat from the tares; that allows us to discern the *worthless nature of the ECSTATIC elations we are so reluctant to part with or are searching for!* Those who have ears to hear, let them hear.

We are not the ego who professes to experience the sundry feelings. Living (being) Tranquillity is to let go the desire (and search) for illumination, ecstasy, light, so that we may consciously BE all there is to illumination, ecstasy, light. Standing as Tranquillity (to the best of our ability) is to discover ourselves less and less involved with all that is *not* Light. We find darkness, depression, sickness, sin and age no longer a part of our experience.

III

QUESTION: Surely you are not advocating that we give up our search for Truth!

ANSWER: I do not advocate that anyone do anything except follow the dictates of his own Identity. I can tell you, however, there came a time for me when I gave up the search for Truth in order to BE Truth consciously. I asked myself, "How can I ever be what I search for? Why should I search for what I am?" Therefore, I ended the search *to be*.

QUESTION: Isn't it better to keep on searching for Truth than to revert to the practices of the old days when we were completely ignorant of it?

ANSWER: Surely the search for Truth is a high road as opposed to the low road of spiritual ignorance, but it is not the narrow way. Like the low road, the high road is a most deceiving "wide road" that many follow, only to plunge into the agony of a personal experience that ever alternates between the dualisms of his fluctuating opinions.

The "narrow way" is the way of Tranquillity, the calm Center, judgless Awareness, the finished, present and only Identity-being-I. Few there be who seem to have the courage to let go their desire for "good" as willingly as they turn loose their abhorrence of "evil." Ah, but for those who finally do, the tranquil Center of Peace becomes their conscious Shekinah, their Christ-comforter, tangibly at hand, never leaving them, never forsaking them! "Behold, I am with you always," says this Tranquillity.

WHO CAN USE THE TRUTH?

One cannot use God, Isness, to cure the ills of the old man, to fulfill the desires of the judge. One must either *be* the "new Identity" or go on playing the fatherless bastard, suffering all that seems to be part of that distortion. It is "necessary" to make the break!

The break *made* is *to be* Tranquillity itself; *to be* motiveless, unjudging pristine Awareness in action, the opinionless witness of That which is.

BEYOND PROFESSION

To stop acting as the old man constitutes the "only acceptable sacrifice," but this alone is not enough. One must identify and *act* as the Tranquillity he is. There is no other way to have done with the worry, woe and want of the imposter.

There comes a time, you see, when we stop looking for an inner peace, stop talking about it and commence *being* Peace, Tranquillity, Harmony and Happiness itself—which we are already in fact! This is the foundation upon which one may stand and know the Real as Reality is Self-perceived.

IV

A DISCUSSION USING THE TELEVISION ILLUSTRATION

The feeling of Peace is a "within" experience. On the other hand, images, objects of perception, things, appear "out there." Mankind keeps feeling (his within-experience) at the constant mercy of the outside objects of perception. "I'd be so happy (feeling) if John (image) would just do such and so! When I saw that bent fender on the new car (image) I was sick!" (feeling)

This sort of judgmental action is the superstructure of the dream. Even humanly speaking, feeling is not really at the mercy of images; the reverse is true. Only through the eyes of serenity are things seen as they are.

Suppose we liken the within-feeling to the inner warmth of the television set and the "sights and sounds without" to the images on the screen. This illustration points out that the images on the screen are being just what they should be *because* the inner warmth of the perfectly functioning television set is already a fact. We see that images on the screen have no power to alter the warmth of the functioning identity, no matter how their conduct is judged.

On the other hand, the inner warmth of the tubes appears to have a definite influence on the screen's images. If the tubes are not working properly, incomplete inner warmth or too much warmth is reflected in a poor picture. But, an eternally perfect set *has* proper inner warmth and the screen has the images it should have in exactly the way it should have them. So it is, even here and now, that images of perception appear as they are when seen through the eyes of Peace, the "Center-White-Light."

QUESTION: Mr. Samuel, this is interesting, but will you please tell me what it has to do with my present situation that seems so filled with frustration?"

ANSWER: It has a great deal to do with it. Let us see exactly how. We are saying that Tranquillity is not beholden to sights and sounds. Therefore, let our objectives be to maintain inner peace first, without so much concern for the picture out there; a first obligation, so to speak, to the inner sense of Tranquillity, and a secondary concern about the sights and sounds of awareness which, you say, are lack, limitation and anger. As a matter of fact, when our first obligation is to Peace, we find sights and sounds take care of themselves. "Seek ye *first* the kingdom of God," said Jesus, with great in-sight.

This does not mean we flout the external picture of an approaching cement truck. We do just what appears the intelligent thing to be aware, but without struggling to make decisions, without great thought, without arduous planning, calculating, reasoning and judgment. Like the television screen, we simply do whatever seems proper under the circumstances—while remaining full mindful that Infinite Intelligence alone is the "Doer" and that there is no other Identity to be than the infinitely intelligent, all-inclusive One being I. *This* is to "acknowledge God in all our ways . . . with all our heart." This is to "listen to the still small voice"; this is to

Identity Is the Center of Being

"walk in the paths of righteousness . . ." listening, watching, expecting, and joying in the fullness of Being. And as an added gift, *this is to be totally unaffected by the sights and sounds of Awareness!* This is to "be a passerby"! This non-action *taken* is to see the nothingness of that which professes the ability to change Tranquillity into non-tranquillity.

"My experience is presently filled with dire forebodings and indications of financial collapse," you say. Well, so what? If it were filled with tons of gold coins, stacked to the ceilings of thousands of private rooms all belonging to "James," it would make no difference to the Identity being James, an identity that already includes the universe in its entirety.

The "kingdom of heaven" is "first"—tranquillity, serenity and peace are first; and when they become our chief consideration, *then* we watch the picture and all it includes, *without fear. Then* we see the storm clouds vanish.

TRANQUILLITY IS DEITY'S SELF-SATISFACTION

When Tranquillity is lived, despite the appearance of things, experience will be seen for what it is: Deity's witness of the Deific nature.

This is not to say there is not a time when events may appear to make every effort to destroy the new-found sense of Peace, such that one is sorely tempted to doubt his unchanging Identity. For me, events appeared to force a decision as to which identity I would choose to be. "Choose this day whom you will serve" was the admonition! Choose!

One choice is broad and leads to the maintenance of a personal judge-role, which perpetuates the pains of the judge's own ignorance. The other is very narrow and exclusive, because it excludes "things" as a power or value. But it does not try to explain "things" away; it leaves them just as they are—things. It leaves the Identity-I-am, the feeling of Peace-within, the Christ Presence, a much greater importance than the opinion holder's picture of poverty. It is recorded that Jesus said, "If you do not know the Self, you are in poverty, and you *are* poverty."

THE INSIDE AND THE OUTSIDE ARE A SINGLE ONE

God is being this inner-Tranquillity we are writing about, and God is the only Being responsible for it; people, places and things, have nothing to do with it. The only reason they are judged to have the power to make one happy or sad is because Isness is being all there is to them also, just as It is being all there is to feeling. "Feeling" and "things" are both within Awareness, *as* Awareness itself.

Jesus told his disciples they would not be conscious of Perfection until they made "the inside and the outside become as a single one." This "single one" is Awareness; the "inside" is "feeling"; the "outside" is the appearing scene.

FEELINGS

For some strange reason, we graduate from the attempt to manipulate things, but continue the foolish attempt to rule and regulate the feeling "within," as though we were its lord and master. We made excuses for our external manipulations on the metaphysical basis of their inclusion within "our" awareness; now we are wont to use the same reason to "handle" feelings.

Well—it *is* within our province to handle the pendulum extremes that judgment appears to make of serenity, but *by ending judgment,* and not by manipulation. We have no say-so

Identity Is the Center of Being

whatever about unjudged serenity *itself*. Serenity is Identity, already established, and we have no personal responsibility for it.

For me, there was a great temptation to search for Peace as though it were not present. This was to be fooled into accepting lethargy, boredom, fatigue, depression and so on as a *real* feeling I was presently entertaining.

And there was another dilly: I believed the Center-Peace (Tranquillity) was the good feeling that comes from doing good works for others. The subtle temptation is to cherish the good feeling as though *IT* were the sought-after Tranquillity within, the Center-Peace. Hogwash! Tranquillity is *Identity*, and it does not hinge on anything done or not done. It does not "come and go, ebb and flow between serenity and sadness."

This is not to say that we do not engage in charitable activities, or that there will be no sense of satisfaction from such acts. This is to say that one does not do for others with the idea of "feeling good." We let go the nonsense that the sense of satisfaction is either desirable or undesirable in itself. We do for others what seems to be the tender thing to do, with the acknowledgment that the "other" is in actuality an aspect of our Self!

There is nothing wrong with the joy that comes from Self-discovery, but neither is it wrong if one is not aware of such a sense of joy. That is the monkey on the judge's back from which his dissatisfaction, restlessness and annoyance spring.

"Be content with contentment," it has been written. This "contentment" is "My peace" the Christ spoke of—tranquillity, serenity, tenderness and love.

THE CENTER-PIECE ILLUSTRATION

A woman sets a beautiful table for her guests. The table setting is built around a central theme. She calls it the center-piece. There is another center-piece, but it is spelled p-e-a-c-e; my peace I give to you; peace beyond understanding. This Center-Peace is the very center-tranquillity of Life, the Heart within. It, too, is a central theme from which springs an endless experience of satisfaction.

The judge looks out on a world of images, giving *them* the authority *to give him* health, wealth, happiness and wisdom. Having bestowed this power *to give* upon his images, he finds he has also given them the power *to withhold* or take away.

Tranquillity does not make this mistake. It could not care less about the academics of "value" and "things." Why? Because Tranquillity knows Isness alone has value, and knows that Isness is being all there is to the consciousness of both "things" and "the feeling of tranquillity."

Tranquillity is the Self-satisfaction that *Deity* feels. There is no other feeling going on. One could sooner blow out the sunshine than he could entertain a real sensation other than pure Self-satisfaction! We are not responsible for acquiring such a feeling. It is ours already; it is "us"; it is I; it is Me!

TRANQUILLITY IS TRANSCENDENT

The misidentification works his head off endeavoring to bring "things" into his personal ownership, believing the acquisition will produce happiness. This (to use the illustration of the lady's table) would place the center piece at the mercy of the accompanying dishes. Can *they* change the center piece itself? They merely alter the judge's many judgments of it. We stop playing the judge to awaken to the fact that *we are* Center-Peace!

This Tranquillity cannot be changed by the many emotions that appear to swirl across its surface, any more than the surface foam can alter the identity of the sea.

CHAPTER XXII

Selections on Supply

I

The intellect utterly fails to understand the admonition, "take no thought" concerning supply. Exactly where fear is greatest, the Truth of the frightening situation and mindkind's judgment of it seem farthest apart; and right there the judge is most determined to listen to his intellect instead of his Heart. The Heart reveals that Supply is not a matter of effort and concern. "Who are you kidding?" asks practical mankind with his "common sense." The Heart says, "Consider the flowers in the field; they toil not, neither do they spin." "Toil not? Don't be a fool! I must plan and calculate carefully, lest I not have enough. I must make this contact or that connection. I must sell this or buy that; close this contract; finish that deal. I must manufacture, produce, supply, stock, maintain, invest, etc., to infinity. And if I don't? If I toil not? I would surely be wiped out! I would be a fool soon parted from my money." But to the bewilderment of the misidentification, the Heart says, "Supply is already supplied and already acknowledged. There is naught here but Sufficiency." Let me explain this.

Consider the actor again. Misidentified as Macbeth, the more he worries, suffers, frets, plans and calculates, making judgments and exercising great programs to bring about a better supplied experience at his castle, *the less apparent is his "real" identity,* which, in this illustration, is his "supply," protection and comfort—even his existence itself. The citizen acting the role of Macbeth doesn't have to *do* anything to be the well-supplied one he is *already*. So far as the play is concerned, supply is a matter of effortlessness; of motivelessness; of doing nothing about supply *but being!* Oh, how the intellect argues with this!

The worried one concerned about sustenance, whatever the appearing situation, is an actor unmindful or uncertain of his greater identity. He does not quite trust the Heart's declaration that tells him he is not *really* bound by the limitations of a play. It is plain to see that every effort to manipulate the externals is self-defeating. On the other hand, the *less the actor contends with Macbeth's many problems,* the better he is able to go about the business of doing all the play appears to ask; and he can do this knowing all the while that the play *itself* includes (is) a sufficiency of everything *necessary* for the play.

Disenchanted with the human drama, one re-awakens to his honest Identity, the happy beholder of Infinite Being's being. What is beheld is the greatest production of all, every bit pure and perfect, beyond an *actor's* comprehension!

Dear reader, when the press of circumstances begins to seem terribly real and shouts for recognition, it is well to remind oneself of the Real Identity who is not beleaguered at all. For a time, this may also be a reminder of the old identity you are not. It was to me. Many times I have shouted aloud to what appeared an oppressive situation, "All right, then, lay on Macduff! If it appears I must, then I'll just play the devil out of his particular scene." Yet I knew all the while that the perfect Identity-being-I cannot be affected one whit, neither bothered nor troubled, despite the action on the stage!

This is the assurance that allows one to "be about the Father's business" while giving only the lightest touch to Macbeth. This is the way to "be a passerby"; to be "in the world but not of it." This is the way to end worry. Not worrying, we can joy in the well-supplied affluent Identity we be, expecting and finding every need accommodated.

THE WOODCUTTER AND SUPPLY

You will remember the woodcutter who labored and starved. His trials and tribulations were all caused by the ignorance (ignore-ance) of his honest identity. He was king all the while; indeed, even as he cut logs and sold kindling, he owned the entire forest and everything in the kingdom. The *tangible* difference came with his acceptance of who and what he was. He could have contended with the incorrect woodcutter identity until doomsday and, in his own eye, never have been other than a good or bad, successful or unsuccessful, laboring woodcutter. The instant he acknowledged his kingship and acted it, however, *that instant* he effortlessly put aside every trial and tribulation that came from acting the prodigal woodcutter. The moment he accepted his honest Identity and acted it, he tangibly and practically received the homage and respect due his kingly identity. That very instant, the Kingdom was *consciously* his, and what is more, he could see it had been his even while he acted the beleaguered beggar. All the time he had been wealth itself; yet, he played the role of the woodcutter and the woodcutter starved. His punishment was dream-inflicted, not something that God did to him in order to refine and prepare him. It was not the fault of another. It was not meted out by fate. He suffered in the practical realm of a woodman's daily experience because he *lived* that identity and failed to identify as who and what he was; failed to believe it when he was told; failed to act upon it, until such time as his Christ-Heart told him, "It is so! It is true! I *am* the King!"

So it is with all of us.

EFFORTLESS SUFFICIENCY

I recall that Tranquillity once seemed an elusive commodity as long as I attempted to do something to experience it, but it was experienced effortlessly the moment I stood firmly on the ground that Tranquillity itself is this present Identity being "me," an established fact already—not something to be earned like a star in a crown; not something to be put on like an overcoat over an untranquil identity I misjudged myself to be.

If one wishes to experience a tangible and practical Sufficiency, he simply stands effortlessly on the rock of his own Identity *as* Sufficiency *already established,* as tangible Wealth *already a fact!*

The contesting (testing) appearance to the contrary is the old habit of feeling we have to do something to help the ego's affairs along. I ask you, must we wait to be the Identity we already are? Must we wait to realize what we already know? When Identity is Sufficiency itself, must we struggle to attain it?

The intellect will never understand what is written here. It would not have the courage to practice it if it did. The ego has equated reward with effort, payment with work for such a long time that the new revelation of Identity-as-Wealth-itself means nothing to it. "Isness" means nothing to "becoming." Old habit appears to argue vehemently and viciously with the Fact that puts it out of business.

The Awareness that Infinity entertains of Itself cannot behold insufficiency or lack any more than one can see a weed in a weedless garden. Sufficiency, Tranquillity, Serenity, Light and Love are all flowers inescapably included within Awareness. Their perception is as effortless as breathing, as effortless as being, as effortless as finding the creek when we are swimming in it!

INSUFFICIENCY IS A LACK OF GOD

There is no shortage of God, Isness, so there is no shortage of anything that constitutes "supply."

Selections on Supply

Isness is all Isness needs to exist. In other words, God has an infinite supply of His own Being—God has all God needs to be God. So just who is the critter who professes to need something? A fearful mortal called Bill or Mary?

Isn't the unsupplied mortal always the one who says he contains life (God) within himself? Isn't he the illegitimate one who presumes to co-exist with God? Isn't he the one who looks at perfection and calls it imperfect; the one who attempts to manipulate the universe and create a better future; the one who says he is the recipient of life? Ask yourself if you are foolish enough to identify as that one.

Who *are* you, anyway? Understand for yourself: there is no denial that I am aware, so I can get off the stump and identify as Awareness rather than the fearful, lying judge who is *being* aware. AWARENESS am I! I am it! It is "me"!

Awareness is the activity of Mind. God is Mind; consequently there is but one Mind for this Awareness-I-am to be the function of: the Divine Mind, the only Mind, God's Mind. "I" am this function itself, not a personality who possesses it. I am God's Awareness!

Now ask yourself, can God's consciousness of God be in a position really to need something? Does sunshine need something in order to be sunshine? No personal possessor-me exists to need anything. Awareness-me exists, and it is my happy privilege to behold the infinity of being! It has been the Father's good pleasure to give "me" the Kingdom, the universe, and all that is in it!

This has the "problem of supply" over and done with; this ends the belief there could be a lack of God. The Awareness-I-am needs nothing to be complete, any more than the sound of an explosion needs anything to make it the sound of an explosion. The "sound" and the "explosion" are one; exactly so, God and this Awareness-I-am are the same one God in action. Explosion is being sound; God is being I.

GOD is being this Awareness! There is nothing I must do to keep supply "rolling in." There is nothing I must learn to be better supplied. There is nothing I must come to understand in order to be what I am already!

What is "supply"? Supply is that which is "necessary" for Awareness to be aware. Supply is *not* that which seems necessary to maintain the status quo of an object within Awareness, be it a body, business or home. The supply of a body appearing within Awareness is the Isness that is being aware of the body. The perception of the body is its automatic supply. *The conscious knowledge of this is all that is ever necessary for the tangible evidence of a body being supplied!*

Any body-object is Mind's own Self-conception, hence its "needs" are contained in the substance Mind is being. *The body-object-image-thing, including this consciousness of them, has no personal responsibility to supply itself.* All responsibility rests with Mind, forever concerned with being Self-cognizant, aware of its own beauty, health, happiness and completeness. Yes, and affluence!

There is no short supply of existence. Existence is God, and this Awareness-I-am is God's Self-appraisal. This Awareness simply cannot be filled with real pictures of insufficiency.

Spirit is to the appearance of "things" what alphabet is to the appearance of letters, or what arithmetic is to numbers. One accustomed by habit to think in terms of letters is apt to forget that alphabet is the entire basis for letters. One educated to attach values to numbers is apt to forget the arithmetic principle that is the substance of numbers, and hence, that numbers have no value of themselves.

For a time, out of habit if nothing else, we are prone to continue an educated concern for the objects of perception, to continue a judgment of them and an attachment of value to them, thus forgetting That which is being complete and perfect Perception itself—Spirit. To remind ourselves of That *ends* the misjudging mind and its pictures of poverty.

SUFFICIENCY is infinitely above the poverty-wealth dualism that a judgment of Sufficiency creates. Sufficiency is the *enough;* not too much, neither too little. Sufficiency is the "just all that is necessary" to take care of the NOW.

SUFFICIENCY

There is just enough ground for the pebble to lie on. There is just enough gravity to hold things on the earth. There is just enough earth to make up the world; just enough ocean, lake, stream, verdant field and arid plain to be the intricate balance called nature. There is just enough moon to make the tide; just enough centrifugal force to hold the earth in its orbit; just enough solar system to keep the sun in its galaxy; just enough galaxy for the Milky Way to spin its way through the universe; just enough universe to be Infinite and All. There is no plethora—no excess of anything. Sufficiency is the word; there is sufficiency of everything.

So, it isn't happiness where agony is; it isn't health where sickness seems; it isn't wealth where poverty and insufficiency are. What is there? To human sense it is that which appears to lie between the judgmental extremes, but it is actually that which is infinitely more than judgment. Peace is where agony appears. Isness is where sickness and death are judged to be. Sufficiency is where either poverty or wealth seem to be.

And, by the same token, Isness, Sufficiency, Peace—all the

Identity being I—is that which is exactly where wealth, health or ecstasy appear to be.
Moderation is the practice of Being.

II

ON BUSINESS AFFAIRS (THE ISNESS OF BUSINESS)

So you think your business is hopelessly muddled? **Too** much anxiety? Too much pressure? You're tired of the **rat** race? I tell you that every untoward judgment of one's personal affairs simply requires rededication to principles professed. It calls for the conscious "return" to Identity, and for "withdrawal" from the practice of making judgments and attaching values. Acting one's professions is the only honest profession.

God is the head of this household, this business. God is the purpose of this adventure. God is the labor and the product, inventory and profit. Furthermore, God is the customer, the sale and the cash exchange.

From the viewpoint of humanity, man labors to earn the money necessary to sustain himself and his family. He labors to maintain his home and his position in society. He labors to provide the comforts that make his leisure more enjoyable.

Ah—but from the standpoint of Identity, Isness, every *action* is God's *benediction to Himself; every* action, from breathing to the bat of an eyelash, is Nowness renewing itself!

It seems hard to remain mindful of this fact very long when we first begin to comprehend and live it. Out of old habit, we may go afield into the dreams, desires and considerations **of** our daily activity; but this does not gainsay the fact that **God** is the All in all and that *actually* all labor is Deity's, despite our peregrinations and circuitous sojourns into fantasy land. Identity is established now and forever, whether we think about it or not.

Selections on Supply

Consequently, what happens to your business or mine, whatever events occur, no matter how they may be judged, all is in the tow of a vast over-riding principle. Perfection remains the eternal fact.

So it is, we make the subtle shift from a concern with the finite as the finite, to the comprehension, acknowledgment and trust in the Supernal, eternal Principle which is being all, whether it appears to be sale, transaction, labor surplus or shortage, inventory, money problem, or anything else! We look "above" the judged, valued thing-of-the-moment to the real Value *being* the *unjudged, nonvalued* thing-of-the-moment.

This does not mean we forsake the "thing"—we do not stop paying attention to the sales effort. We do not stop usual business practices necessarily; we do not ignore customers or employees; we don't pooh-pooh work or stop doing all our job appears to require; but we do these things while remaining mindful of superlative ISNESS and aware that *all* activity is Isness's *Self*-activity.

QUESTION: Does this mindfulness mean that our business difficulties will be straightened out, that errors will be corrected?

ANSWER: As appearances go, yes! Miraculously so! But Perfection will not have been altered; merely the judgment of imperfection vanishes, because a judgment has no place to exist within the judgeless Being.

We find the minuscule does not have the significance once given it. We find events appearing to have a "purpose" never dreamed of, and we find ourselves nevermore calling situations helpful or destructive, no matter how they appear.

ABOUT MONEY

It is because the presence of money is judged "good" that the judge writhes in such agony with his inevitable experience of the opposite of that judgment—the absence of money.

Money is just being money. Whatever there is to it, as with anything, exists by virtue of the fact that Isness is being money, exactly as "alphabet" is being m-o-n-e-y. The alphabet is not going to stop being those letters, nor run out of them; neither is Isness going to stop being all Isness is as money.

Identity is being total Affluence, including all the money in existence; therefore, one is never in short supply of dollars. Proof of this, however, is not to be construed as dollar bills running out of the ears. *Sufficiency* of affluence is the "real."

As appearances go, Sufficiency is the "center" between poverty and wealth; exactly as Tranquillity rests "between" elation and depression; just as Now abides between past and future; as "here" exists midway between infinite distances in all directions.

There is, and forever will be, a sufficiency of everything necessary for Identity to continue being the Self-perception of Deity, whether it is called "money" or something else.

There has never been actual value in money. Eternally, "value" is the Isness, God, being everything.

SUFFICIENCY AND TRANQUILLITY

Sufficiency is the fact of Tranquillity. This means enough labor, enough merchandise, enough money, home, love, enough of all that may appear necessary for Tranquillity.

Tranquillity is Identity and it doesn't need anything. It needs neither the presence nor the absence of images. The perfection of the television set is not impaired when certain programs are not being televised. Neither is this Tranquillity-I-am affected by the absence of any person or thing. The "show" is going on yet; another view perhaps, another scene, another act, but the show is going on, and it is Perfection's show, *not "mine."* I am not the director; neither am I an actor. Most especially, I am not the re-write man. Rather, I am being the awareness of a perfect production. It could not be otherwise.

I look outside at the swirling water in the lake; there sits the biggest, fattest dove I have ever seen—and a robin! The sun is shining. There is nothing imperfect there—only a day being a day, superlatively!

ABOUT THE "DEMONSTRATION" OF SUPPLY

The fruits of Being are not necessarily a plethora of personal possessions—big homes, fat bank accounts, fancy automobiles and all that goes with the fulfillment of humanity's desires; but the fruit *is* "happiness." The "proof" is always joy and contentment. Overflowing Tranquillity is apparent to all, despite the old automobile, the modest apartment or the income that doesn't put one in the upper bracket. Yet, these happy and peaceful ones are always, and in all ways, filled with an unspeakable power to all who come their way.

Jesus observed, "Your Father knows you have need of these things even before you ask . . . seek the Kingdom of Heaven and its righteousness first and they shall be added unto you." Does this mean a big bank account, two automobiles and an electric toothbrush for every member of the family? Are these the "added things"? Not so at all, despite the fact that many prosperous practitioners, practicing metaphysicians, and an entire materialistic society are forever tossing this biblical remark into the air as the only proof of one's "finding." A bank account "spiritually arrived at," and a "successful human existence" are the "fruit," they say, the only "proof." Folly!

The proof is not things! Never! If it were, the United States would be overflowing with saints. Doctors would treat only the poor. The judgment that the presence of "things" is "proof" of one's understanding is only the other end of the same dualistic nothingness that claims a *lack* of health, wealth or harmony is real! Do not be trapped into believing that the presence (or absence) of "things" is either proof or disproof of Sufficiency, Tranquillity, Being.

The fruit of living the Identity is always evident and as apparent as a million candlepower light atop a tall bushel. It is manifest as happiness, not as a personality rolling in money; it is apparent as Joy-overflowing, not as a big car and chauffeur; as Calm and Tranquillity even if all else seems to be coming apart at the seams. It is apparent as all that is ever necessary to meet the demand of the moment; as the absence of fear even while newspapers bellow and belch world-wide hysteria. It is apparent as one to whom others listen with respect; with whom others delight in being, feeling uplifted and inspired after having been near; as one who speaks with authority. It is, inevitably, an effortless Self-satisfaction! It is *beyond* human understanding! It is the "Peace I give unto you that your joy may be full." *Tranquillity* is the "proof"!

"Mr. Samuel, I have a great indebtedness before me. I need money to get me out of a bind. I have comprehended that money is a 'thing' within consciousness; therefore, there is as much money in consciousness as there are letters in the alphabet. My trouble is that I haven't been able to demonstrate enough tangible dollars to pay my debts. Will you help me?"

This is par for the course. If one appears to lack health, he wants to see health. If he appears to lack dollars, he wants to see dollars. But we are not in the magic business attempting to produce the objects of desire via sleight of hand, magic or metaphysics.

In order that the agony of fear may be lessened, we point out the valuelessness of "things" first, then explain where they exist: within consciousness. However, we go to great lengths to state that THERE IS NO PERSONAL RESPONSIBILITY FOR *WHAT* APPEARS AS CONSCIOUSNESS. This also means that we have no responsibility for what does *NOT* appear within consciousness. The one caught up in the agony of "not enough" usually wants to produce the images he thinks will solve the appearance of lack, and he is willing to do this by whatever means he thinks will work: magic, metaphysics or mumbo-jumbo. Then, when he finds out that many of his appearances appear as they do because of his own manipulations, the idea grows that he is in the manipulating business, and he sets out to heal the world. This state of affairs is worse than the first and leads to an agony of whatever proportion is necessary to bring him to forsake all personal effort *and to surrender the identity who makes it.*

I have been able to communicate this subtle and "difficult" point in our face to face discussions with others, particularly in the "Lollygog Lectures."

THE POTENTATE AND THE BULL

Reader, it is all well and good to read about Wealth, Sufficiency and supply, because this is something that pertains to our veritable Identity. It is fine to listen to these things and talk about them, but if one is to *let go* the appearance of lack when it seems present in his experience, if one is to *have done* with an apparent absence of health or wealth, there is much more to it than reading about it, more than listening to tapes and lectures. There is to gather these facts into the Heart where they are accepted without intellectual reservation and where they are revealed to be in accord with one's concept of himself *and with his here-and-now-actions!*

Let me put this into a simple illustration. If one should be the affluent potentate of a prosperous country, he surely doesn't wander through his garden viewing the flowers through a thick, inner haze of worry over money matters, because one of the many attributes of his identification as potentate includes an elephant load of silver and gold. The potentate does not walk through the forest or marketplace or visit his friends while despairing at the heavy, internal feeling of poverty. He does not allow such a noxious grind in the belly to remove the edge from all he says and does. Does he? No! And why not? Because there is nothing about poverty even remotely connected to the station of his identity.

If, for an instant, he should worry about the price of something he appears to need for his well-being, all he needs to do is remind himself of the affluence that exists as the natural (and effortless) fact of his identity as potentate of the land.

But, reader, what good does it do to *proclaim* the affluence of Identity, even though it is an absolute fact, if we continue to go about our daily affairs as though we were impoverished, as though natural, normal sufficiency were not the birthright of our Identity? Why do we continue to wander through the garden with the grind and grate of "look at the terrible obligations facing me" bending our enthusiasm to the ground?

Why do we do this? I'll tell you why: because we want the dollar in hand first! We want the "healing" first! Because we do not believe the Deific Identity is being all there is to this Experience-I-am and to the sufficiency thereof!

What does it *take* to make us believe our Identity without mental reservation? It only takes *being* Sufficiency and *acting* the role of Sufficiency with just enough tenacity to knock a single judgment of insufficiency in the head! Just one. But we must act this role openly, and not only within the cloistered confines of our study, or merely during those cherished moments of high inspiration and "Illumination." We must act this way *out in the arena of daily experience,* exactly where the appearance of insufficiency exists. *This much honesty is required!*

Does this take courage? Human courage, yes—who will deny it?—but courage comes automatically with the conviction that the Godhead of Perfection, Tenderness and Love prevails as the only present Reality and the only Reality present. The *doing* brings its own strength.

To end the first claim of insufficiency may be likened to one standing in the midst of a field where wild bulls are charging at him from all directions. The fearful agony of cringing and dodging has never allowed him to see that the charging bulls are not bulls at all, but mere whirlwinds of dust and leaves, harmless and incapable of hurting anyone. Girding up his loins *and standing erect,* even for a moment, he discovers that *he* has given the whirlwinds a name, power and importance *they do not possess!*

He has been told this many times, but in order to be firmly convinced, he must actually *do* it. He must stand erect *out in the field where the bulls appear:* not only in the sequestered confines of his study (this is not the "uttermost farthing") ; not only in the lecture hall or before a tape recorder, holding a metaphysical book in his hand. He must stand and face his former concepts right in the field where the thundering bulls appear—in daily experience.

Does this mean he will no longer see the whirlwinds? No. He continues to see them, *but as harmless whirlwinds, not bulls.* Then, in the absence of self-distrusting fear and consternation, he discovers how to cross the fence into other fields where the wind doesn't blow.

So it is, we come out of our escapes and retreats from a misjudged, foolishly empowered personal experience and go out into the daily affairs of experience and THERE think from, act from, feel from and rejoice from the Identity *as Sufficiency,* not as lack; from the Identity as *Sufficiency,* neither as poverty or wealth; from *Sufficiency* instead of the agony of poverty and fear. We walk through the same garden, but this time we walk without the grind in the belly.

Do this, reader. Discover what wonders an erect, honest view of the universe brings. See how quickly fear flees in the face of Equanimity, in the face of Identity *stood on as though it were real,* and not merely an ivory tower speculation wherein one closes his eyes, pinches his nose, recites a metaphysical pronouncement, and hopes to escape his own misjudgments.

This NOW of Awareness is eternally Self-Sufficient, including everything "necessary" for Tranquillity to remain tranquil. I do not look for the "thing" supposed to resupply my own Identity; I stand as the unchangeable Tranquillity-I-am and discover the absurdity of that which, by being "absent," is *supposed* to alter my Identity; supposed to make me NON-Tranquillity; supposed to make me fear-full, hence, Substance-absent.

But it appears we must *stand up* to the absurdity right where it persists, and *treat it as an absurdity* rather than as something to be feared and conquered.

Oh, as much as this may sound that I am foolishly (dualistically) advocating that one do battle with a nonexistent devil, I am not saying this at all. Insofar as words will permit, I am writing that, for myself, it was not enough to *proclaim* the powerlessness of the seeming while rejoicing in "the allness of God"; that for me, in the once-upon-a-time, the "seeming" persisted until *actions replaced protestations*, and until absurdities were reacted to as *absurdities*.

THEN it was done—and THEN I knew!

"DEMONSTRATED" SUPPLY

We appear to be stumbling along within an economic system wherein pieces of paper must be exchanged in order to have meat on the table. This implies that without enough paper dollars we won't have the meat; without enough dollars or other things of value we find ourselves in a state of lack, limitation, insufficiency. Those finding themselves in such a bind will sooner or later tackle the job of "supply" by metaphysical means. They will attempt to "demonstrate" the dollars or other valuables in order to have the meat on the table and take care of the obligations that are pressing.

Selections on Supply

But, this simply is not how Sufficiency is! Not at all. Metaphysics does its good work when it points out that "things," including dollars, are contained within mind, but it goes afield when it indicates that a "demonstration" amounts to *dollars* metaphysically produced to meet the demand.

We do no such thing. While we are happy to discover that dollars have no actual value, that they are contained within consciousness, that all that is necessary is "within," and not "outside" this Identity I am, *we go another "step."* We insist that this very Identity I am, here and now, is IMMUTABLE PERFECTION ITSELF, and that no sight nor sound has the authority to do aught to it. THEN we perceive that Identity, this one, right here, right now (the one that may have been complaining about not enough), is SUFFICIENCY ITSELF, TRANQUILLITY ITSELF—against which *nothing* can prevail! HERE WE MAKE A STAND! We simply BE Sufficiency and Tranquillity. We perceive that the picture of poverty does not have the power to alter IDENTITY, *and we let go the harsh judgments we have been making of the picture.* We hold this position with the determination of a soldier against a threat of encroachment; we hold this line as surely as the one who, gritting his teeth, *stands up and faces* the charging bull. Then, then, THEN, we discover that SUFFICIENCY is, really is, *actually is:* this IDENTITY-I-AM!

Does this discovery appear as dollars coming onto the scene or as meat on the table or as obligations settled? I can in no way tell you how you will experience this knowing, except to say that it comes in a language you will comprehend without doubt and view with wonder and awe. Always, our "answer" is more than we could ever outline.

THE PRICE

"Mr. Samuel, I am puzzled by what appears to be a mercenary attitude by many practitioners and teachers. It seems strange to me that one should be expected to pay to listen to a lecture about Love or about the valuelessness of money."

If we call our images of perception "mercenary" (or anything else), *that* is *our* problem. I fought this battle too, and I was ruthless with the mercenaries! Then, one day it occurred to me that I was very freely receiving but was not so freely giving. In a moment of honest introspection, I found I was quite willing to pay for everything on the face of the earth I wanted and could afford except the most important thing of all, the pearl of great price.

Isn't it strange that we do not expect to enjoy the services of anyone or anything without paying the price that is asked, and yet when it comes to the many hours someone spends writing a letter to us, or a book, or a poem or a melody about Isness, the most magnificent thing of all, we wonder why we should pay for this!

Inasmuch as it appears that writers, teachers and "practitioners" abide by the social amenities and pay for their pencils and the trips they make, it is only fair they be given a remuneration equal to that so unhesitatingly given to others whose wares are not half so meaningful. Even Jesus insisted, "Give me what is mine!"

It may appear that the price we pay to purchase the Pearl is "dollars," but I tell you that all the dollars in the universe cannot buy a knowledge of Identity. Identity cannot be bought with "things," even if we "go and sell all things whatsoever we own." The uttermost farthing must be paid—which is not money at all! We pay the price of the old identity, the old man, the ego, the personality—we surrender up *that* one, loose it and let it go. There is no other price that makes room for truth, no other payment that reveals Self as Self is. The real price we pay is surrender of the old man. Surrender! Not money. Surrender of old opinions, ideas, notions, concepts and dreams.

Nearly dearest (and so most tenacious) among the notions

Selections on Supply

to be surrendered is the belief that images have value. They do not; and this means that "dollars" and the goods and services they purchase, have no value either. But as long as it appears that dollars are the script with which images pay for purchases, it would be foolish to pay the storekeeper with pebbles or letters of thanks. We give to images that which is image's. Jesus gave the tax collector gold when gold was demanded, not a dissertation on the valuelessness of gold or the presence of Infinity; but He gave them that too—for free—when it appeared the thing to do.

Isness is being the Sufficiency-I-am, and we have no personal responsibility for the language of that appearing. The Value being Identity is neither increased nor decreased by monetary transactions.

The real giving, the "payment" that matters, is not "mine" to do; it is the action of Isness being Self-sustaining. This sustenance ever appears to Isness as Awareness sufficient unto itself. The exchange of silver certificates has nothing to do with payment. Payment has to do with the surrender of the old identity. So reader, you can see for yourself, as I have, when the expenditure of money is viewed in this light, our purchases will be found to be infinitely more rewarding.

And then, somewhere is a proverb that says, "Man leaves half of charity's dole, but not one crumb of a purchase."

Isn't it apparent that humanity cherishes what it pays for with its own blood and tears and disregards its gifts? Why, it has been the good pleasure of Being to "give us the kingdom," but it seems we have paid it no mind! We have *given* it no attention! We have freely received, but haven't so freely given.

We see many images which do not appear to give us what is ours, but we are mistaken if we think our sustenance *must* come from images. It is not up to the screen to determine and dictate where images appearing as dollars come from. It is up to the screen to be a screen, period, and even that is the happy responsibility of the television set, not the screen. How much more, then, is Deity's Self-awareness? We do not *give* God much credit, do we?

CHAPTER XXIII

Ending the "Seeming"

THE DARK NIGHT OF THE SOUL

Dear Mr. Samuel,
 In the last few years I have been suffering from terrible depressions. The harder I try for an understanding of Truth (I belong to the _____ Church), the worse these depressions become. My only consolation is the fact that I am also experiencing more frequent illuminations which seem to follow the depressions. Someone told me "the darkest hour is just before the dawn." This has been comforting because it lets me anticipate the Light that follows the darkness. But how long will this go on? I am becoming awfully tired of the black depressions.

Sincerely yours,

Dear Mr. Johnson,
 We swing like pendulums between agony and ecstasy as long as we attempt to hug the Truth to ourselves as something to understand rather than something to be. The search was well and good, but there comes a time when. . . . well, let me use this illustration.
 There is the story of an old man who was freezing to death in the depot until someone showed him the red-hot, pot-bellied stove in the middle of the room. At this point, the old man realized that his misery was his own fault, in direct

proportion to his distance from the stove. After this discovery, he enjoyed the wonderful "sweet in the mouth" experience as he "returned" to the stove. Ah, but at the other extreme of that journey came the "bitter in the belly." There he stood trying to hug the red-hot stove to himself, all in the name of oneness, singleness, allness, atonement. He still had the stove and himself, the basic dualism he began with and which he was attempting to unite.

For the traveler, this second misery is worse than the first. Can you see, there is naught to do but *end* the attempt to be an entity which coexists with the pot-bellied stove? There is to let the stove—ISNESS, GOD—be the all and only it is, even to the shadow and the shadow's dream called the "old man." Do you see this? The stove *and* a man are the basic duality from which the poor prodigal's wanderings proceed.

THEOLOGY'S MESSAGE IN THE LIGHT OF THE POT-BELLIED STOVE ILLUSTRATION

Theology tells the old man in the depot that his lot will be much improved if he will behave himself. "Stop stealing, cheating, lying, drinking and carrying on like the profligate," it tells him. "It will not be easy and you will be sorely tempted, but behave yourself," it councils, "and people will treat you better. Furthermore," it tells him, "your exemplary conduct will earn a starry-crowned passage to a warm and wonderful Heaven which awaits you after you freeze to death in the cold depot. But let me caution you, friend, if you do *not* repent of your sinful ways, woe is you," the weary traveler is warned, ". . . eternal damnation and hellfire!"

It is interesting to note that theology, relentless custodian of the prodigal's morality, has its own irrefutable proofs of the accuracy of its message. Who will deny that the old man fares better when he stops stealing?

THE MESSAGE OF METAPHYSICS IN THE LIGHT OF THE DEPOT ILLUSTRATION

This illustration also makes the distressing end results of metaphysics particularly clear. Metaphysics commences by telling the old traveler about the red-hot, pot-bellied stove in the middle of the depot.

"Do you mean I do not have to die first and go to heaven to find God?" inquires the ecstatic wanderer.

"Absolutely not. Its perfect warmth is available this instant, but you are holding yourself aloof. You are creating your own ills by your own ignorance of it. Your chilblains are in direct proportion to your self-imposed distance from the stove. My goodness, man, get on the ball! Stop wandering as a profligate! Find out about the Stove. Study the Stove. Love the Stove. Make the Stove first and your chilblains last. Watch what happens!"

So the profligate, tired of his misery, turns from the far corner and begins his journey homeward to the stove. "Eureka!" he shouts upon the discovery. "I'm getting warm!" Healing after healing occurs; cold fingers, cold toes, cold bottom and nose are warm again! "Wonder of wonders, I'm healed!" he shouts. "Oh, what a very present help in time of trouble! Indeed, there is no good but the good the Stove bestows! From sense of cold to the sole Stove my pathway lies before me," he sings.

And like theology, metaphysics has its irrefutable proof of accuracy. Indeed, it measures the pilgrim's progress by his healings. Who will deny that the old man's fingers and toes become warmer as he moves toward the all-encompassing, red-hot, pot-bellied stove? And colder if he withdraws?

But reader, these are the "successes" that make the final surrender seem such a sacrifice. "Why in the world should I question the methods and procedures that have worked such wonders in my experience?" asks the metaphysician. "What do you mean 'let go the me who is traveling to the Stove?' NEVER! Does not my salvation lie in becoming *one* with the stove?"

Impossible—utterly impossible. Who can hug a red-hot, pot-bellied stove? Those who have not become so entangled in the meshes of higher education discover peace more quickly.

But most of us try to hug the stove and from out the vain attempt (*this* is the mystic's mysterious maze; *this* is the wonderous nightmare the poets have called that Dark Night of the Soul) comes forth the new recognition found only when the prodigal gives up and surrenders himself, completely, totally, honestly. To the one willing to confess that the old identification which *returns* is less than dust and ashes, and then, in more than lip service, *forsakes* that identification, comes the old-new light revealing that the "Stove" with open door has been the all and only all the while. It is revealed that the old man, the depot and all the sights and sounds in it, all the words every traveler has ever uttered and all the feelings of coldness and warmness, are all but sparkling reflections of the pot-bellied stove just being a stove—stove, Isness, comprehending its own being—Isness, beholding its own warmth and perfection, Isness, being neither judge nor judgment—ISNESS being all and only!

Dear Mrs. Prim,
    I did NOT say God has a pot belly!
Sincerely yours,

THE REFINEMENT AND PURIFICATION-BY-FIRE FLAPDOODLE

We have all heard of the tests one is subjected to once he begins his search for Reality. It is generally believed these tests

Ending *the "Seeming"*

are to "try our metal" and "temper the steel" and that we will emerge purified and spiritualized. These tests, all education tells us, are the refining process. Every trial is followed by another more difficult and takes us, we are told, nearly to the "breaking point," but "there is within us all that is necessary to withstand these purifying pressures, no matter *how* wretched the experience." We have all been taught this action-reaction bluster from the beginning.

To play the role of a liar is to play the role of a liar suffering from his lies. What appear as purifying ordeals are not to purify the ego as we have been taught; they are magnificently inherent in the futility of attempting *to be that ego* and serve to insist that we stop trying to do the impossible. The purifying cause-effect, action-reaction business of karma is applicable to the misidentification alone; it is that which shakes it out of its own "seeming" and explains it away. Therefore, the karmaic purification-by-ordeal is very real to the one who travels the path from the depot's cold corner back to the pot-bellied stove in the middle of the room. The journey back, attempting to become one, is like the moth attracted by the flame, darting in and out of the darkness, eyes ashine, finally singeing its wings and falling.

One may experience this sweet-at-the-start and bitter-at-the-end *return* if he wants to, for just as long as he can take it. One may walk the long years of study and devotion back to the red-hot stove to finally burn away the last vestige of the old man in the final stove-hugging experience if he wants to; but he does not have to! He does not have to make such a pilgrimage to Mecca or a slow return to the Father's house. He may, once he sees it for what it is, *instantly* let go, leave, stop playing the role of a separate ego who is turning (or has turned) and is now returning. He may awaken in an instant BY *BEING* THE ONE WHO HAS NEVER BEEN AWAY.

THERE IS THE PROFESSING AND THERE IS THE DOING

It seems there is a long while when we say, "I know there is no such thing as a separate, Awareness-possessing personality," while we continue to play the part of one still making the long journey to the promised land. Still rearranging the sins of a sinless world we say, "Lord, Lord . . . have we not cast out devils and . . . done many wonderful things?" And we hear the clear answer, "I do not know *who you are;* depart from me, you that work iniquity."

Reader, must we walk the full cycle? Must we suffer the agony of the entire trip? Once we perceive the misidentification, why cannot we *leave* it? We can! We can! We may forsake that one immediately, no matter upon which landmark, out of Nod, we appear to be standing. Using the language of the illustration, instantly we may let the stove be Alone and Only on the scene, perceiving that the glowing *stove* is being all there is to every flickering shadow and to this consciousness of them. Reader, this is possible to do simply because it is a fact already; but it takes the doing in addition to the professing.

IDENTITY IN THE LIGHT OF THE DEPOT STOVE ILLUSTRATION

Exactly as the stove in the illustration is the only "real," so "God in the midst of us" is the Real. The one who holds himself in a dark corner is a ghost, a phantom, a mirage, a dream, a nothing claiming to enfold the consciousness of images. The one who has been "cast out," the one wandering in a far country, the one who has "fallen," the one professing to be the judge of good and evil IS NOT REAL, but is merely a role we are playing—an *assumed* identification. The Center Light, the red-hot, pot-bellied ISNESS is the Real and the All. This ISNESS is the only identity, being all there is to the light, the warmth, the snap and crackle, every image, every "thing," every feeling and thought.

To identify Self as the cold shadow of impoverishment groveling its way toward the Light, is to identify as the ghost, as the phantom, as a sputtering spectre and spook. Only to *that* one is there a law of action and reaction, a move back and forth, a coming and going, an ebbing and flowing between serenity and sadness. Only *that* one must endure the ordeal of having to plan and calculate every move back to happiness and the Center Light.

Let such an absurd one go. How? Discover Self to be God's very own Awareness of Being. In the language of the stove illustration, find Self to be the glowing light of the stove itself, not one attempting to find it. Indeed, exactly as the Christ declares, we are the Light of the world.

Those who mistakenly identify themselves as the old man—that silly spectre—inevitably spoof themselves into playing the role of Spook Inspector. In addition, they find themselves being the spurious spectator of *other* Spook Inspectors; Spook-self, self-spoofed, or, Spectre-self completely spoofed.

Of course, all of this is a fantastic fantasy of farcical foolishness, false from the first, and powerless—but funny, *after* it is seen for what it is.

METAPHYSICS IN THE WORLD

The metaphysical schools at one point or another in their instruction would have the troubled one seek out the specific "thought" that has made them sick at heart and dis-eased. Then, in general they teach that the OPPOSITE of that thought is the one "to hold in mind" as the "Truth" to heal the situation. Undeniably, this karmaic approach "works" *at the level of the apparent problem* (and this is the arena wherein most of us begin the search for Reality), but this method is not the final answer.

These metaphysical procedures have had their day in court. Their influence has already been felt around the world; their results presently appear as a world experience divided into a self-attracting duality—positive-negative, real-unreal, white-black, Eastern-Western, wealth-poverty, good-evil, spiritual-material, God believing-God denying, liberal-conservative, free world-Communist world completely divided and sub-divided against itself, within and without. Though we find ourselves knowing what will appear to happen to this positive-negative mess, it is of little consequence because *neither* of the apparent divisions has to do with the Transcendent Isness, the undivided, unjudged Kingdom existing exactly where refracting PERSONAL judgment-making and its spectrum of agony appears to be going on!

A CONVERSATION ABOUT THE PENDULUM AND JUDGMENT

When a pendulum swings, the motion beyond the still center in either direction is energy stored to send it swinging in the other. Back and forth it goes, from mountain to valley, extreme to extreme in slowly lessening arcs until we give it another boost to another swing.

The "mellowness of age" is time's lessening of the swing; but we do not have to await the year's slow work in this regard; we do not have to continue our contention with extremes of feeling; we do not long have to continue the metaphysical ploy of countering negatives with positives. We can stop all of this foolishness immediately! Duality's pendulum stops when we stop making judgmental evaluations!

Why? When we stop making judgments, we stop playing the judge, and the judge *himself* is the pendulum! The pendulum is the judge whose actions are *re-actions* based on his own evalued images. His actions-reactions send him winging into greater movement; *non-action* allows him to find the quiet, peaceful Center at rest!

Jesus said, ". . . it is a movement and a rest." Human evaluation is the movement; the pendulum stilled is the "rest." This is the Secret Place, the Shekinah, the Sabbath to keep holy, the Center of Being!

"But Mr. Samuel, how do I stop making judgments?"
By making no more judgments.
"But I cannot stop!"
You will stop when you see that only the judge suffers from his own judgments, and when you perceive how *lifeless* and how *nothing* is his role!

MORE CONVERSATION ABOUT THE "SEEMING"

There is one mind and it belongs to Isness, God. There is no assemblage of little minds arrayed against us; no cabal intended to overthrow you or me; no ogre, demon or devil attempting to do us in, despite the beliefs we may have had before.

There is but one mind functioning; that mind is being this here-and-now Awareness I am (and you are). This Identity-I-am, therefore, is Deity's Self-awareness.

Because Isness is perfect, the Holy is not conscious of trials and tribulations within its nature. God and Perfection are ONE. Inasmuch as God is Self-aware (what exists outside ALL for the Holy (whole) One to perceive?), and as the Self that God beholds is Perfection *itself, there is no perception of imperfection going on, now or ever, here or anywhere!* Awareness, aware here and now, is an evident fact. Consequently, this activity is God's activity and naught but perfection is being witnessed.

QUESTION: But what is the seeming imperfection I see?

ANSWER: It is the light-refracting *judge's opinion* that a particular set of images, a certain picture on the screen, a specific color of the spectrum, is *not good*. It is usually something the judge sees as a threat to himself.

QUESTION: Then is this to say that whatever mankind calls bad is actually good?

ANSWER: Images are neither; they are just images—perfect, but valueless. They are qualities and attributes of the Holy, that which God knows God to be. Evaluations of them, good, bad or in between, are personal misevaluations.

QUESTION: Does a knowledge of this change the seeming into a better situation?

ANSWER: When one stops playing the role of an evaluator who is *acted upon* by the images he values, he experiences the *actuality* of no-value in the object of perception; THEN, the situation that seemed bad *to the evaluator* is seen *in a new unrefracted light* by the new Identity. The new view does not call the situation bad; but it doesn't call it good either. When it is seen as neither, it is recognized for what it IS and KNOWN as Isness being (beholding) Isness. This is always much more wonderful than any personal judgment of good could have been.

QUESTION: Is this what is meant when it is said "when the two become one" we will experience the Kingdom?

ANSWER: Try it and see!

QUESTION: How?

ANSWER: By ending your judgment of the feelings, images and thoughts within consciousness.

Ending *the "Seeming"* 257

QUESTION: How can I do that when I am constantly being called on to make decisions?

ANSWER: By judgment is meant *the attachment of values* to the things we see, most especially the value called good or evil. It is meant that we stop *giving authority* to that which has no authority except to be what it is—an image being an image, a thought being a thought or a feeling being a feeling. When we stop delegating the authority that belongs to God-being-this-Awareness-I-am, we are enabled to stop reacting to appearances as if they had such value, power and authority. We find this Deific Self-Awareness-I-am actually *does* "have dominion over every creeping *thing* . . ." as we have been told from the beginning.

QUESTION: You mean I will still make judgments concerning my business and daily affairs, but I make them from the position of *no value in images?*

ANSWER: Yes; from the position that ALL Value is in *that* which is *being* images! The "That" is ISNESS, REALITY, the SUPERNAL. Perhaps I should point out again that by ending our evaluating *judgment* of Awareness and all it contains does not mean the end of *distinction*. The tree is a tree and the mountain is a mountain. Each is distinctly what it is. Our ability to *distinguish* "increases" enormously as we stop the attachment of *values* to that which is valueless. This "expanding" aliveness is one of the many wonders of this work.

Jesus observed that "there is nothing hidden which will not be revealed; there is nothing unknown that will not be known." Awareness is where the unknown becomes known; so when we end the silly practice of making this Awareness-I-am tributary to the images it includes, we begin to see what misevaluation and misidentification have hidden. It is as simple as that.

QUESTION: You said that one "experiences the actuality of no-value in images." What is this experience?

ANSWER: It must be *lived* to be known. What can Macbeth be told about Shakespeare? It is infinitely varied because it is Deity's view of Deity's infinite selfhood. If it is not realized to be one's present view of things, then he needs only to stop theorizing, to let go the old man and start acting the unjudging Awareness he is.

QUESTION: Then, in a nutshell, despite all the world has to say about it, this present experience is not really a bad experience or a good one; and God is being all there is to these sights, sounds, thoughts and feelings?

ANSWER: Yes—by being this Transcendent Awareness of them.

QUESTION: Then I must think and act from the standpoint that this consciousness-I-am is God's activity, God perceiving what God knows Himself to be?

ANSWER: Yes.

QUESTION: In God's name, how do I do this?

ANSWER: In God's name, effortlessly! By knowing that you-as-Awareness have no personal responsibility in the matter. Isness is; Isness is already Self-aware. There is nothing unpossessed Awareness must do, or not do, but reside in (as) this Perfection, doing whatever appears the thing to do. We find the doing effortless, full of Thought, empty of thinking, and wondrous indeed.

CHAPTER XXIV

Simplicity

Dear Dr. Adams:

When one seeks the "secrets" of life, the secrets of the universe, the secrets of science, mathematics, God or anything else, in reality he is searching out the vistas of his own Identity. Those who know this are the ones who find the true answers; and all they find is simple, not complicated, arcane or abstruse. Those who do not know this search for the Truth in ever more complicated places and ways of their own making.

The experience of mankind is growing more frustrating every day. Human pressures are mounting on every hand. As various segments of humanity find themselves unable or unwilling to keep up the frantic pace or longer battle the self-imposed frustrations, the man-made lids are beginning to pop off.

When will it end? Apparently not until misidentified mankind is forced out of himself in a self-wrought Armageddon. However, you and I are not waiting for the world "out there" to awaken. We leave every bit of it behind. We let it go. We rise above it, so to speak, by the simple willingness to put God first and let God, Isness, the One Identity, be the all and only of us.

This is not an impossible task. It is only from the standpoint of a judgment maker that it even seems necessary, much less a difficult job to be undertaken. The fact is, God is *already* being the all-we-are.

It is not difficult to stop judging everything after it has been discovered that judgment is the cause of apparent suffering. It is not hard to stop cherishing the things the world calls valuable when it is found they have no value. It is not impossible to stop feeling a sense of personal responsibility when there is no real personality to feel responsible.

When the final statements concerning God are made, they will be supremely simple. When the last words about Reality are written, they will not be an academic presentiment or a mysterious metaphysical maze requiring much musing, meditating and persevering study. When finally it is made clear to humanity what it must do in order to come out and be separate from its frustrations, the doing will not be difficult; it will not be an arduous path to follow; neither will it be a step-by-step overcoming. It will neither be a putting off nor an awakening, though it is difficult to *speak* of it in any other way.

It will be an utter *simplicity* that excludes no one and no thing. The last instruction for a doing will be a quiet, simple, undemanding demand for no more effort at all. The simplicity of Reality, Deity, is the effortless being of total Perfection, here and now, *the exclusive* fact of already-existence.

At the moment, mankind believes the knowledge of God is limited to very few, if any. According to the religious systems of the day, "the blessings that a knowledge of Truth bestows upon suffering humanity" are experienced only by those who belong to this or that church or study this or that philosophy, only by those who overcome, struggle, strive, contend, demonstrate, experience illumination or take drugs. Hocus-pocus!

We *leave* the human sense of things, the judged sense of things, and happily discover that we also leave complexity. We return to the Deific Identity and find ourselves in a garden of tender simplicity where there is no concern for "good" or "evil" and no talking serpent who makes us give values to everything. Things that are seen are simply seen, without critical analysis and misevaluation. Here, "experience" and "awareness" are one activity belonging to God. Here, Awareness is God's Self-perception, hence, God's responsibility. We feel the weight of the world taken from our shoulder. We recall the promise of old, "Come unto me, all ye who are weary and heavy laden and I will give thee rest."

HAPPINESS COMES WITH LETTING GO

Deity is a paradox to man who cloaks his measly bits of wisdom with an aura of profundity to impress others and feed his insatiable ego. But to those sincerely interested in ascertaining Reality, there is an area of breakthrough available. Where is it? We are in the fertile center of that area the instant we stop playing the judge, the great evaluator. Here in Judgeless Being tribulations are rooted out, smothered and returned to their native nothingness within a burgeoning Tranquillity that exists where the elations and depressions of personal judgment seemed before to hold sway.

God is not a complexity, far off and unattainable. God is *available*, else Reality would be a plum pluckable only by the plucky few who have the wherewithal to plow through many volumes of witchcraft and transcendental lore, and even those scholars but touch the hem of Truth's garment.

Reader, the Presence is felt as an enlightenment, as a "breaking through," as a lifting, as a rest, as a rolling up the scroll, as the lessening of a load, as peace and happiness. These words are but poor sounds to signify the simplicity of God—not the complexity of God, not the mysticism of God, not the paradoxes of Truth—but the tender simplicity of the Presence.

Happiness comes with a letting go, not with taking on; by ending concern, not developing more. The Unencumbered, like children, enjoy the Now without worry over yesterday or tomorrow.

CHILDLIKENESS

How children joy in fragrances and colors and moving things! Their sweet simplicity is why the world is so wonderful to them. Their enjoyment of the Now is why the flip of a cricket or the silent plop of a pudgy frog is a momentous event. Credulous innocence is their entry into every activity with gusto and why their imaginations run so freely from fancy fairy tale to wondrous dream; why the sounds they hear seem so sharp, sights so exciting, the air so crisp and filled with all it is filled with!

This childlike simplicity appears to become veiled by the processes of education. "Growing up" is to become brainwashed, conditioned and accustomed to playing the pseudo-identity: "adult," adulterer, chief evaluator and judge. Ah, but the Unencumbered, with the freedom of angels, remain unconcerned with the world's evaluations, even while remaining hyper-aware of every "thing" in the universe! Our simple childlikeness continues! Our alertness remains undimmed!

Who doesn't speak of the innocence of youth? Who doesn't wonder at the idyllic credulousness of childhood? Who hasn't longed for the exhilaration and exuberance of youth again, for the health, happiness and carefree excitement of childhood? And, who hasn't heard the Christ say, "Except you become again as children you will in no way enter the kingdom?"

Reader, you can become as a child, and do it without appearing foolish, without ignoring home and family, without withdrawing from society. We become childlike in the most effortless way imaginable: *as we stop making vain and unnecessary evaluations and live the instant called NOW!*

Dear Mr. Samuel,

The way my daughter acts (she reads your work), everything on this earth is just peaches and cream and perfect. To

Simplicity

hear her tell it, you would think this place is heaven. You should be ashamed for causing her to act like there just isn't anything wrong with anything.

Yours truly,

Dear Mr. Samuel,

I am writing to complain about the idiotic nonsense you write in your letters. My daughter has read your books and the letters you have been writing to her personally, and I can tell you from looking that it hasn't done her a bit of good. Before she read your stuff she was perfectly miserable, *but at least she was doing something about the causes of her misery.* Now she has just turned her back on those causes and isn't doing a thing about them anymore! She just *thinks* she isn't miserable and unhappy.

I know that one of these days she will find that all her problems aren't just going to continue to melt away, that one of them is going to rise up and smite her in the face as they used to do. Then she will be as bad off as she was before she started listening to you instead of me. She has just simply become *inhuman* the way nothing bothers her anymore! I think it is terrible!

Yours truly,

When we finally get smart and let go the complexity of education and its struggle to understand, we discover there *remains* the tender, simple, single Awareness of Being which is even now beholding these words. *This* is the Singleness *as which* we have always been aware and conscious of being. Perfection beholding itself is this Consciousness of Being I am and you are. God's *beholding* is the Identity Bill is, Jack is, Nancy is and Julie is.

The "only acceptable sacrifice" is the surrender of the complicating, personal ego, the judgment making intellect, the old man who says "I," "me," "mine," and creates his own misery with "I like" and "I don't like."

PEOPLE, CHURCHES AND PHILOSOPHY

Teachers, books, leaders, philosophies, practitioners, religions, theories, bibles and holy books of the world may be likened to leaves on a tree. When the wind blows, the leaves make sounds—some loud, some soft, some high, some low. The pine needle that makes a strong sound, like a tuning fork, sets those of the same note into sympathetic vibration. This is as it should be, but surely it must be understood, the Value isn't in the leaf, the pine needle, or the sound they make. The importance isn't in how many kindred images vibrate in sympathy, in how many agree or disagree. The task is not to find the sweetest sound or the softest sound; neither to find the truest sound, the "authorized" sound, nor the "most absolute" sound. The task—if it is a task at all—is to recognize one's own identity to be—TO BE—all there is to the tree, the leaves, the sounds and even to the gentle wind that moves them!

The value isn't in the religion, the holy book, the leader, the authorized literature, teacher, philosophy or system, not in the images within Awareness or in their beliefs as countless as the needles on the pine. No! The Value Supernal is "in" *That* which is *being* the Awareness I am (and you are, Reader), perceiving the religions, holy books, leaders, teachers, philosophies and systems within Itself.

"Samuel," mere image of awareness, is nothing of himself. Samuel-image is but a leaf on the tree. The eternal Isness *being* "Samuel" (plus all other images) is being the entire tree, every leaf and every zephyr that animates them. It is downright silly to admire or disparage one of the leaves, a single image of the Self, as being the only authorized leader, the straightest line, the least or the most absolute statement,

Simplicity

system or approach. This is judgmental foolishness, unnecessary twaddle, the tinkling of cymbals, the whisper of new leaves whose sounds mellow as they grow in the Light.

We enjoy the sounds of many leaves. We do not close the door or turn a deaf ear toward others. We will continue to read books, give and listen to lectures and discuss ideas as long as it comes to us to do these things. But we know the value isn't there. The importance isn't the book, lecture or speaker, even those authorized by the board of directors or the high priests at the temple. We maintain an unshakable equanimity in the knowledge that Eternal Allness being the Identity-I-am is the Value. We joy in the simplicity of Allness's all!

We remain wary not to be drawn into an attack on what others say, or a defense of what we say. The Truth stands as its own monument with beauty, simplicity, tenderness and an unjudging love that makes the Heart sing and does astounding things within our experience!

> "I listen to the Holy Councilor only, who teaches me directly—here, right here in my Heart."

CHAPTER XXV

A Discussion of Church Membership

QUESTION: I am finding it increasingly difficult to abide the mamby-pamby stuff I have to listen to at church. I no longer agree with so much that is said there, but I can find no other organization that states the unadulterated Truth, either; so should I withdraw membership from my present church?

ANSWER: Who is "Samuel" to tell "Mary" what to do? We are not in the counciling or decision-making business. "We" are in the *being* business whose business is judgeless, motiveless beholding! *How* this appears is not a Bill-responsibility or Mary-responsibility and there cannot be a *necessary* Bill-struggle or Mary-struggle to make a decision about it.

Whatever "decisions" appear to be necessary to be who and what we be are made for us. They come about in their own time and way in an effortless manner, and seldom as Bill or Mary would have determined personally. They arrive "on time" and if it should be they establish a course that leaves old landmarks behind, there will be no regrets. On the other hand, if we should continue as we have been, there will be no lingering frustrations or doubts about it. There is a humorous illustration in this regard:

Once upon a time there was a man who became interested in fish. He studied goldfish for a time, then freshwater fish, then *fat* freshwater fish, and finally, tiny *tropical* fish.

Ultimately, his studies led him to join that august and aristocratic group known as the Pottsburg Society for the Propagation and Preservation of Infinitesimal Tropical Fish.

A Discussion of Church Membership 267

They met at the town hall every Wednesday evening. The meetings were made up of brief business sessions followed by considerable testimonial periods during which the visitors (and sometimes members) spoke of their accomplishments along the lines of the propagation and preservation (and on occasion, the proper paternal care) of their infinitesSssimmal fish. (He *loved* the way they said it!)

However, our man soon became interested in *astronomy* (which he preferred to call Celestial Physics), but he continued his membership in the Pottsburg Tropical Fish Society and attended their meetings regularly.

At this point, he began to notice an interesting phenomenon. As his interest in astronomy grew, he heard less and less that interested him during the Wednesday evening meetings of the tropical fish society. As a matter of fact, he soon observed as to how they were having nothing *whatever* to say about Celestial Physics. Astronomy—that wonderful science—seemed to be the *last* thing on the face of the earth they were interested in! Why, they wasted every bit of their time talking about—of all things!—the silly, propagation, preservation (and sometimes proper paternal care) of a bunch of fish, runty ones at that. "Why do they palaver about fish," he wondered, "when there are so many comets, planets, gaseous galaxies, exploding quasi-stars and asteroids zooming right over their fat heads?"

Well, during one of the solemn Wednesday evening meetings, the man rose to his feet before the imperious Society for the Propagation and Preservation of Infinitesimal Tropical Fish, and there, to the thunder-struck fish lovers of Pottsburg, delivered an impassioned testimony *about gaseous galaxies and zooming asteroids*. His arms were still waving when they led him lovingly from the town hall and threatened him with excommunication. Out on the sidewalk he was given the precise page, paragraph and line numbers from the organization's rules pertaining to such unseemly conduct.

There is a sequel to the story. Our friend continued attending the meetings for a time. "After all," thought he, "I owe it to my friends to tell them of the vast universe of hot gas and comet tails they could see if they would but lift their heads from the fish tanks," but nothing was accomplished and only argument resulted:

"Waddaya mean, your gaseous galaxies are better than my red-tailed pirrhanas? You are surely full of meteors."

"On the contrary, my friend. You seem to have guppies where your asteroids should be."

And so it went. He succeeded in convincing no one. Anyway, who is able to survey the vistas between the Pleiades and the Milky Way while he is arguing with members of the Pottsburg Tropical Fish Society down at the town hall?

Inevitably, the decision of circumcision from "organization" is made *for* us. We *know* if and when to pack our duds. There is no tearing the hair over the matter.

Now that we have put this matter of church membership into its proper perspective, would anyone care to ask specific questions about it?

QUESTION: What church are you a member of?

ANSWER: None.

QUESTION: Is it *profitable* to withdraw from the church?

ANSWER: This question was asked centuries ago in almost exactly those words. Then, as now, it was motivated by a revolt against intransigent tradition. In the early days of historic Christianity, it was spoken of as "circumcision."

"If circumcision were profitable," Jesus said, answering the very question you have asked, "their Father would beget them circumcised from the womb." Then He concluded, ". . . but *the true circumcision is profitable in every way.*"

Church membership is not UNnatural; it is neither "good" nor "bad," and it is tributary to "the true *circumcision*" from

A Discussion of Church Membership

the misidentification. Withdrawal from the old man, the liar, the deceiver, the opinion holder, is of more moment than the withdrawal of our names from a membership list. To come out and be separate from the misidentification is the withdrawal that is profitable in every way!

This may or may not appear to include a termination of membership in a social organization, but as attention shifts from value in images to *Isness*-the-Value, there is a growing knowledge ("expanding Awareness") of what images are all about, including those called organizations. We become less involved with the intricacies of personal politics and all that appears to be the man-manipulated machinations of those institutions. We are infinitely more concerned with Isness-being-images, by whatever their appearing and whatever they are called.

One thing more! The sundry religious movements are neither good nor bad. They are not the ogres they are increasingly being pictured as, and they are not the paragons of virtue they have pictured themselves to be. To think that a certain religion (like a color of the spectrum) contains the power for good within itself, makes inevitable the appearance of another religious group we think has the power for evil within it. Why should we continue to do this to ourselves?

There is no real power (or authority) for good or evil in churches; not even in the priesthood, the hierarchy, the board of directors or the Supreme Court. ISNESS ever remains the only authority—the same Isness being this Identity-I-am ("we" are).

In this light we are able to see that the "true circumcision" is to cut ourselves away from the judging, opinion holding *misidentification* that looks at the very organizations he creates and then calls them good or evil. (But listen, listen: even *that* act of judgment by the old nature is neither good nor bad, right nor wrong! It is no more "wrong" than a flower is mistaken before it blooms. And who is to say the cicada is wrong because it lies still a-wallowing in the earth and speaks of the eternal nature of darkness all about? When the cicada climbs into the sunlight it is no longer writhing in the damp dirt, and when it wings its way through the bright colors of the summer scene it is no longer philosophizing about the reality or unreality of darkness. *It was neither good nor bad while it was happening,* however; and this impartiality is a fact which, when finally admitted, opens large windows and massive doors to tranquillity on earth.)

ABOUT GIVING COUNSEL TO OTHERS

Awareness is not in the business of telling images when to come and go, when to enter and leave or on which side of the aisle to sit in what church, any more than the television screen is in the business of ordering the scenes within it to fade in and out.

Now comprehend this: equally, Awareness does not *ask* images what it must do to be opinionless Awareness either, any more than the television screen asks the soap commercials how to be a brighter picture. The conscious awareness reading these words needs no advice and does not need to give any. Infinite Intelligence is being this Awareness-we-are.

MORE ABOUT GIVING ADVISE

Look at the trees along the shore there; just trees being trees, without regret for where they grow—or why. Do they ask the sunshine and the rain when to bloom? Or do they just bloom?

Suppose you were one of those trees—and the Self you are

A Discussion of Church Membership 271

includes every tree in the universe—would you ask the sun and the rain and the wind and the birds winging in the wind when to blossom? I hardly think so; but suppose you *did* and the rain told you to bloom on the twenty-seventh of March and the sunshine said to bloom on the tenth of April, while the wind and that little flock of birds there told you not to bloom at all. What would you do then? It would be chaotic to follow all the external advice you were given, wouldn't it?

Now turn this around. Do you tell the wind when to whistle and the flowers when to bloom? Do you tell the leaves when to fall from the branches? Would you tell the falling leaf wig-wagging its way to earth on which side of the path to rest? Of course not.

The mystery is, since we would neither give nor follow such advice, why are we always doing it?

QUESTION: When someone asks me for advice, what am I to tell them?

ANSWER: When *I* am asked, I tell them who I am and who "they" are (it is the same Identity), and sometimes I tell them how I came to know it. I am ever mindful that the one I speak to is the Self-being-I; consequently, discourses are not only eye to eye, but "I" to "I." I have no responsibility for the appearance and action of images out there, and therefore, I can tell "that, out there" (and often do) "You have nothing to do but *be*."

Now, I say again: I tell "others" who "I" am and, mayhaps, how I have come to discern it, but I have no business at all, at all, telling others what to DO. Images are not obligated to us to *do* anything. This is the indebtedness we "forgive" *if we expect to enjoy an experience wherein we are not indebted to a flock of demanding images!*

WE STOP WORRYING ABOUT WHAT *OTHERS* DO.
THERE IS NO ONE *OUT THERE* WHO MUST
PUT OFF THE OLD MAN!

In spite of all and everything, most especially despite the personal proclivity for judging the sights and sounds that come as "experience," a very perfect, "good" Reality remains the fact; Reality continues being all existence; ONE Self-mindful Reality exists; only one MIND is present. There is not a multitude of little minds running around "out there" with the ability to dream up diabolical schemes or Machiavellian intrigues intended to sink a personal concept of "me," or attempting to make this Awareness-I less than tranquil. The little ego that suspects such silliness is the little ego that sees what it expects.

Reader, it is well to repeat, we are ever concerned with *one* Awareness: *THIS* ONE RIGHT *HERE*. When we speak of the personal judgments of this or that, we are not talking about the judgments, opinions, and evaluations the world-*out-there* makes; we are talking about those made right here as THIS-AWARENESS-CALLED-I—if I am foolish enough to do it. When we speak of the "old man," we are not talking about the misidentification of our friends and relatives or the people down the street, or about the incorrect opinions *they* appear to have of *themselves;* WE ARE TALKING ABOUT THE MISIDENTITY ONLY *WE* CAN PRESUME *OURSELVES* TO BE RIGHT *HERE,* RIGHT *NOW.* To "put off that one" is not for OTHERS to do, but for ME to do, right here. *Others* have nothing to do with it. The picture of the world, including others, is HERE and NOW, THIS-AWARENESS-BEING-I—*not another!* Seest thou this? The fabled "last judgment" takes place *here* AS I BE I, instead of the *container* of I.

A FINAL WORD ABOUT TEACHING

I think perhaps the last thing to be understood about "telling others of Reality" is this: the way to tell is to be. When we be it, we tell it with the most wondrous effectiveness; and when we be it, we are not concerned with the details of why, how or even "if," lest it be we are asked—and then we know.

As Awareness, Awareness-I includes "others," who appear as animate, immaculate images "within." As Awareness-I, I did not put those images there (here) and I am not responsible for them except to continue the honest, unjudging consciousness of them, perceiving them as the myriad, magnificent qualities ISNESS knows Isness to be, and knowing it is Isness who is being this Awareness-I-am.

If it should or should not appear that images come into an understanding of God, this appearing (or non-appearing) is the perfect activity of Isness; this is God, Self-revealing and Self-comprehending; this is Isness being this Consciousness-I —Self-comprehension in action! This is the Identity of the same (only) consciousness reading these words.

I tell you this: those who end their attempt to be a manipulator and a judge inevitably find themselves being the sunshine from which "others" appear to derive "their" nourishment. Then "they" too, as appearances go, blossom one by one into brilliant New Orbs, being and doing likewise for those they perceive.

ABOUT PURPOSE AND PROFESSION

QUESTION: Do I have a purpose for being on earth? That is, do I have a mission?

ANSWER: In plain words, without attempting to exclude or preclude "words that imply duality," I can tell you that *I* have a mission, and that it appears to this I that "you" have the same mission. It is to apprehend the Identity being I and then to live it and be it.

QUESTION: Where does my profession as an artist fit into this?

ANSWER: In the most natural of all ways. Living and being the real Identity inevitably appear as "others" coming to comprehend "their" Identity. This rightful Identity-we-be is the only true artist . . . and our "medium" is not limited to canvas or music or words. It includes all art forms, and it includes a great depth in whatever medium we may enjoy at the moment.

The real artist irresistibly and effortlessly "communicates" his self-discovered Identity. His artistry is the appearing of the communicating going on. It is doing its "good work" by "putting eyes in the place of an eye, hands in the place of hands, and feet in the place of feet"; it is like the roadside periwinkle looking out and finding itself surrounded by itself, from seed of its own kind given to last Summer's wind.

A FABLE

Once upon a time there was a wise lantern and a foolish lantern. The foolish lantern wished for a hundred bugs to shine its light upon. To fulfil its desire, it set out chasing moths in the night. Swinging over fields and fences, darting and circling from moth to moth, the foolish lantern tried very hard to make the bugs see it.

Pursuing a particularly vivacious moth one evening, that lantern smashed against a fence post and broke. The wise lantern, however, motiveless and very still, sits safe atop a stone wall, ministering to thousands.

CHAPTER XXVI

About Love

"Love is the key to the Mystery; Love is the astrolabe of Life."

Love, as Love is, remains unperceived until one puts aside the personal sense of self; until he lays down the "life" of the pseudo-identity and lets go the actor who believes himself to be Great Judge and opinion-holder.

What joy is known when we awaken to perceive that Love is our Identity! This Self-I-am is Love itself. Love is being all there is to "me." Love is being this Consciousness here and now!

WE ARE NEVER TO BE CONCERNED WITH THE "LOVING OR UNLOVING" ACTIONS OF OTHERS! Rather, we are to understand fully that Love itself is THIS Identity! Love is Identity being "I." Love is our continuous identification.

LOVE IS NOT A WAY TO ACT, BUT AN IDENTITY TO ACCEPT! I went about for such a long time thinking Love was a way I was supposed to perform, that I was to act "loving" and that others were to act loving toward me. But, once I accepted the Self to *be* Love, I found there is no way to act but *as* Love. We awaken to see there is no other love but *this* Love being "me."

There are no objects of perception we must rush out and love. The "neighbors" we are to love as ourselves are *within* the Self, within Awareness, not separate nor apart from it. Awareness is forever, tenderly, gently beholding the Infinity being all Identity is.
Isness loves the infinity Isness is. This is the only love going on. God loves the Reality God is; there is no other reality. One-Only-Reality "loves" (knows and is aware of) *Itself*. That Love in action is this Awareness-we-are.

Love is simple. Love is tender and effortless. Love is pure, motiveless Awareness that makes no judgments and clutches no opinions. Love is forgiveness. Love is humility. It wrestles with nothing because there is naught outside Identity to be contrary to its nature. It simply is. It is the Identity we are, not an act we must perform.

Tenderness is the hallmark of love. It accomplishes more in an instant than force does in an aeon.
The lover touches the face of his love with an open hand and a tender touch. Love speaks with a soft voice. It has no need of pressure or coercion. The tender touch and the soft sound warm the coldest appearance.

Why does mankind resort to ugliness when it surely compounds his problem? Why doesn't he try gentleness and tenderness when its effectiveness is so apparent? Here is why: he interprets love as something he must do or something someone should do for him. But Love is not a doing; it is a being. It is effortless, because it is the Identity we are.

With a fragile blossom, the flower tells of love; but it does not dictate the form and color of the bloom nor put a price on its fragrance. It does not judge; it simply blooms, without regard or regret. It blooms even if no one is there to praise it. It blooms with a tenderness void of pretention and selfishness. It gives itself without anger; without force. It gives with honesty and simplicity. The flower doesn't love by "doing," but by *being* the flower it is. THIS is the love to be: acknowledgment that God's Love is the love we are.

The stars will fall before we can be *given* love! It is foolish to *expect* someone to *give* us affection, to show us gratitude or in some way be "loving" *to* us. Inasmuch as Love is what WE are, it is *being* all there is to every image within awareness. Furthermore, it is being the very action images appear to be engaged in, no matter what opinion personal judgment holds.

Churchdom has the cart before the horse when it speaks of love as though it were a duty; as though one were to be punished if he acted otherwise; as if the crown had no jewels until we do such and so.

This is not to disparage kindly deeds, but there is only one way to act loving, and that is to see that the only Identity in all existence is Love *itself*. *That* Identity is *this* one-I-am (and you are, reader.) Identity is unceasing Love in action.

Love is exactly where the consciousness is that reads these words—that feels the wind, rain and sunshine of a Summer day! Yea, this very awareness we call "me" is the *presence* of infinite affluence, health, holiness and love. This is how close we are to all we might have thought necessary for happiness! How close can we get? ALL is here, right now, closer than breathing. It is our Identity, awaiting Self-acknowledgment.

Do you think Identity is one thing and worldly wealth another? Let me tell you right now: Identity is not a Spiritual Realm away out there somewhere, attainable only through strict intellectual practices or arduous in-breathing and out-breathing of metaphysical exercises. When one finds himself ready to let go the imposter, and does it, to *rest* in the warmth of the Already Only, *that* one finds whatever he appears to need, dumped right in his lap effortlessly, unavoidably. He finds love and companionship to be what he is—Identity.

Identity—which is the perception of Totality—cannot look upon itself as poor, needy and without love, can it? Love sees Love! What else? Love is what you're looking at, neighbor—and it is the looking!

Dear Mr. Samuel,

My husband and I are not always together in our search for Truth. Very often, my interest in Truth appears to mean nothing to him and to cause antagonism. Will you comment on this?

Dear Mrs. Love,

The Truth-we-be appears continually as new ideas we are coming to comprehend. It is natural to share our delight and enthusiasm with someone else, but we let go the notion that we must see *them* indicate their understanding, acceptance and approval of these new ideas. We are in the *beholding* business, and not in the business of judging how certain images are supposed to act or respond. To free *them* of such obligations is to find *ourselves* free of any dependence upon them for our happiness. Why should we limit our pleasure to the actions of others? When we stop this, we see no more antagonism "out there." (See the selection *The Basis for Action* and the one following, page 102.)

It is frustration and folly to attempt to determine and arrange for the proper appearance of the images within our seeing. The Identity we are and have always been, is *Perception itself*. Awareness is perceiving, not dictating what is to be perceived nor how it should appear. The attempt to arrange the affairs of the objects within Awareness is the "effect" of desire, the "cause" of misery. This is unnecessary activity that we can stop immediately and effortlessly, because Perfection is the finished fact already.

A LETTER ABOUT HARMONY IN MARRIAGE

Dear Mary,

You write that your husband does not understand you, doesn't do little things for you as he once did, doesn't know you exist, isn't attentive to the children, doesn't do his share toward raising them, and "doesn't think about anything but his business."

Also, you write that you have been "very diligent and specific in attacking each of these problems," yet all the work you have done to overcome them has been to no avail and now you are "completely miserable." (Little wonder!)

There is the story of a man who dreamt every night he was being chased by a bevy of lovely ladies. Before the girls could catch him, a vicious tiger suddenly appeared in the dream and jumped on his back. At this point he always awakened in terror. Night after night, the same dream repeated until the man went to a psychiatrist and told him the story.

"Yes, I understand," said the doctor. "You want to get rid of the terrible dream."

"Oh, no!" the man replied. "I want you to get rid of the *tiger* so those ladies can catch me!"

To do battle with a specific set of images within Awareness is just such senseless manipulation. It is the effort to have the picture turn out the way Mary wants it to, or as Mary thinks it should. It is an effort to be rid of the tiger in the dream—*all of which still leaves the dream going on.* Perhaps a well-directed, well-manipulated dream is to be preferred to a nightmare, but it does not compare to the Tranquillity in which there is neither sleep, dreamer nor dream.

Sooner or later, often in desperation, we are forced to forsake every value attached to the picture. This is never done while still doing battle with a specific aspect of the picture.

If Mary believes something is wrong, the wrong lies with the one called Mary and her personal sense of Self. There is nothing wrong with husband "out there."

Surprised? Don't be. The instant you recognize and acknowledge your actual Identity, which is not Mary at all, Mary's present hurts and frustrations will stop bothering you; and when you start responding to Mary's opinions as *valueless* opinions (instead of power-full opinions) they will stop appearing to attempt (tempt) to bother you!

You cannot be Mary *actually,* no matter how hard you try. No matter how much you may love her and enjoy playing her role, Judge-Mary is not your Identity. Who, then, are you? You are Awareness itself—*Awareness.*

But who is Mary? She is the Judge and the opinion holder; she is the dream-ego, the phantom, the nothing, who acts as though she contains Awareness *within* her as her personal possession. (Now, *listen!*) Your *actual* Identity is this *selfsame* Awareness, but it is not possessed, has never been contained within a body and, indeed, couldn't be!

Poor, suffering Mary is an impossible identity, a man-made personality, who believes she has a will and mind of her own, a

About Love

mind that is being aware *for Mary;* a mind which *she* says owns the consciousness of these words. Is this not what the intellect says? "I am someone who is aware and conscious. Awareness is the activity of my mind, and I, Mary, (or Bill) want it to be aware of what I, Mary, want so see and hear. If I do not see what I want to see, I call its absence 'bad' and I am upset about it. When *my* mind doesn't show *me* a husband who is attentive to *me and mine,* I, owner of that mind, am completely miserable. I cannot be happy until I see my husband do such and such, or *stop* doing such and so."

Dear one, since "your" Identity *is* Awareness, undeniably the activity of Mind, this Awareness-we-are is the awareness of the Divine Mind, God! What greater birthright could we have than to be God's own consciousness of Himself?

There is *one* God; hence, one awareness, holy and divine. *That* one is *this* one, conscious of these words. You are it (this) and this (it) is you—not a possession of Bill's or Mary's. Awareness (you) belongs to God! And (listen!) *God is responsible for it!*

We stop making demands of all seen and experienced within Awareness. We stop playing the judge of everything included within the Identity being this Consciousness-I-am. We be what we are—Awareness! Dare to be Awareness only! Behold as Awareness—without judgment, without opinion, without motive! End Mary's say-so in the matter!

(The one to whom this letter was sent now has the happiest home that can be imagined, as all who visit her know.)

To define Love in one word, we might use Tranquillity.

Inasmuch as Love, Tranquillity, Joy, is God, Self-identified, we can be certain that Love, Tranquillity, Joy is universal—everywhere!

Love is an inherent aspect of every object of perception included within (as) Awareness. The appearance of the broken pencil sharpener in disarray and dust is as Joy inducing as the sight of sunset and still water from Lollygog's window. The spattered bucket and wrinkled papers about my feet are as lovely and awe inspiring as the leafy slopes along the silent Coosa. Why? Because Isness, Deity, Reality, is being all there is to *every* sight and sound, every leaf and berry, every footprint and fleecy cloud within this Awareness!

Tranquillity is not a seldom induced *feeling;* Tranquillity is Identity! Tranquillity is who and what I am, always! Tranquillity is not dependent upon what is seen or experienced; it is one's very own presence and being; it is one's *Self,* one's *Identity!* I cannot escape from myself; neither can I escape from Tranquillity.

What is there to do? Only to stop looking for things to *trigger* happiness; to stop looking for certain people or experiences to *give,* or *induce* a feeling of serenity and love. Why should we keep on giving images the authority to give or withold *that which we already are*—our own Identity? When we "begin to end" this monkey business, we are not far from the continual *conscious* experience of Tranquillity, Peace, Joy and Love everlasting.

God, alone, total and all, is the Lover! The Love my bounding heart "feels" for all I see is God's love for the universe—Reality, self-identified!

To "love God with all thy heart and all thy soul and mind" is simply to be honest and stop playing the part of another who attempts to co-exist with God.

To love is to claim Awareness to be our Identity. To take this true Identity to be the Self-I-am is the Holy Matrimony for which marriage is the appearing.

Conclusion

Listen, those who have ears to hear: the intellect and the intellect's comforting institutions simply will never put the intellect out of business. Metaphysics is not going to explain itself away. Education is not going to educate itself out of existence, and religion is not going to stop binding back its concepts of fallen sinners to its especial notions of Truth. But the intellect will never derive the comfort it seeks from its self-created foundations, sandstone every one. If we are to have done with the world's fears and phobias, we have no alternative but to come out and be separate from the personal intellect which has made its troubles and its troubled institutions in the first place.

Ah, but here comes the intellect's ace in the hole, its last bastion of hope. *"How,"* we puff up ourselves and ask (the fabled snake was surely a puffing adder), *"how do we surrender an identity that does not exist?"*

The scholasticism behind this question and those like it is the ego's jewel encrusted sword upon which so many of us hang self-impaled, wiggling like a worm in hot ashes. Without doubt, this is the verbal dalliance upon which William Samuel choked the longest. To me, the most insidious of intellectualism's many convincing arguments was woven around this imposing pronouncement of "enlightened common sense" that "it isn't possible to put off a non-existent misidentification." Oh, how I excoriated those who, in the name of Truth, dast say we could!—and then had the audacity to call their message "absolute!" "Duality and double-talk!" I labeled any such mention of a non-existent identity. Said I, "Talk of a mortal man makes a reality of a non-reality," as if such a thing were possible.

No indeed, we *cannot* put off an identity that does not exist, but (listen! listen!) if we seem to be suffering a phantom's seeming, *we are playing the phantom's role;* and, though such an identity has never been real, it seems very much so to those who play its part. If we are to discover the Tranquillity that is already our here-and-now-Identity, we simply must—and effortlessly can—stop attempting to play the part of that stumbling, fumbling, bumbling, trembling, untranquil, phobia-filled phantom called the "old man," the judge.

Those of us who shout the loudest about "duality" have not discovered the precise nature of its ridiculous, rhetorical role and have not stopped attempting to enact it. When we actually do, we no longer battle with words; we see through, *and end,* the ruse of attempting to be a misidentified ego *professing its own impossibility! Then* ends the experience of being a contending, swinging pendulum, ever wavering between its truth and error, real and unreal, absolute and otherwise.

Therefore, we pinpoint the pseudo-phantom and understand it for the farce it is. We unmask that proud intellect, ego, opinion-holder and judge; we uncover it and let it go! We stop theorizing about doing this; we stop speculating about it, stop pondering, studying, meditating, talking and arguing about its possibility or impossibility, *to do it*—actually to do it—to act! We stop hiding behind that desperate ploy of self-righteous erudition that entraps us with "I cannot let go something that doesn't exist," *to stop trying to be that "something that does not exist!"* We break with city hall.

We have written about the Heart; we have spoken of "my" Heart within "me," but who is this me? Who is this one who says *"I* will listen to *my* Heart within *me?"* Who is this I, my and me who professes to be the great recipient and custodian of something within himself so wonderful as Infinite Aware-

Conclusion

ness? Who is this one who makes himself a *container* for the Secret Place and says, "I am the possessor of Life?" *There is no such one! That* is the non-existent identity we surrender; *that* is the fatherless *nothing* we stop playing at being!

Though it seems Truth is felt within a "me," though this is the "place" of the Christ-Heart, the immaculate conception, the virgin birth of Truth, we shortly discover our identity is the Heart, Christ, Truth *itself,* and the container-ego professing to *feel* the truth, is the devil, satan, the deceiver, the nothing, who is claiming to be the lord and master of this Awareness-being-I.

The stirring of the Heart once seemed dishearteningly infrequent to me, and I did not know why, but now I do. I went about foolishly proclaiming, "I will listen to my Heart; the Heart is in me!" Great ego-Bill and his personal sense of self said, "The Heart is mine," and, without realizing it, actually set out like Herod to destroy the Christ-spark within the manger.

There seemed to me, for lack of a better way to say it, a time of argument and struggle between the Heart and the ego-personality who said, "I am the one the Kingdom of God is *within;* I, Bill, am the one who listens to the Heart; I, Bill, am going out into the world to tell everyone about it." All the while, *that* one was an impossible imposter; and, all the while, as recorded in the Bibles of the world, the Truth within was going right on about its Father's business, destined, as time and appearance go, to "grow and develop apace."

Because Truth cannot be possessed, the I-possessor is a stark *nothing,* whose role we simply stop playing! We can do this nearly effortlessly because Reality is already *all*—and is being "I."

Once upon a time we looked out on experience and saw it divided into a good and evil world. We took sides; we chose to fight with the "right" against the "wrong"; we took up the cudgel and, as valiant soldiers marching to war, undertook to slay the dragon and heal the world. We shouted, "This is the way; walk ye in it!"

Now, the circle nearly closed, we see that all we see is precisely as it should be; we see that the levels of education, even as they appear, are neither right nor wrong, good nor bad, material, spiritual, real, unreal, a dream nor any other such thing.

What are they? They are perfect images just being perfect images; Isness being Isness is what they are!

But who am "I"? Nothing of myself! Awareness is being aware of all Isness is mindful of, and this awareness—right here, right now—is busily perceiving the infinity of perfect Being being. THIS is WHO I am, WHAT I am and what I am DOING—nothing else. The consciousness reading these words is the selfsame Awareness! Comprehendest thou this?

MAN IS NOT GOD—GOD IS BEING ALL THERE IS
TO THAT WHICH IS CALLED MAN!

Within this world-scheme of things, there is found no demand to stay lost in the field of healing, changing the picture and attempting to make over the universe. One day the appearance of world turmoil, individual or collective, will be understood for what it is: the misidentification's negatives and positives aligning themselves for their inevitable confrontation and neutralization. Out of this comes the inescapable recognition of the New Identity, neither positive nor negative, and infinitely more than both. This has been the Identity all the while.

If there is any choice—free will, as the philosophers say—it is that in the final confrontation going on even this moment,

Conclusion

in the fiery dissolution of personal judgment's opposing forces, we have the ability to choose *not* to suffer nor be disturbed by these events.

Who is spared the personal agony of these "last days" of the old man? Those who know the Truth? Those who belong to this or that church or metaphysical organization? Absolutists? The answer is straight and simple: only those who stop attempting *to be* the old man can escape the agony of his last days. There is no more suffering, neither shadow of tribulation, only joy unspeakable and unending for those unpretentious and credulous enough to actually *stop* evaluating and *end* their personal judgments of good and evil. These are the ones who will no longer side with either extreme in the explosive confrontations of the old nature's judgmental dualisms.

Who can do this? Only those who give God *all* the power and glory; who give God that which is God's and "appearance" that which is appearance's, and Awareness that which is His! Only the one who, in utter simplicity and humility, like a child taking off his clothes without shame, *surrenders* to the Being which is being Awareness and does not continue in his vain attempt to make Awareness into God.

Yes, God is ONE and ALL, but this Awareness-I-am is not God. A monumental gulf separates the statement "The Self-I-am is God" from *"God* is this Self-I-am." Most writers of the day, daring their profoundest metaphysical "paradoxes" declare, "I am Truth; I am Life; I am Love" or "God is all and I am that all," but a vast dark night of apparent agony hangs like a veil between those pronouncements and the ones that say "Truth am I; Life am I; Love am I! The All is being this Consciousness I am!"

Yes, we may state, "I am the Awareness of God"; *but it is God who is aware,* not we, not me, not I. I am Awareness itself, God's awareness of God! I am God's own Awareness in action, beholding the infinite nature of the Divine Selfhood which is being all I am—BUT I AM NOT GOD! The Awareness

[handwritten at top: Prepositions are relational and play havoc with "reality"]

called "I" is not God. Awareness is the *action* of God, but not God.

Oh, foolish and perverse generation I was. How long I argued with this! How long it seemed to make that final surrender and stop attempting to be God! How tenaciously the ego held on, insidiously masquerading as the One. "I and God are one," it maintained. "I am God and not man," it wrote, it whispered, it prayed, *but never was it so!*

Indeed, the old man says these things, and more. "I am Awareness," it professes. "I am Consciousness," it deludes itself into believing. "I am God and not man," it can say. "Images and objects of perception are within *ME*—they ARE me—and the way I see them, interpret them, react to them, is *how* they *appear* to be"; *but the old ego is there yet,* attempting to see as God sees, earnestly working to heal its erring conceptions of perfect Isness *when Isness has never misperceived itself and Perfection has never seen itself imperfectly!*

Someone has written (even as I did in times past), "I am ALL in all." While this concept did its work for a time, now we see a new pronouncement which states "The All is I! The ALL is I! The All is all I am!"—but never am I the all!

It has been taught: "I am all the Life and Mind there is or can be." Not so, not so. Nearly, but not so. Life and Mind are being all there is to the Awareness I am—and Awareness includes all things—but never, never is this all-inclusive Awareness the *all* of Deity, the eternal Godhead!

Reader, listen carefully: After the dreamer has devalued his images, his dearest, most valued belief, his last bastion of hope, becomes a tenaciously held belief of *his own Deific grandeur.* Under the guise of supreme devotion to God *as all of all,* the unsurrendered ego proclaims *I* am God and not man.

But the glory of the final honest letting go! The relief of *giving up!* The liberation, the joy, when finally *honesty* prevails, when the Finished Kingdom is acknowledged! In a flash, in a twinkling, effort is over; healing is done; demonstration, manipulating and thought guarding are finished. Planning and calculating are things of the past! Effortless Tranquillity from glory to glory becomes the acknowledged, unending, *experienced* fact of being.

As appearances go, the ones least willing to make this surrender are those who derive the greatest personal satisfaction and delight from their metaphysical manipulative mastership and their great scholastic knowledge of the world—or of "Absolute Truth."

But all the while, like a child, this Awareness-we-are is in the tow of Already. Like a child, Awareness is simply being what Perfection is, in the process of tenderly and effortlessly being aware of Itself. Like a child, Awareness is motiveless living in the Now of Eternity—without regard, without regret, unblemished, pristine, pure, trusting, confident and happy beyond measure. Like a child, Awareness is Tranquillity being This-I-am, forever!

EPILOGUE

Reader, this is an unusual volume and it ends with an unusual request. *I ask that you begin to read it again without delay;* this time with the idea in mind to try it out, test it out, and find out for yourself if its precepts are honest; to see if they are practical and applicable to you. They are!—but this means nothing to you until you are willing to try them out and discover what they will do within your experience.

Finally, I ask that when you begin to discover the monumental Peace and Tranquillity which your Identity is, and when "others" come to you and ask about it, wondering how you are able to maintain such poise and equanimity, such serenity and calm in the face of their "seeming," that you *tell them who they are, who you are and how you came to know,* even as I have tried to do (no one will ever know how earnestly) within these pages. This, as I understand it, is to give as we have received—and, of a certainty, this is to look out like the hickory tree, like the periwinkle, like the eagle, like the dove, and *see* the Peace "that passeth understanding" everywhere. This is the reason and the purpose of our existence!